Financial Times Pitman Publishing books

We work with leading authors to develop the strongest ideas in business and finance, bringing cutting-edge thinking and best practice to a global market.

We craft high quality books which help readers to understand and apply their content, whether studying or at work.

To find out more about Financial Times Pitman Publishing books, visit our website:

www.ftmanagement.com

HARNESSING STRATEGIC BEHAVIOUR

Why personality and politics drive company strategy

TONY GRUNDY

FINANCIAL TIMES
PITMAN PUBLISHING

FINANCIAL TIMES
MANAGEMENT

LONDON · SAN FRANCISCO
KUALA LUMPUR · JOHANNESBURG

*Financial Times Management delivers the knowledge,
skills and understanding that enable students,
managers and organisations to achieve their ambitions,
whatever their needs, wherever they are.*

London Office:
128 Long Acre, London WC2E 9AN
Tel: +44 (0)171 447 2000
Fax: +44 (0)171 240 5771
Website: www.ftmanagement.com

A Division of Financial Times Professional Limited

First published in Great Britain in 1998

© Financial Times Professional Limited 1998

The right of Tony Grundy to be identified as
Author of this Work has been asserted by him in accordance
with the Copyright, Designs and Patents Act 1988.

ISBN 0 273 63094 6

British Library Cataloguing in Publication Data
A CIP catalogue record for this book can be obtained from
the British Library.

1 3 5 7 9 10 8 6 4 2

Typeset by Northern Phototypesetting Co. Ltd, Bolton
Printed and bound in Great Britain by
Biddles Ltd, Guildford and King's Lynn

*The Publishers' policy is to use paper manufactured
from sustainable forests.*

ABOUT THE AUTHOR

Tony Grundy graduated from Cambridge in Philosophy and Social Sciences. He became a Chartered Accountant and worked in general management and in finance with BP and ICI. He has consulted with KPMG and PA and continues to work with major clients independently with his company, Cambridge Corporate Development.

He has an MBA, MPhil and PhD from three Business Schools and an MSc in Organizational Behaviour from London. He is now also a Reiki Master and Seichem Master of the subtle human energies.

Harnessing Strategic Behaviour is Tony's sixth book on strategic management. He is Senior Lecturer in Strategic Management at Cranfield School of Management.

CONTENTS

INTRODUCTION

Name one company not facing considerably more external and internal change than it was 10 or 15 years ago. You might be struggling to come up with one.

It is a brutal reality that managers are facing increasing levels of change while also coping with increased complexity and, frequently, reduced levels of resources. Primarily tactical styles of managing are now outmoded and companies are awakening to the imperative to think – and act – strategically. Still, however, they find themselves held back by the quagmire of organizational politics.

Strategic management has become an expectation, not only on the part of the company but also the individual, who often feels as if they are clinging to a fragile and precarious management structure. At any moment, the fact that their own roles can disappear into an organizational black hole generates a good deal of defensive, political behaviour. That same behaviour undermines the capacity of the organization to behave strategically. Thus, there is frequently a huge gap between the expectation and the reality of managing strategically. Although managers know they are expected to act strategically, they frequently don't know what this entails – in short *how to do it*. Is this merely a case of lacking the necessary strategic thinking skills or is it something more fundamental?

I shall argue that managing strategically very much involves managing the behaviour associated with strategic management. It also demands a move beyond organizational politics.

To illustrate why I believe strategic management is much more than a matter of strategic thinking skills, consider an example from my own experience of a strategic thinking programme for a major technology group. This involved working with 40 senior managers to give them the necessary skills to put flesh on the strategy being developed at Board level, and to prepare them for its implementation. After one of the workshops, I was given an off-the-record debrief by the Human Resources Director about a particular senior director:

> You wouldn't believe it. After the programme, Joe (Director of X Division), who was on the programme, came up to me and said, 'I want to do an MBA'.

He was the last person in the company I thought would say that. He is just purely tactical.

You know there is more strategic thinking and behaviour in the average gerbil than he could ever have – with or without an MBA, but I'm sorry, that might be an insult to those furry creatures.

At the time I was taken aback by this comment. I felt conflicting things about what was said:

- I felt sorry that a senior manager had shown enthusiasm for strategic thinking, but was regarded as inherently lacking competence in that area
- I wondered whether or not the Director was right – Joe was never going to be a brilliant strategic thinker, but this did not prevent him from achieving reasonable competence in that area, actually he was a bright manager
- maybe the biggest constraint Joe faced was the way in which his behaviour was constrained by that of the top team of which he was a member, and the behaviour of the wider organization, especially that which was political in nature.

So, if there was a strategic disability here, it was certainly not just down to Joe. This was not simply a case of a specific individual creating their sustaining strategic thinking in a relative vacuum. No, the main blockage appeared to be a behavioural one, and not just some impairment in individuals' management skills. In short, the problem was one of how the managers behaved strategically.

Joe is not an isolated case by any means. In fact, he is typical of many thousands of extremely well paid, but occasionally very stretched, senior executives. Whenever I have worked in senior teams to facilitate strategic thinking, this impression is consistently reinforced: behavioural issues are both the most important and frequently the most difficult to overcome when trying to manage a team or an organization more strategically. Truly strategic behaviour seems to be an absolutely central part of the critical path in managing an organization strategically.

By 'strategic behaviour' I mean those behaviours associated with the management of strategic issues within companies. The topic of strategic behaviour is not one that comes up often in management theory, even though it is clearly very important in practice. My perceptions of management practice and the awareness of the lack of theory on strategic behaviour at a team level led me to begin a fascinating study of these behaviours in 1995. Over the next couple of years I was able to study this behaviour both as a management researcher and by means of my consulting practice.

During my research study, I was able to shadow managers as they debated strategic issues and observe their patterns of behaviour. These yielded some most interesting insights that I have been able to turn into recipes for management practice, as you will see later on.

In this book on strategic behaviour, the focus is specifically on small, overlapping groups of individual managers rather than the organization at large. It therefore stays primarily at the human level, rather than at the level of the economic behaviour of firms within their competitive markets (which is the main concern of competitive strategy). This is because it is at the human level that strategic decisions occur, and where strategic action is initiated.

In managers' strategy making the focus is also on the social interaction between individuals on the small scale – that is, in their everyday strategic behaviours. These individuals also bring their own cognitive abilities, perceptions and assumptions to the 'strategic party'. To make matters more complicated still, the assumptions made by managers are heavily influenced by their personal agendas.

Why is strategic behaviour important?

So, if we now take it as read that strategic behaviour is the behavioural context for strategy making, why is it important?

Strategic behaviour is important for the following ten key reasons.

1 **Informal decision making**   Too frequently, one (or more) manager is more vocal and dominant in a team than the others, resulting in the arguments and concerns of other members being marginalized or in them not even being expressed at all. This creates an unbalanced political climate within the team. Where strategic behaviour is managed well, then there should be a more favourable climate for informed decision making.

2 **Speed of decision making**   Relatively turbulent strategic behaviour is very likely to slow, or even halt, the progress of decision making in

a team. This reduces the strategic responsiveness of the team, which has a knock-on negative effect on the responsiveness of the rest of the organization. It also gives an opportunity for the wrong kind of organizational politics to thrive.

3 **Decisions are actually made, not deferred**   One of the biggest problems in senior management teams is actually coming to a decision, even once the strategic issues have been thoroughly explored. This was described graphically by the Head of Strategy of a well-known financial services group:

> When our management team gets together it is just like Heathrow. More and more aircraft [strategic issues] are coming in and the air traffic controllers seem to have given up. They just get stacked up and nothing ever seems to be landing.

4 **Creativity is encouraged**   Where a team's strategic behaviour is consciously orchestrated, there is perhaps a greater chance of its full creativity being harnessed. This applies both when a team is full of very creative individuals and when it is relatively deficient in that vital, creative spark.

5 **Discussing the undiscussable**   Many management teams find certain issues particularly difficult to deal with. These may be associated with strategic projects or programmes that are drifting or appear likely to fail. As soon as this occurs, the ripples of organizational politics begin to spread, building one on the other until they become waves. Otherwise, they may be concerned with the competence or behaviour of individuals outside the team or even within it. Where a team finds it hard to harness its strategic behaviour, these kinds of issues are likely to remain in the realm of the undiscussable.

6 **Mental maps are enriched**   Managers in established teams sometimes tend to assume that everyone in the team sees the world in more or less the same way. The reality is, however, that, even in a mature team, they often do not. Managers may need to work hard in their interactive behaviour to explicitly share and compare their mental maps. Otherwise, they are likely to run into unduly (and often unnecessarily turbulent) strategic behaviour. Much of what we know as organizational politics is probably caused by mental maps being only partially exposed, thus generating either artificial or exaggerated areas of disagreement.

7 **Frustration is avoided and energy accumulated** In a management team facing many intractable strategic issues, and where team behaviour is not really under control, frustration can mount and mount. Energy then dissipates as problems are not solved, everything appears to take two or three times the time it should and, very quickly, in these circumstances the team's behaviour becomes fractious. However, where the team can helicopter out of its behavioural difficulties, this can resolve the more business-related complexities and dilemmas. Where frustration builds unduly, top managers may be inclined (in their desperation) to 'drive through' strategies. This sets up waves of (political) resistance, some of which could be avoided.

8 **Team commitment is increased** Even a relatively strong and open team may struggle when it has to deal with painful options, such as putting a major project on hold, refocusing activities or embarking on a significant downsizing. By being able to steer around the more awkward behavioural blockages, these decisions can be made not only with less difficulty but also with a better balance of evidence and judgement.

9 **Creating a platform for influencing** Many business teams find that they need to influence thinking and feeling about strategic issues elsewhere in the organization. Unless the team's own strategic behaviour is well aligned internally, it may prove difficult for the team to exert its influence in the rest of the organization. In such instances, being able to focus strategic behaviour reduces the political disadvantages of a department or business unit relative to its organizational peers.

10 **Internal politics are channelled more effectively** Although every team has to deal with its fair share of internal politics, if unchecked, political activity can debilitate it severely. As will be seen later in the book, many of the dysfunctional aspects of internal politics can be channelled into a more constructive debate. (This channelling can help alleviate the kind of effect on the organization that is normally associated with inadvertently driving a car with the handbrake on.)

Strategic behaviours thus unquestionably have a big impact on the effectiveness and performance of an organization. How though can they be more effectively harnessed? The challenge is to unravel the complexity of strategic behaviour to a point where we can define points of leverage over team behaviour. These points of leverage are opportunities for steering behaviour from a more tactical track to one that is genuinely operating at a strategic level and can be brought out in a number of ways.

First, Chapter 2 contains a case study on Champneys Health Farm, with pointers for both managing strategic behaviour and strategy facilitation generally. Second, in the core of the book (which details a case study of British Telecom) some key pointers are brought out at the end of each section. Third, in Chapters 7 and 8, the implications for managing the dynamics of strategic behaviour are examined.

Part I thus deals with discovering strategic behaviour. In Chapter 1 strategic behaviour is defined in detail. Following this, there is an exploration of how important strategic behaviour is within the strategic management process. Then the sources of theory about strategic behaviour are examined and some time is taken to look at some practical illustrations of strategic behaviour in action.

Part I

DISCOVERING STRATEGIC BEHAVIOUR

STRATEGIC MANAGEMENT AND STRATEGIC BEHAVIOUR

The one who figures on victory at headquarters before even doing battle is the one who has the most strategic factors on his side

Sun Tzu, *The Art of War*

INTRODUCTION – WHAT IS STRATEGIC BEHAVIOUR?

So far I have said that strategic behaviour is those behaviours associated with the management of strategic issues within companies. However, whose behaviours are these, when do they occur and how are they different from other kinds of behaviours or, if they do not differ totally, how do they develop or interrelate?

Let us now define 'strategic behaviour' as:

the cognitive, emotional and territorial interplay of managers within (or between) groups when the agenda relates to strategic issues.

A 'group' here can be two or more managers – it does not have to be a large team.

'Strategic issues' are now defined as:

Issues concerned with setting the longer-term direction or path of change in a business in relation to its key stakeholders.

However, most importantly, mere 'behaviour' has been expanded to encompass 'the cognitive, emotional and territorial interplay' of managers. This stresses that there are several factors at work here and that these are extremely closely interwoven. In the case study on BT later, it will be seen that these interrelationships between cognition, feelings and territorial interplay are appropriately called 'the behavioural cocktail'.

However, before looking at the origins of strategic behaviour, let us first examine the influence of corporate strategy on management thinking.

CORPORATE STRATEGY
AND 'THE EMPEROR'S CLOTHES'

Corporate strategy has had a pervasive influence over many managers for the past 30 or more years. Ever since early works such as Ansoff's *Corporate Strategy* (1965) fired the imagination of managers, corporate strategy has been seen as a major way of achieving growth, profitability and, ultimately, management reward. However, to be genuinely effective, corporate strategy can only reap these rewards if the behavioural and political issues generated in its wake are managed well. And dealing with that behaviour can be very hard indeed.

Corporate strategy has thus been at the apex of management theory and is very much the centrepiece of business school courses, whether these are for MBA students or for experienced managers. As a lecturer myself at Cranfield School of Management – one that is proud of its practical focus – I sometimes experience mental strain on reconciling the theory of corporate strategy and its actual practice. Because corporate strategy has to be written or talked about in a structured way, this can give it the 'look' of being a very disciplined and orderly process. However when this structured process is compared with the behavioural realities of corporate strategy practice, frequently there is little form and process. Managers obviously place huge weight on their intuition and judgement – and fluid interaction within the group. There is at times an almost awesome reliance on individual and collective gut-feel, even when dealing with the most complicated of issues.

A more haphazard strategic management process has its attractions. It feels natural to most managers. It gives full rein to divergent management debate, feeling infinitely elastic, as managers dart from issue to issue. At the same time, though, it may be frustrating, unproductive and superficial. However chaotic, managers appear hooked on it. Ultimately, it can be responsible for key strategic decisions being made that are inappropriate, and go 'pear-shaped'.

So, returning to prescriptive management theory, what happens when managers experience 'Strategic Encounters of the Third Kind' at a business school, coming into contact with the alien technologies of strategic management? Even more experienced managers frequently come to business schools with the mindset that there is a ready-made conceptual process that can simply be plugged straight into their organization when they get back. However, corporate strategy is never like plugging more memory into your PC – it involves a fundamental change in how managers manage and – very important this – behave. Strategic management needs such new sets of behaviours to be adopted in order for it to be effective that, almost invariably, attempts to introduce new ways of strategic thinking falter or fail.

In many organizations, corporate strategy is thus very much a case of dealing with 'the emperor's clothes' syndrome. Corporate strategy is something that managers feel they should have – otherwise they feel they will be embarrassed ('we have no story to tell') – but, largely for behavioural reasons, strategic thinking hardly seems to permeate management action on an everyday basis. Although this results in there being no well-articulated corporate strategy, managers still go around pretending they have one.

Corporate strategy thus falls between two camps – one of being a 'nice to do', if only we had time and being a 'must do'. Like doing a tax return, it is seen as being complicated, messy and not obviously rewarding – something to be delayed as long as possible.

Because of its concern with content – and, ultimately, with the strategic plan – corporate strategy is depicted by the majority of readily available strategic management books as being largely strategic analysis and strategic choice. (There are notable exceptions – for example, Johnson and Scholes, 1987, who explore in depth how corporate strategy is shaped by organizational culture.) Thus, the main task of corporate strategy is often perceived to be an analytical one, not a behavioural one.

Corporate strategy has made some major achievements in providing managers with analytical frameworks, but, as will be seen later on in this chapter, the 'analysis' part of strategy is only a part (and perhaps a small part) of the whole picture, which is peppered with behavioural issues.

Try answering the questions in the worksheet 'The strategic emperor's cloths – have you a corporate strategy?' to start your thinking on the matters touched on here.

The strategic emperor's clothes – have you a corporate strategy?

To test whether or not you have a well-articulated corporate strategy, ask yourself the following key questions.

- For the businesses we are in, do we know why we are in them?

  _____

  _____

  _____

- Do we have a good idea of which businesses we do not want to be in, and why?

  _____

  _____

  _____

- Does the corporate centre have a clear idea of what value it is adding to the business units?

  _____

  _____

  _____

- Does each business unit have a plan to develop strategically, and know how this will generate shareholder value, and when?

  _____

  _____

  _____

- Does the corporate centre have an overview of both organic and acquisitive opportunities across and beyond the business portfolio?

  _____

  _____

  _____

- Does the group have a clear plan for dealing with opportunities for divestment, unbundling or turnaround?

_____

_____

_____

- Are there any common ways of doing things across the group or other genuine synergies that provide the strategic glue for the group?

_____

_____

_____

Corporate strategy analysis and story-telling

Corporate strategy is a most satisfying intellectual discipline, but this aspect of it can be a trap, as it can become little more than a strategic fantasy. The worst kind of strategic thinking is that which enjoys strategic analysis for its own sake and so fails to move into the more behavioural domain, which is where it needs to move to if it is to produce action and change.

Undeniably, corporate strategy is an enjoyable intellectual pastime. Perhaps the most intellectually satisfying frameworks for corporate strategy are to be found in Michael Porter's two earlier books, *Competitive Strategy* (1980) and *Competitive Advantage* (1985). My ten-point guide to creating competitive strategy summarizes the content of these books.

1 The five competitive forces (buyer power, supplier power, entrants, rivals and substitutes) determine who gets the lion's share of the value created in an industry.
2 The intensity of these competitive forces is the major force behind longer-term profitability generally in the industry.
3 The five competitive forces are frequently more important in determining longer-term market attractiveness than the growth rate of that market.

9

4 As an industry or market develops and matures, the competitive forces themselves will change and only highly adaptive firms will survive.

5 To understand your strategic position, you need to understand which set of players you belong to (your 'strategic group') and how you can threaten or be threatened by other strategic groups.

6 You do need to choose how to compete – seek a distinctive positioning.

7 One way of competing successfully is to differentiate yourself from your competitors by adding distinctive value to your target customers. (This is then rewarded by a premium price.)

8 Another way of competing successfully is to seek a 'best cost' position. This involves you becoming the lowest-cost player in a particular strategic group (or even in the industry).

9 Trying to achieve a 'differentiation' and 'best cost' strategy simultaneously (and with equal priority), is unlikely to be successful as you will confuse your customers – and even yourselves.

10 You need to align all the activities (within your 'value chain') to achieve an effective competitive superiority.

Porter's achievement lies in his providing a way of analyzing external opportunities and strategic options for competing in a carefully structured way. Sadly, Porter did not continue his work, providing us with an equally helpful way of understanding managers' strategic behaviour – his main interest being in business economics rather than behavioural psychology. However, this gap can be remedied by extending Porter's work ourselves, at least into the land of competitive behaviours, as follows.

Porter's five competitive forces are typically used to understand the attractiveness of the different markets in which a business operates. Sadly, their relevance to management action and behaviour has been underemphasized.

Listening to a presentation by a team from Oxford University Press triggered the idea of refocusing the five forces principally on the implications for management action and behaviour. This can be achieved by means of two steps. First, each of the five forces can be used to generate a number of 'competitive success factors'. ('Critical success factors' are more often than not confused by managers with more localized, operational imperatives. A 'competitive success factor' is defined more strategically to mean those things we have to do to become more competitive and to avoid becoming less competitive). Table 1.1 shows an example of this analysis applied in the case of the UK supermarket industry. Second, for each of the five forces, we need to examine the key strategic behaviours that are required in the organization. Table 1.1 also shows an example of how this is done.

Table 1.1 Competitive forces, success factors and strategic behaviours in the UK supermarket industry

Porter's five forces	Relative attractiveness of industry	Competitive success factors	Strategic behaviours
Bargaining power of buyers	Medium – buyers have some loyalty but will switch	Build brand awareness and loyalty to increase switching costs with excellent service and loyalty schemes	Adopt an obsession with 'customer first' – at all organizational levels
Entrants	High – entrants need critical mass and brand awareness	Avoid creaming price to dissuade likely entrants and attack them vigorously	Adopt the mindset of a new entrant in developing new business areas/ changing old
Substitutes	Low – supermarkets dominate customers' mindsets	Avoid manufacturers going direct via Internet/direct delivery	Challenge own ways of doing things – is there a better way we can achieve via substitutes?
Competitive rivalry	Low-medium – few sustainable competitive advantages, but only a few big players	Avoid a price war and erode competitors' share gradually, but insidiously	Challenge the mindset of the industry, which dictates the rules of competing in the industry
Bargaining power of suppliers	High – suppliers are fragmented and private label partly displaces brands	Exert bargaining power against suppliers and discourage collaborative behaviour by suppliers as a collective	Question existing arrangements for sourcing and collaboration – what supplier network should you have as opposed to what you do have?

Returning to Porter, his two books deal primarily with business unit-level strategies, but they also raise issues at the corporate level (particularly what businesses a group should be in and how these should be coordinated to add value). A more recent attempt to synthesize what is known about corporate strategy is Goold, *et al.*'s, *Corporate-level Strategy* (1994). This book's main theme is that collecting a set of businesses together as a group is not necessarily sufficient to generate shareholder value. (Goold, *et al.* contend that, frequently, groups of companies actually destroy shareholder value by, for example, collecting businesses that do not fit the group's parenting capability – that is, what it is distinctively good at.) As with Porter, Goold, *et al.* provide an excellent framework for diagnosing the logic (or the absence of logic) for strategy at the corporate level. However, the key question remains – how do managers begin to behave more strategically, thus aligning their thoughts, feelings and ambitions with delivering a common strategic goal? In short, how does their strategic behaviour provide the engine for driving the corporation in more or less the right kind of direction – one that creates shareholder value?

Whatever the intellectual merits of showing that you have an official corporate strategy, much of the practical benefits are to be found quite simply in 'having a strategic story to tell' (both internally and externally). This strategic story describes where the organization is, where it wants to go and how it proposes getting there. 'The story' is important precisely because it gives shareholders comfort that the organization knows where and how it will make money – now and in the future. It also helps management and staff to coordinate their efforts in a strategic way, rather than merely tactically. It also helps customers and suppliers to understand what the organization is trying to achieve and anticipate what it can offer in the future and will need itself. Where some strategic clarity exists, there is at least some broader frame of reference to help cope with organizational politics.

Although it is no easy task to assemble a robust corporate strategy, it may come as a surprise (to some) that many organizations operate with a relatively sketchy one (taking us back to the emperor's clothes syndrome). This may be the result of a combination of time constraints, difficulties in collecting data or simply a reluctance to spell out the story (for fear of being proved wrong). Whatever the problems of arriving at a sensible corporate strategy, there are many attractions in creating a comprehensive and clear story about how an organization can migrate into the future (its 'strategy'). A major attraction is that this story provides a clear focus for aligning managers' strategic interactions, so that their conversations have a common purpose. Their personal ambitions can then become more aligned rather than becoming rampant politically.

So, what is this strategic story-telling about? It is about telling a story of a journey as it unfolds, a journey up a corporate mountain.

Strategic mountaineering

If corporate strategy involves strategic mountaineering, we should begin in the foothills – particularly with business planning. Prior to the advent of competitive strategy in the 1980s with Michael Porter, strategic management was primarily associated with long- and short-range business planning. Business planning is the manifestation of corporate strategy for managers at an everyday level, and business planning is frequently conducted in a tactical style. In many more financially driven organizations, business planning could be excused as something done by accountants for accountants, for the pleasure of accountants, and sometimes to the detriment of non-accountants. So much obsessive emphasis is put on the financial numbers, and forcing them up to achieve corporate financial goals. (I speak myself as an 'FCA', or 'former chartered accountant', but one still paying Institute fees.)

Moving somewhat beyond the foothills, it becomes a hard task to expect managers to adapt their strategic process to incorporate Porter's more external and competitive perspectives. Indeed, for the last ten years, most of my consulting time has been spent doing precisely that. Even more difficult, however, is to make progress on the behavioural frontier in strategic management. Here we probe into how managers feel (as well as think) about how their businesses are positioned. (For instance, when I am shifting yellow Post-its about on flip charts at business positioning meetings, I feel like a surgeon operating without anaesthetic – apparently minute movements produce noticeable signs of anxiety in the managers.) We therefore need to ask explicitly how these positionings affect their territorial concerns and hopes for the future. Climbing the strategic mountain is very much an emotional task.

To many managers, corporate strategy is like trying to climb a very *high* mountain. Managers have been told about the merits of climbing the strategic mountain (especially that they will gain a very clear strategic vision), but how to reach the summit of the mountain remains unclear. So, each year, they repeat the ritual of trying to climb the Mount Everest of corporate strategy, without the mountaineering skills – both strategic thinking and strategic behaviour – they need to do so. They appear unaware of the fact that Mount Everest is exceedingly high and they will have to manage in a very different way if they are to get to the summit (their mindset is perhaps one of the UK's Snowdon mountains, which at over 4000 feet hardly counts as a mountain at all). So, each annual planning cycle, they only get as far as the tops of the foothills (tactical and financially led business planning), then find the ascent too difficult and come back down again, having not achieved any real strategic vision at all.

Sometimes the more adventurous managers do begin to scale the higher slopes, but they set about it with both the techniques of climbing that are only relevant to the foothills and the team behaviour associated with the level plain. They then wonder why their strategic efforts fall apart when they encounter unexpected hazards, apparently intractable constraints and sudden, hostile changes in their environment (often of a behavioural nature). Rather than set about behaving strategically in this situation, more typically they will then argue, become defensive and fragment as a team. While some of the managers' problems in scaling the Everest of corporate strategy appear to be due to a weakness in strategic thinking, a more difficult, fundamental problem lies in managing their strategic behaviour. For, as managers ascend the mountain, they see more, they may suffer from vertigo, fears are amplified and the team spirit breaks down. Then organizational politics really sets in. Sadly, the higher they go, the more cohesive they need to become as a team. However, what actually happens is that the higher up they go, the less effective is their behaviour towards each other, resulting in the odd casualty or fatality.

A particularly good way of picturing the strategic mountain is shown in Figure 1.1 – the Pyramid of strategic thinking.

The base of the strategic thinking pyramid is made up of strategic analysis (including SWOT analysis, the five competitive forces and other techniques). Frequently managers and students of management alike (maybe 50 per cent) fail to ask themselves the 'So what?' question, which is the next level of the pyramid.

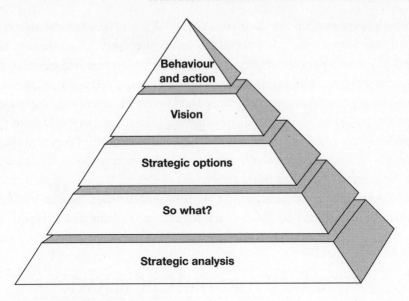

Fig 1.1 The strategic thinking pyramid

Then, perhaps another 50 per cent of the remainder fail to generate some truly radical and creative strategic options. These strategic options should include not only:

- the 'what' – the strategic positioning externally
- but the 'how' – the implementation strategy.

One of my favourite workshop illustrations is an acetate of the front cover of the *Kama Sutra* – the lesson from this being that there are frequently a hundred ways or more of implementing a particular project, whether it be sensual or strategic!

The next level up from that of options is vision. Perhaps another 50 per cent of managers are too shy to really distil their strategies into a singular picture or message. Finally, perhaps another 50 per cent of those still left fail to translate this into clear action plans, and perhaps a 50 per cent of these fail to adopt strategic behaviour. So, in summary, our overall success rate could be:

$$\text{Success rate} = 50\% \text{ (so what)} \times 50\% \text{ (options)} \times 50\% \text{ (vision)}$$
$$\times 50\% \text{ (action plans)} \times 50\% \text{ (behaviour)} = 3.1\%$$

15

which helps explain the poor success rate of many strategic plans.

However, if you now want to look for help in exploring the behavioural aspects of strategic management, then you will quickly run into problems. While strategic thinking is covered relatively extensively in existing management texts, there is relatively little written – especially at a practical level – on the behaviour associated with strategic thinking and action – or 'strategic behaviour'. The purpose of this book is to show precisely how strategic behaviour influences management action, and how it can be managed more effectively.

To begin our exploration, let us first take a brief look at existing management theory on behavioural influences on strategic management.

THE SEARCH FOR STRATEGIC BEHAVIOUR

How do top teams behave strategically?

My attraction to the idea of strategic behaviour resulted from doing some strategic mountaineering myself (helping managers, as their 'strategy guide' – hopefully, to avoid the precipices). I then developed a deeper interest in it as a result of my investigations into strategic decision making (Grundy, 1992) and strategy consulting experience. My research into strategic decision making (with BP, GrandMet, London Underground, The Post Office and Rolls-Royce Aeroengines) taught me that managers are frequently overwhelmed at a psychological level by the complexity of strategic issues. However, my consulting experience also led me to believe that management behaviour was an even more important factor, causing mental overload. When you put both the mental demands of strategic thinking and the behavioural stress that comes from dealing with strategic issues together, you have the recipe for strategically overwhelmed managers.

Despite such awareness, I had not realized the full significance of the role of managers' feelings in shaping what seemed to be rational management behaviour. Often these feelings were only implicit and lurked beneath the surface of behaviour. These feelings became interwoven and cognitive and behavioural forces. They became a kind of 'strategic soup' that managers fall into each time they begin to deal with a strategic issue.

Then I looked at the hundreds of books and journals on strategy and organizational behaviour, but found very little written on the specific topic of strategic behaviour of top teams. Although there was a lot written on the interactions of top teams generally, little described that team behaviour associated specifically with strategic issues.

I began to conjecture – could it be that the primarily analytical (or cognitive) focus of many contemporary efforts within strategic management to provide strategic thinking was overdone, and possibly even misguided? Perhaps this implied a profound shift from concern with analysis to concerns with behaviour. If so, this might suggest an alternative route towards managers acting strategically, a shift away from such actions being based primarily on cognition and strategic thinking.

I then set off to discover what I could learn about the real insights into managers' strategic behaviour.

The realities of strategic behaviour

As we have seen, although much has been written about strategic decision making, relatively little focuses specifically on strategic behaviour. For example, Johnson (1986, p59) says:

> It is perhaps surprising that ... there are so few systematic studies of *the way in which the interaction of individuals* contributes to strategic decision making. (my italics)

Much of the previous thinking on how managers actually make strategic decisions is concerned with attacking rational and analytical models of strategy rather than actively creating new frameworks for understanding strategic behaviour. For instance, Mintzberg criticized the process of 'strategic planning' and the 'design school of strategic management' that promotes the development of strategy as an analytical process (Mintzberg, 1994) as simply not being what managers actually do. Strategic planning is also thought by some to be of very limited utility because of the sheer uncertainty generated by fluctuating economic and market demands, competitive activity and organizational change. This acute uncertainty crystallizes in chaos (Stacey, 1993). Most managers will recognize the havoc caused by uncertainty and chaos, but at the same time would clearly like to avoid seeing chaos as being inevitable.

Other major strategic writers have experimented with the idea of strategic behaviour, but only in a relatively limited way. Ansoff (1987) describes how paradigms (how the organization unconsciously reacts to things) determine how organizations adapt to crisis in terms of their reactive behaviour. Sadly, however, at no point does Ansoff actually define strategic behaviour. Also, Dixit and Nalib's book (1991) asks in the opening chapter, 'What is strategic behaviour?' but then, unfortunately, does not actually define it. Strangely, managers themselves recognize it immediately. One wonders then, 'is strategic behaviour self-evident?' – certainly for us it warrants definition.

Because writers have so far been less than helpful about the significance of strategic behaviour, we are probably better looking at some of the rather immediate and obvious problems and frustrations that occur in everyday strategic life. Let us look, therefore, at the following short example. (Sometimes, when I am working with senior teams, I find myself reflecting on the vast amount of literature written about strategic management and how complicated it seems to make things. Yet, in practice, managers' main concerns are not fundamentally complicated, and more often than not, the major areas of complexity boil down to behavioural issues.)

Managing complexity – at Multi-Multi Services (MMS)

A substantial services company with 13 business areas had begun to review its range of businesses (and their strategic priorities) in 1996. By 1997, it had developed relatively good prioritization of its key strategic priorities, but was still struggling to decide which business areas to run down or pull out of. However, at least part of the management team was unwilling to 'let go' of a number of business areas, because a lot of effort has been expended in the past or due to the internal embarrassment of pulling out or market changes might make these businesses more attractive in the future.

MMS is part of an even larger group, the head office of which has a major influence over the targeting of business performance goals over the forthcoming three years. Although some indicative targets had been set earlier in the process, it was only when the group had looked at the sum of their business submissions that they firmed up their specific expectations. These particular profit targets became so tight that expenses had to be capped to make the numbers work. These constraints meant that the company could not (physically) resource its existing plans for strategy development across all of its business areas. There was therefore pressure to simplify the business portfolio of MMS division while simultaneously achieving the sales growth projections already submitted (which assumed that the 13 business areas at the beginning of the review would still continue).

If this did not provide enough problems there was worse to come. During the strategic review, the full extent of the extra investment in IT that would be required to address the year 2000 issue (so that MMS computer systems would remain viable after midnight, 31 December 1999) became apparent. This meant that – along with the financial constraints on cost – the company could not possibly support its diverse development plans across all 13 businesses. There was therefore no choice but to narrow the portfolio of businesses, even if this might imply a future (strategic) opportunity cost.

It may be obvious to say that making the decision to narrow the focus of business was a most painful process behaviourally, but it is important to note that the main drivers of the eventual decision were more intangible and behavioural than many of the theoretical accounts of the strategic management process described in textbooks on the subject. The drivers included:

- MMS's management trying to do an 'honest' job in defining the business goals that it felt were do-able, given a quite thorough external analysis of its markets
- head office management tightening targets to deliberately stretch management – perhaps beyond the 'do-able'
- too few resources were available to actually achieve the strategy – people and money – unless the 'way we do things around here' and 'what we do' philosophies were fundamentally challenged
- senior managers wished to cling on to their existing strategies, even in the face of overwhelming pressures and constraints
- there was great uncertainty about how each of the strategies would pay off, making it very hard for the company's Chief Executive to cut back the portfolio without appearing to have 'gone tactical'.

MMS's situation highlights the influence of the strategic tennis game that is often played between a company and head office's management, the business targets and what resources will be available. These more brutal, behavioural realities make it seem as if elaborate, analytical strategic management is less relevant to our understanding of what is really going on beneath the surface. This is not, however, to say that strategic analysis is unimportant – simply that it may not sit at the centre of strategic management.

However, before taking a look at our own study of strategic behaviour (see the BT team example on p. 71), let us now take a more detailed look at what writers have said about strategic behaviour in decision making in the learning and change literature, and on politics and contention.

Strategic decision making

Many managers have a somewhat schizophrenic view of decision making. On the one hand they see the ideal process in very rational terms – there needs to be a careful weighing up of alternatives prior to making a strategic choice, and then the whole must be dealt with rather than merely a part of the issues. However, actual experience is one of decisions made reactively in response to pressures and constraints. These pressures and constraints are frequently handled by compromise or by deciding to deal with only part of the issues or by simply delaying the decision.

Constraints are a key barrier to making 'strategic' decisions on a more holistic basis. (So frequently do constraints seem to dominate managers' thoughts that I am reminded to write a, hopefully, future best-selling management book on the 'joy of constraints' – somewhat along the lines of *The Joy of Sex*, but showing managers 100 ways of escaping constrained situations.)

So, there is very great tension between the rational model of strategic decision making and managers' everyday experiences. The rational model is a set piece approach to dealing with the fundamental messiness of strategic issues. However, before we throw it out as being unrealistic, let us first examine what it suggests, so that we can distil what is good about a rational perspective. Figure 1.2 explores how the key model assumes a deliberate and linear progression from thought to action, strategic decisions being the filter of strategic options and strategic resources being absorbed in the process.

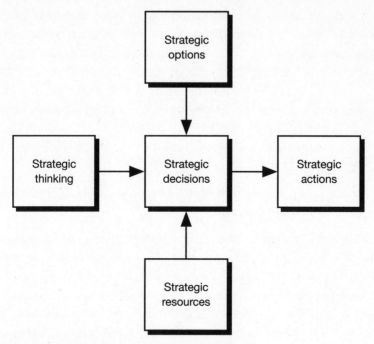

Fig 1.2 Linking strategy and action – a rational model

However, as earlier discussions have highlighted, strategic decision making is, at best, a part rational, unpredictable, fluid and haphazard process. Some decades ago, Cyert and March (1963) called this 'satisficing' behaviour (to draw attention to managers' tendencies to avoid the worst outcomes rather than seek the best outcomes). In everyday terms, we call this avoiding cock-ups.

Cyert and March also suggested that management decision making is effectively 'bounded rationality' – in bounded rationality some strategic issues were dealt with rationally while others are not. Indeed, Cyert and March described the decision-making process more colourfully as 'the garbage can model' (Cohen, March and Olsen, 1972). Another writer, Brunsson (1982), went even further, suggesting that apparently 'irrational' decision-making procedures play a key role in shaping actual decisions. Turning Cyert and March on their heads, strategic decision making could be regarded as a case of 'bounded irrationality' – in other words, the main influences on decision making are non-rational (and may therefore be primarily rooted in the emotional and subjective) with an occasional glimmer of rationality creeping in. Many managers – and not necessarily pure cynics – might recognize that their own organizations are primarily governed by non-rationality and subject to only the occasional constraint of being rational. (Of course, this rational/non-rational distinction is potentially misleading, as something that is highly rational for an individual may be less rational for their organization – for example, pursuing a pet project.)

Brunsson now helps us to understand the strategic decision-making process:

> Some actions are not preceded by weighing of (strategic) alternatives, evaluating alternatives or choosing.

Brunsson achieves a considerable understatement here. As a management consultant, I have often been asked to introduce the most basic of decision-making methods into senior teams. Sometimes it is not at all easy even to define decisions as Mintzberg suggested because of the fluidity of the decision-making process. It may not even be fruitful to study 'decisions', as they are actually so hard to locate. As Mintzberg (1978) says:

> It occurred to us that we were in fact not studying streams of decisions at all, but actions, because those are the traces actually left behind at organizations.

This suggests once again the need, perhaps, to shift our concerns from strategic decision making to understanding and managing strategic behaviour. However, if the situation managers face in strategic decision making already seems hopeless, now let us throw in the additional problem of incrementalism (Braybrooke and Lindblom, 1963).

Incrementalism has been described as being 'the science of muddling through' or of dealing with one problem at a time, even though these problems are inextricably linked. Quinn (1980) highlighted how strategies tend to evolve in disordered steps that build on (and sometimes detract from) each other. These steps are frequently made without holistic, pre-design. So, not only do we have partially formed, loosely defined and partly rational strategic decisions, they are also disjointed. They do not come together over a period of time to generate a coherent strategic vision, but represent many substrategies that are being pursued. Those substrategies are sometimes in conflict with each other, producing a state of 'stratophrenia' in managers (defined as being the confusion that occurs when two or more opposing strategies are pursued simultaneously).

Besides the problems of disjointedness in strategic decisions, we also have the final problem – that strategic decisions are often weakly implemented (which one could call the 'wimp' syndrome, standing for *w*eak *imp*lementation). The problem of weak implementation is well documented. For example, Butler writes (in Hickson *et al.*, 1986, p12):

> An interesting question is why some decisions achieve a greater degree of implementation than others … [perhaps] the original intention was only weakly implemented [or the gap] could arise when the implementation was of a completely different substance from the original intention.

In other words, implementation bears an almost accidental relationship to the original strategic decision (or, if a strategic decision is actually implemented, it might be because it is a fluke).

The strategic decision literature therefore suggests that it is the fluidity and disjointedness within the strategic decision-making process that makes it so hard to gain real clarity in strategic thinking and equally focused action. This underscores the need to explore how strategic behaviour can be harnessed more effectively to stabilize and direct the strategic decision-making process.

In summary, then, strategic decision making is:

- at best, a partly rational process
- frequently based on avoiding worst, rather than seeking best, outcomes
- entails carefully weighing decision alternatives in a systematic fashion only in exceptional cases
- often occurs as a continuous stream of discussion, without producing specific, tangible decisions
- generates strategy incrementally, rather than as an holistic pattern
- is frequently weakly implemented.

The incremental and disjointed nature of the strategy process means that managers may be carried forward by the momentum of their own strategic behaviour and into action. This can occur without any discernible events that could be called discrete 'decisions' actually taking place. As will be seen later, creating and sustaining this strategic momentum is a key challenge for senior teams.

Figure 1.3 shows a momentum-driven model of the linkages between strategy and action. It depicts external and internal events influencing strategic behaviour. These events crystallize strategic action. Notice that also included is a zone of strategic inaction. Strategic inaction is not necessarily a weakness in the process – it allows management the space to do further strategic reflecting.

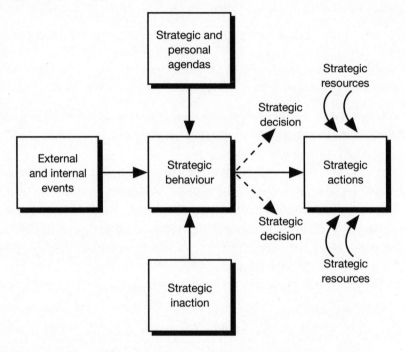

Fig 1.3 Linking strategy and action – an emergent, momentum-led model

In Figure 1.3 you will see a number of differences from Figure 1.2, which was a more artificial, rational model. Figure 1.3 suggests that:

- events themselves (rather than strategic thinking) are the prime drivers of strategic action
- agendas (personal and strategic) filter strategic decisions on a go/no-go basis, rather than a careful, rational weighing of strategic options – particularly their advantages and disadvantages – taking place
- strategic inaction plays an almost equally important role to that of strategic action (strategic inaction can be either intended or unintended – you can either decide not to do something deliberately or drift into it)

- strategic resources are typically allocated primarily tactically rather than in a carefully programmed way
- strategic behaviour is the power-house of the strategic management system (in my view, it is frequently more crucial than the cognitive processes associated with making specific decisions, indeed, decisions themselves become almost secondary, even a by-product of the mobilization process).

Organizational learning and strategic change

Organizational learning and strategic change also offer us additional insights into strategic behaviour. More recently, organizational learning has received a resurgence of interest, principally because of Senge's work (1990), which looks at things from the perspective of systems theory. However, the main contributor to linking learning and strategic behaviour is Chris Argyris.

Argyris' theory (for instance, 1991) is fundamentally simple: managers protect themselves from error by means of a set of explanations (or 'espoused theories') of what they are doing and why. These espoused theories (their reasons for action) often differ dramatically from how they actually behave.

Besides helping provide us with useful theories of strategic action, Argyris also helps us to understand the role of errors in the strategic management process. Error-making is linked to organizational learning because managers are supposed to learn from their mistakes. However, Argyris again puts us right with his notion of 'self-sealing errors', which is another way of describing organizational cover-ups. Things that go wrong and which are then covered up might therefore be a key ingredient of strategic behaviour (see Figure 1.4). Argyris sometimes calls this phenomenon the 'dead cat syndrome', likening it to finding a dead cat in your back yard. Instead of burying it and trying to find out why it died, you simply throw it into someone else's back yard. They discover the cat and repeat the process, throwing the cat into someone else's back yard. This results in a profound waste of energy.

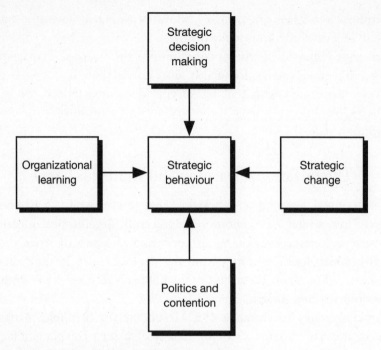

Fig 1.4 The ingredients of strategic behaviour theory

When working with one services company as a consultant I was drawn into saying:

> Sometimes there are not just one or two individuals playing the game but whole teams. Thus they are in the organizational back yard with rackets, trying to get the dead cat back over someone else's wall – or effectively playing 'dead cat tennis'.

In the most extreme case, the 'dead cat issue' can become highly dangerous, characterized as being the 'nuclear dead cat' – one that is due to go off unless someone manages to defuse it.

Janis' (1989) work links with Argyris' by focusing on errors that are especially damaging (the nuclear dead cat again). Janis lists a variety of sources of biases in judgement leading up to errors. For instance, he chronicles gross omissions in setting objectives or surveying alternatives, poor information, selective bias (misprocessing of information), failure to examine risks and, finally, failure to work out detailed implementation steps and devise contingency plans. When managers are under a lot of pressure, their strategic behaviour defaults, according to Janis, to a 'wow, grab it' mode – they jump at the first plausible solution (or alternatively, in the case of a dead cat, 'wow, get rid of it').

The role of strategic errors is shown in Figure 1.5.

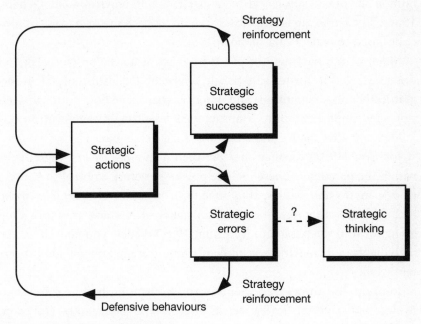

Fig 1.5 The role of strategic errors

However, is Janis falling into the trap of adopting an (economic) rationalist perspective – depicting managers who exercise limited rationality as being 'foolish'. In reality, managers are buffeted by behaviours of others, their own feelings and perceptions that they have limited power and influence over events. Then, they might be acting quite 'rationally' – following the easiest (if 'erroneous') course of action.

Argyris describes many instances where espoused theory diverges from theory in use. For instance, during his study of the behaviour of strategy consultants (1986) he found that, on numerous occasions, they projected difficulties that they were having in interacting with their clients as 'client incompetence'. Argyris' point is that, far from being aloof from defensive routines, 'professional people' are actually more vulnerable to indulging in defensive routines (Argyris, 1991).

27

Turning next to organizational change, the idea of paradigms appears. A 'paradigm' is defined as the deeper level of basic assumptions and beliefs that are shared by members of an organization, ones that operate unconsciously. These assumptions define in a basic, 'taken for granted' fashion an organization's view of itself and its environment (Schein, 1986). The paradigm is also closely bound up with the management processes used to make things happen.

Much of the paradigm in practice works at an unconscious level in organizations. It forms a network or 'web' (Johnson) of taken-for-granted beliefs, assumptions and practices that shape both strategic decisions and implementation. Managers are unwittingly caught up in this hidden web that shapes and constrains their behaviour.

Johnson (1992) distinguishes between a number of key ingredients within the paradigm. These include power, structure, controls, routines, rituals, myths and stories, thus ranging from relatively tangible to the intangible. Johnson describes the importance of ceremonies in providing living form to the paradigm (Johnson, 1992). Unless you consider these ingredients in formulating or implementing strategy, you will almost certainly fail.

Johnson also draws our attention to 'momentum building' (see also Miller and Freisen, 1978) versus inertia-type behaviours (Johnson, 1992). Clearly, creating and maintaining a momentum is a key part of the management of a senior team, and this momentum is threatened by apparently intractable strategic issues and dilemmas. Virtually every team has some concern with achieving progress (although I have been involved in some more intellectual teams where debate was an end in itself – thankfully, such teams are not overly common because of the pressures of the real business world). The idea of momentum building naturally leads us into the land of politics.

Politics and contention

Organizational politics is an inevitable ingredient of strategic behaviour. When individuals interact strategically, this is necessarily attended by extensive political influencing. We are inescapably drawn into analyzing and interpreting some of the key patterns of influencing behaviour that surround the strategy (Pettigrew, 1977). Strategy making is a highly political process (Johnson, 1986) and requires extensive bargaining and negotiation between subgroups.

A helpful way of surfacing political influences (which we will explore in depth later) and agendas is the use of stakeholder analysis (Piercey, 1989). Stakeholder analysis not only identifies the key stakeholders (on a particular strategic issue) and their likely position (in terms of both degree of influence and attitude), but may also help to surface agendas, as will be explored in more depth in Chapter 7. Although attempts were made to expose managers' thinking about stakeholder influence during our own research, these were not explicitly and specifically brought to the surface. Again, it would seem that managers prefer to reveal these influences obliquely.

Stakeholders may also reposition themselves significantly in times of crisis, depending on their perceptions of the crisis, their ability to understand it and their capacity to respond to it in appropriate ways (Chilingerian, 1994).

Politics can be a positive force in freeing up essential debate. For instance, both Kanter (1983) and Pascale (1990) emphasize the role of unleashing contention as a positive force in organizations. Unfortunately, these suggestions appear to be prescriptive rather than based on any well-grounded, empirical study. In the wrong hands, they can be an excuse for a specific individual in the team to be disruptive and destructive, with the intent of undermining the leader and becoming the centre of personal attention. However, if contention is suitably directed – and if managers can cope with the heat of challenge without going into Argyris' defensive routines – then there may be some real breakthroughs.

Before we leave our quest for strategic behaviour, let us remind ourselves that strategic behaviour is not something that is remote from our everyday contact with organizations. Where an organization begins to suffer from behaviour rigor mortis at the top, the effects may be found right down the organization and outside, in the customer base.

To illustrate the indirect effects of strategic behaviour on competitive activity everyday, I went in search of an example of 'organizations behaving badly'. I looked not for the learning organization but for the careless organization.

Selecting the best example for inclusion here was really difficult – not because of a lack of examples, but because of the sheer glut of them. The top few were the following.

- A telephone company that cut my telephone line off for nearly two days. It still insisted that my line was playing a nice message saying 'This line is temporarily down' when, in fact, there was the sound that I normally associate with 'he was unable to pay his bills'.
- A leading international airline that had checking-in queues of 50 minutes. When I got to the front of the queue, I was told the flight was 'closed' and so I might not have a seat because I was late (potentially messing up my day trip to San Diego, California, in a big way). When I began to gently voice my anxieties, the clerk turned this into an argument, culminating with her suggestion that I 'fly Virgin Atlantic next time'. (Thankfully this company saved itself as the cabin staff were so shocked by my story that they volunteered a complimentary bottle of champagne.) The next time I flew by the same airline (from the same airport), precisely the same thing happened. By coincidence they were doing some market research at Heathrow. Proactively, I offered myself as a volunteer. When I said 'Virgin Atlantic have minuscule queues relative to your airline' the response was, 'Well, perhaps they have fewer customers than we do', to which my response was 'Well, you might have one less next time'.
- The 'Hotel from hell'. A hotel at a major airport served a senior management meeting cold club sandwiches and chips (twice), making us all slightly unwell. This was followed by trapping us in the hotel car park while pretending that there was nothing wrong with the barriers, despite intensive, cross-questioning.
- A TV company.

The award goes to the TV company – an array of leisure channels that we will call Alien TV. This case study adds a lighter ending to our first chapter.

Strategic behaviour and customer value, at Alien TV

Does the way in which an organization behaves strategically have an impact on customer value? I think it certainly does, as we all meet instances of value destruction on a daily basis.

In 1997, a friend of mine moved house. His new house required substantially new furnishings and, on the day of the move, a caravan of vans delivered – on schedule – his new sofa, chairs, bed and other furnishings within an agreed 2.00–5.00 pm timeslot.

However, one particular new service was not delivered. My friend is an avid football fan who supports Arsenal. He desperately wanted the array of leisure channels, now available in addition to the UK's channels 1 to 5, to be installed as soon as he moved in. He was told:

Oh, we can't say when the engineer will call – it might be any time between 9 am and 5 pm.

My friend was initially patient, seeking a more specific fix on the timing of the visit, but the customer service person at the other end refused to be budged.

No, I can't say when the engineer will arrive – it is our customer policy not to give any more specific time than that.

His patience reducing, my friend said:

But this is nineteenth-century coach and horses service, I am a busy person, I can't be in all day, hanging around just for Alien TV to come.

The customer service person was unmoved – it was a take-it-or-leave-it situation.

My friend thus spent the next 15 minutes trying to problem-solve with Alien TV. Presumably, he argued, at some point, a real human being would make their plans on the day of that visit and, presumably, could telephone to at least say whether it would be morning or afternoon.

Well, no. Unless you are lucky and the engineer has a mobile phone, we can't tell you

was the reply.

So you mean that some have a mobile phone and some don't?

said my friend.

Yes

said the Alien TV man.

But why is it that other companies can say that they'll come in the morning or afternoon and you can't

said my friend.

Because our engineers plan the route that best suits them – it reduces our costs

▶

31

said the customer services person.

So it is Alien value 5, customer value 0

said my friend – thinking about a forthcoming football match that he was now looking forward to missing. There was no comment from Alien TV.

Reluctantly admitting defeat, my friend acquiesced and decided to wait in for Alien TV. As he had his own business, there was a considerable cost to him of doing this – either £400 of lost work or a day's holiday (take your pick how you value it). However, as noted earlier, he is a religious Arsenal fan and nowadays most matches are shown via the new satellite TV sports channels on Alien TV so he felt he had to do it.

Well, the day of the Alien TV installation came and went. No engineer came. No calling card dropped through his letter-box. 'Have they gone to another galaxy this week?' my friend thought.

Finally, my friend rang Alien TV. They could not explain why he had not been visited, but he could get his Alien TV installed that Sunday as the engineers were working overtime prior to Christmas.

Sunday came. My friend stayed in all day. He missed seeing his 11-year-old son play football. The man from Alien TV never came. My friend missed seeing Arsenal beat Manchester United 3–2. This was aggravated by the Sunday time-slot for the installation being between 8 am and 8 pm, which meant 12 hours of incarceration. Monday morning, his ansaphone was hit by its first message:

Your engineer's appointment is now 17 November [eight days' time]. Apparently you thought the engineers visit on Sunday, but they don't work on a Sunday.

By now my friend had spent 19 hours waiting for Alien TV. He also felt a fool, as, once he had moved in, he discovered a cable TV box (a competitor of Alien TV) just outside his house, he rang the local cable TV company:

Sure, we have the sports channels. We can install for £15 between 2 pm and 5 pm on Saturday. Yes, we will be there. No, we won't let you down. No, we don't employ Aliens as engineers who do their own thing

was the cable company's response to my friend's panicked questioning.

The trauma caused by the disappointing experience of waiting in for 19 hours and then getting nothing for it does not fade away quickly. Crudely, if we put a value on the utility destroyed by this incident, we have:

	£
Value of a day's holiday forgone	400
Value of a Sunday being kept in for 12 hours	250
Value of missing son's football match	100
Value of missing Arsenal 3, Manchester United 2	50
	800

Although we do not know what costs Alien TV saved by having a service that didn't differentiate between morning and afternoon, I suspect it would not be more than a small percentage of this value destruction of £800.

However, perhaps the ultimate penalty is paid by Alien TV. If we consider that my friend would probably watch Alien TV, on average, for ten years (before ceasing to be a subscriber), then the revenues forgone by Alien TV would be in the order of:

£30 a month × 12 months × 10 years = £3600.

As probably 80 per cent of this revenue becomes profit (due to the very low variable costs of the transmission technology employed by Alien TV), then Alien TV's own value destruction was, in fact:

£3600 × 80% = £2880.

If we translate that into goals scored (roughly), the result is:

My friend 3, Alien TV 1.

CONCLUSION

Strategic behaviour is not a wholly new idea – at least a few strategic thinkers have already highlighted that the behaviour of senior teams in creating and implementing strategy is significant. However, strategic behaviour appears to have been under-emphasized outside the more theoretical texts in strategic management. Also, even here, strategic behaviour is not something that has been deeply understood, let alone as something that we understand so completely that we can manage it well. Strategic behaviour has thus fallen into almost a Bermuda Triangle where the corners are strategic thinking, strategic decision making, and strategic action.

Strategic behaviour is much more than purely a set of 'softer' management processes. As will be seen later, strategic behaviour is a domain of cognition, feeling and territorial manoeuvring, which are all virtually inseparable from one another.

Strategic behaviour (described in Chapters 3–6), is also highly fluid and emergent. It is dependent on the momentum of senior teams, and this momentum at times seems to lead a life of its own. However, perhaps the time is now ripe to re-establish some sense of direction in this disjointed, and frequently chaotic, process.

In the next chapter, you will begin to see how this challenge can be tackled by examining strategic management and strategic behaviour. Figure 1.6 gives a complete 'road map' of the remainder of the book. While the core of the book – Chapters 3–5 – contains the BT case study, Chapters 6, 7 and 8 then draw out the themes of strategic behaviour. These chapters also highlight how management practitioners and theorists alike can come to grips more effectively with this interesting new area that lies between strategic management, organizational behaviour and politics.

SUMMARY

Strategic management has become increasingly preoccupied with intellectual analysis. Thus, although the 'process' of strategic management has emphasized the messiness of strategic decisions, the importance of the actual behaviour of senior managers has been underplayed.

While strategic management theory is helpful in understanding some of the behavioural issues, what is needed is a more in-depth understanding of strategic behaviour. Until organizations can manage strategic behaviour more effectively, they are perhaps destined to suffer – strategically – the everyday effects being felt by their customers and staff alike.

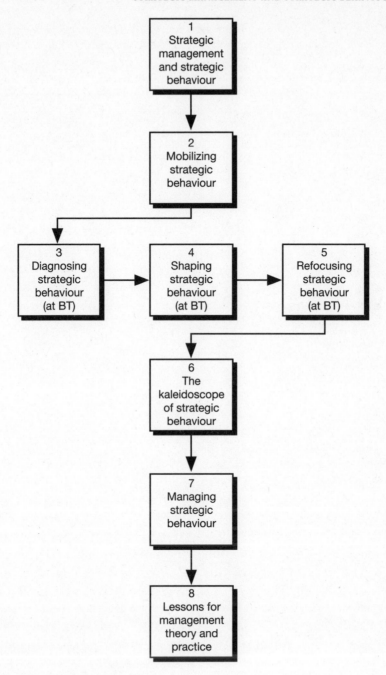

Fig 1.6 The structure of the book

MOBILIZING STRATEGIC BEHAVIOUR

When the speed of a hawk is such that it can strike and kill, this is precision. So it is with skilful warriors – their force is swift, their precision is close. Their force is like drawing a catapult, their precision is like releasing the trigger.

Sun Tzu, *The Art of War*

INTRODUCTION

In this chapter, we look at why strategic behaviour is important and how it can be made less haphazard so that managers can behave more strategically. Thus, this chapter has a more practical and illustrative focus than did Chapter 1.

To illustrate the impact of strategic behaviour, let us look at a perhaps unlikely example – a health farm. However, it is of particular interest as it highlights the extent to which the success of strategy rises or falls depending on how behaviour is managed. I am sure you will find the story of Champneys Health Farm very illuminating.

After the lessons from Champneys have been distilled, in the second part of the chapter the focus is on the practical ways of facilitating strategic behaviour.

Before moving on to looking in detail at Champneys Health Farm, let us just quickly recap what came out of Chapter 1. The main lessons on strategic behaviour were that:

- managers confuse doing some extended budgetary plans and projections with thinking and behaving strategically
- the actual making of strategic decisions typically occurs as a result of a much more haphazard process, one characterized by incremental development
- frequently, even where strategies do crystallize that are clear, coherent and well-articulated, they are still weakly implemented
- the quality of the organizational learning that goes on around strategy development and implementation is often quite weak
- the 'paradigm', or self-concept, of the organization can be extremely strong and may vigorously resist attempts to create a sense of new direction
- the existing pattern of political power may need to be challenged directly.

All of these themes come through strongly in the Champneys case study.

STRATEGIC BEHAVIOUR AT CHAMPNEYS HEALTH FARM

Background

Champneys Health Farm is located at Tring, Hertfordshire. Champneys is a select, rural retreat for its members, who principally reside in and around the Home Counties, England. Traditionally it is a most exclusive retreat, charging near-Savoy prices for its luxurious and relatively exotic services, which are to do with skincare and generally looking after the body.

However, by the time of the recession in the 1990s, Champneys was suffering considerably. Falling demand meant that its cash flow had deteriorated to the point where it experienced an annual cash deficit of a million pounds. Its previous owners decided that enough was enough and sold the business to foreign investors.

In business terms, Champneys was in a strategic turnaround situation. Its new investors decided that a breath of life needed to be injected into Champneys to secure its future. At the same time, Champneys was saddled with a particular set of management behaviours, and these needed to be challenged strongly so that the organization could move forward.

In late 1995, Savoy-trained Lord Thurso was recruited to spearhead Champneys' recovery. As its new Chief Executive, Lord Thurso set about formulating a turnaround plan that would secure Champneys a viable future. At this time Champneys also featured in the series on BBC 2 entitled *Trouble at the Top*. Some of the quotes from Lord Thurso given below are taken from the television programme, some from an interview with myself in late 1997.

Strategic diagnosis

In the tradition of turnaround specialists, Lord Thurso set himself a tight deadline for formulating his turnaround plan – just one month. In the course of that month, Lord Thurso was to spend the bulk of his time listening to Champneys' various stakeholders, particularly:

- its members and regular customers
- its staff
- its current managers.

When Lord Thurso took over Champneys, he was overweight. As a parallel agenda, Lord Thurso also undertook to reduce his weight – co-incidentally, this was in parallel with what became Champneys' own corporate slimming exercise. Most important for Lord Thurso in those early days was to sample Champneys' exotic, health-generating treatments.

Lord Thurso, who at first exhibited a natural scepticism of the worth of these treatments, rapidly became a convert. Admitting to receiving a facial, he rapidly became an enthusiast for the value Champneys offered to its customers.

Lord Thurso's early findings indicated that Champneys suffered from a number of underlying problems (see Figure 2.1, which portrays a 'fishbone', or 'root cause', analysis of its malaise). These included:

- a legacy of under-investment (and decay)
- a decline in standards generally
- an overly-zealous attempt to market Champneys' time-shares, to customers outside Champneys' core customer base
- promises made to members that could not be kept
- a top-heavy management structure
- relatively poor (or inappropriate) management and financial controls
- a lack of a sense of strategic direction generally.

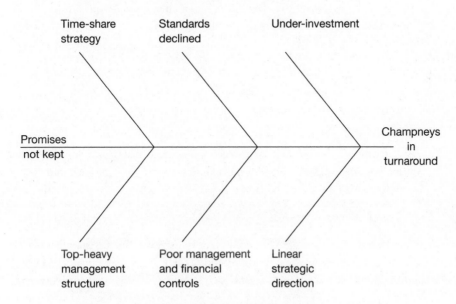

Fig 2.1 Champneys' fishbone analysis – turnaround causes

Lord Thurso, on his first inspection of the property after taking over tells us:

> It is clearly very tired. These rooms would have been considered five star when they were built, but clearly the expectations of five star have changed. It is bland, it is grey, it is a very dead, dull room, it has no colour and it has zero on the excitement scale.　　　　　　　　　　　　　　　　BBC 2

Also, Champneys' strategic positioning itself seemed to be unclear:

> I have asked the question of everybody 'What are we selling?' and I get a lot of long-winded answers; the real answer is that no one has thought about it.　　　　　　　　　　　　　　　　　　　　　　BBC 2

He also reflects:

> And I had also decided – it was as plain as day – that at the heart of the previous strategy, was this wonderful name 'Champneys', which was the great opportunity. But what had been created in the past was the infrastructure for a hundred million pound company, even though it was only a ten million pound company.
>
> It had all these people here who were called brand managers, and none of them understood what a brand was. And that was the extraordinary thing – none of them understood the elementary concept of a brand being a promise made to customers that has values and a character. If you said to them 'What does Champneys mean?', the answer was, they hadn't thought it through.　　　　　　　　　　　　　　　　　　1997 interview

Many of these issues must have been apparent almost as soon as Lord Thurso drove up Champneys' drive. As soon as he arrived, he found a mass of memos from his managers. Lord Thurso says:

> There are piles and piles of paper. It is a fairly classic thing – there are too many managers sending memos to each other. And I am suspicious of any company that is capable of generating so much paper when they are told they are expecting a new Chief Executive.　　　　　　　　　　BBC 2

He also said to me:

> When I arrived here, there were huge reports on everything. I said to them, 'Look, I just don't read them. I don't mind reading a novel by Tolstoy or Dick Francis, but I am not going to read *that*!　　　　　　　　　1997 interview

The following reveals Lord Thurso's quite different management style:

> I tend to communicate by getting up and sitting in someone's office. I loathe
> memos. In my last company I banned them completely for two months. I said,
> 'The next person who writes a memo will be fired'. It was amazing, we didn't
> have a single memo written for two months. It was brilliant, people actually
> started talking to one another. 1997 interview

At the same time, management lacks the fundamental information that it
requires:

> We do not have good financial information. In fact, not only is it not good, it
> is actually awful. The management accounts that I have seen are mathemati-
> cally correct but they are not informative. BBC 2

He said later:

> There was a management structure which didn't work. The management
> reports were gibberish. I asked simple questions: 'Do you know what your cash
> flow is?' and the guy couldn't tell me … . They didn't produce balance sheets.
> They produced huge, thick reports, full of graphs, trend analysis. But the one
> thing that they didn't do was to produce reports where you could find profit,
> where you could find cash flow. I said we will really have to start from scratch.
> I remember sitting on the lawn on holiday wearing my Panama hat and a T-
> shirt and my kilt, and smoking a cigar trying to read through two years of
> drivel, the management accounts … . I can usually work things out and I just
> couldn't make it work. 1997 interview

However, instead of rolling out a turnaround plan straight away, Lord
Thurso spent precious time soliciting the views of all the company's key
stakeholders. This enabled him not only to be absolutely sure that his
chosen path was the right one but also that, in behavioural terms, it was
owned.

This period of listening was also, in fact primarily, so Lord Thurso
could establish a rapport with his new staff. He told me:

> To be honest, I had already made up my mind before I arrived here what I
> would do. I had actually decided before the day that I started that I was going
> to take a million pounds out of the costs. 1997 interview

He continued:

> I wanted them to have thought that I had thought it through. They wouldn't
> have understood that I was capable of thinking it through very quickly, and

43

that it was really clear what had to be done. It was really a very simple problem and it needed some pretty straightforward solutions.

After I arrived I said, 'I will have a month and I will make no decisions until
the end of the month'. It was a good thing. I did fractionally amend certain
decisions but 90 per cent of it was exactly what I had thought [previously].

1997 interview

The above highlights how a leader needs to be able to be a very quick-
thinker, but, at the same time, be able to go at the pace of the organization. This does not come naturally to those senior managers who are
particularly bright.

Lord Thurso realized intuitively that Champneys was the kind of situation that could so easily blow up if a number of stakeholders decided,
rightly or wrongly, that he was 'the wrong man for the job'. Quite
quickly, Lord Thurso concluded from his own personal course of treatments that his operational staff were a real asset – to be retained, nur-
tured and grown:

> The closer I get to the front line, the better I find the troops are. And that is
> very pleasing because if you have good officers and lousy soldiers you have got
> a lot of work to do, but if you have good soldiers and lousy officers, then you
> have to work to train or change the officers. BBC 2

In some contrast, Lord Thurso found the management that he had in-
herited, although up to the task of managing in a more steady state
environment, were not really up to a turnaround. The top-heavy management structure was not only an expense that the business could not
afford, it also impeded the recovery plan.

The change process

However, knowing this posed a major dilemma for Lord Thurso: if he
moved very fast and introduced a new, slimmed-down management
structure, the shock might topple the organization, undermining morale
at the cutting edge of customer service. In these situations, there is probably no single 'right answer'. Arguably, by leaving Champneys' managers
in suspense for one month, he prolonged the agony of uncertainty. On
the other hand, by at least listening to them over this period he ensured
he had a better idea of who was and was not able to make the transition
– and also, in simple, financial terms, how many he could take with him.

Lord Thurso said:

First of all, I wanted a huge change and I wanted that to sink in quickly. I
wanted the troops, the army in the resort, to go 'Hey, this guy might know
what he is talking about'!

I also felt that I only wanted to do it once. I wanted it to be viciously quick
for two reasons: one was to make a point, and the other thing was to say to
people 'That's it. It is done'. And that undoubtedly worked.

1997 interview

Once this first, crucial month was up, Lord Thurso needed to move fast
to communicate and implement the first stages of his turnaround plan.

He reflected, in late 1997, just how serious the problems at the old
head office had become:

And there was a business over there that had been completely neglected at head
office. There was a flip chart in every office, which to me was a symptom of
this very introverted style – the moment anybody had a meeting, someone was
on a flip chart. The whole thing was driven by the processes rather than by the
objectives. If there were objectives, they were tacked onto the process.

People worked hard and interacted and interfaced, and essentially went
around in circles. There was no questioning of 'Why are we here?' or 'What
is the meaning of the universe?'

It was quite clear that I had to make a very definitive statement that there
was a complete change coming. It wasn't quite as bloody as it looked, because
I redeployed quite a lot of the people I had here back into the units. That refocused them on where the action was.

I described it once as 'This head office was once a great black hole which
sucked energy out of the units. Things vanished into it never to be seen again'.
Whereas my idea of a head office is that it should be a tiny, tiny star in the sky,
twinkling light down, completely out of the way.   1997 interview

The above is interesting from several points of view. First, that managers
can mistake brainstorming for genuine strategic thinking. Second, that
strategic thinking may become so divergent that it becomes hard to discern a clear output. Third, this strategic thinking can become uncoupled
from subsequent behaviour and action.

Finally, Lord Thurso highlights the adverse impact of head office's
strategic bureaucracy (of the wrong kind) on business. Indeed, it makes
me think that a more appropriate name for head office would be either
'light office' or, better still perhaps, 'star office'. (In one major inter-

national hotel group, senior managers began to describe 'head office' as 'nose office' – a title more appropriate to its style of activities.)

Potentially, Lord Thurso faced major resistance to his plan. In business terms, there was little alternative but to severely reduce the number of his central management team. Lord Thurso addressed the team as follows at a management meeting:

> Please view my arrival not as something disastrous, but, actually, as an expression of support by our shareholders.
>
> The problem, in a nutshell, is that we are losing money. You are all intelligent people and therefore you will know that there will be a cost-cutting exercise. We have an expression in the fitness centre of 'no pain, no gain', but there will be pain.
>
> We are, with the cost of head office, losing, as a company, approximately one million pounds in cash terms per year. It is my intention and target that, by the end of the next year, we will be cash-breakeven. The direction I have decided to follow is to put Champneys, absolutely and without doubt, at the top of the tree. BBC 2

He had decided to tell them collectively of his decision so that he delivered two clear and separate messages. The first message was that there was an impelling need to restructure and reduce the management resource. The second message was to specific individuals – that they were, or were not, to be members of the future team.

An alternative would have been to only speak to individuals separately – to communicate the need for the change and whether or not they still had a job at the same time. This approach would have had the merit of removing the period of uncertainty during which his managers would have been concerned about their job security. However, equally, it would have meant that, while Lord Thurso was interviewing his managers, some would have heard about the organizational change sooner than the others.

These simple logistics highlight the behavioural implications of making a strategic change in an organization. Whichever way Lord Thurso played it, it would have an effect on individuals' feelings – perhaps one of hurt and fear – and have ramifications for their future and that of the remaining team.

The impact of these redundancies was obviously severe for the managers. Champneys' Property Manager, Willie Serplis, attempted to put a brave face on it as he came smiling to the television interview following his meeting with Lord Thurso. His smile quickly faded as he told us:

> Do you want to ask the question then ... 'How are you?' Not very happy. I just lost my job, which is better knowing, but what can I do? You want to be angry with someone or something, but it doesn't make sense. You can dress it up in all the esoteric bullshit you know – downsizing, redundancy – but the reality is, for no fault of my own, I have just been fired ... .   BBC 2

Lord Thurso himself looked emotionally strained when he was asked how he felt about this part of the process:

> I would find it hard to sleep if I felt that anything I was doing was wrong in any way. I dislike doing it, but it is a necessary operation that has to be done on the company. All that one can do is to do it as humanely and profession-ally as one can.
>
> Most of them have been angry because, at the end of the day, we all like to think that we have a value in an organization and, effectively, when you are made redundant someone is saying that you don't have a value in the organ-ization. When I say that it isn't to do with your performance, it is to entirely do with the financial structure of the company, it actually doesn't help them very much.   BBC 2

It is not hard to imagine what the atmosphere must have been like within the management block at Champneys as the reality sank in that it was the end of an era. It would be hard for those going, but those staying realized that they would be expected to achieve a quantum shift in the level of effectiveness – if the business were to come back into profit.

It was then Lord Thurso's turn to address his operational staff. He appeared to be in a lighter mood as he informed his staff not merely about the severity of the situation, but also of the fact that he was not planning other job cuts:

> The last part of the strategy, and the bit that does concern all of you, is that New Court and the concept of a headquarters is going to be quite radically scaled down. There are 22 people sitting here and we have probably half the number of places actually available. You are intelligent and you will have worked this out. And therefore some people are going to have to be made redundant ... . And I do recognize the pain that this will cause you. I am sorry that some of you will be going, but please understand that it is nothing to do with you and your capability. It is simply about how this business has been run over the past few years and the requirement to put it on a proper cash footing.

Finally, I would like to give you a little thought. All my life I have been involved in giving first-class service to people and I believe it is a wonderful thing to do. Be always ready to say 'yes' whenever a client or guest comes to see you and asks for something and you are tempted to say 'no'. Stop, think, and that will help us to create a level of service unheard of in this country. BBC 2

Lord Thurso's own larger-than-life character was a crucial ingredient in signalling that the changes necessary were very, very real. He reflects:

But the key figure at the top should have a kind of evangelical fanaticism about what the strategy is. Unless you have this, you are not going to manage to convince people. For example, last year I called our plans 'going from good to great'. And we didn't go from good to great, we got better. So I said 'This is good to great part II'. We could be back here next year doing part III or even part IV, but one day we will get there and I ain't leaving here until we do.

I believe that all human beings are capable of change for the better. This may be an optimistic view, but I therefore start from the premise that it is better to work with people rather than change them. I find that the grass on the other side of the fence is not often greener.

When you are sorting out a business and getting the headcount right, yes, you have to cut to get it right. But some people would go in and say, 'I can't work with that General Manager' and fire them and get another one. And then after six months you get another one. Personally, I prefer to say 'Why is this not working? Let us look at it and actually help this person.' I find that you then get staff who are more loyal. 1997 interview

However, this involves recognizing that staff's agendas may not be nicely aligned with the vision. Lord Thurso tells us about the practicalities of achieving the necessary culture change to radically shift old behaviour patterns:

If I am honest with you, I am only a small part of the way through. All the things, these wonderful things that managers do, that is all part of our game. But the guy at the bottom says 'Sod you, I only have 40 hours to do my job'. What he is saying to you is 'If you want me to do this, give me a reason'.

And that guy at the bottom isn't going to say, 'Wow, that guy at the top – he is a "zing", now I will suddenly smile at customers'. There has got to be something in it for him. And part of it is being controlled, led, cajoled, pushed into it. And a part of it is being rewarded, feeling nice, all of the rest of it. It is a huge culture change that virtually every company in this country needs to actually genuinely understand what a customer-orientated organization is. I have grave difficulty in thinking of a truly customer-orientated organization in the United Kingdom. I mean, there must be one somewhere.

Mine isn't yet. It is a tremendous culture change.   1997 interview

Besides dealing with internal stakeholders, Lord Thurso had to manage the expectations of Champneys' members, whose business was needed to secure a successful future. These members had been disappointed in the past by the prior management who had, perhaps, set up expectations about improvements in standards that had not, or could not have, been delivered.

Lord Thurso was quick to realize that the 'Health-For-Life' time-sharing scheme needed to be halted:

> From what I have seen, the constant push-push-push on 'Health-For-Life' has given the wrong impression in the marketplace. I think maybe we should cut that right back.   BBC 2

He also determined that the physical facilities and amenities at Champneys did not provide a sustainable foundation for its future strategy:

> What a great architect friend of mine once described as the 'wow' factor. What we have got here is the 'er' factor. What we need is a 'wow' factor.
>
>   BBC 2

So, besides the organizational changes Lord Thurso instigated, he also set about developing an ambitious project to revitalize the physical fabric of Champneys. This included:

- a major uplift in the entrance and façade to the central building – and to the driveway itself
- conversion of the management block to produce 20 additional treatment rooms. This, Lord Thurso hoped, would provide the spur to expand Champneys' customer base.

These renovations, Lord Thurso hoped, would provide a further benefit – signals to Champneys' employees that the company was genuinely going to be set on the road to a prosperous future.

The turnaround plan

To achieve these plans, Lord Thurso needed to build the confidence of his investors, who might well have thought that a turnaround was possible without major investment of this order. Lord Thurso realized that, to provide the basis for this confidence, he would need to achieve a number of things:

- the restructuring of management had to be implemented successfully
- better financial planning and control needed to be stabilized – with the help of its new Finance Director, who Lord Thurso had brought in
- his restructuring would need to have delivered the required cost savings
- although a gap still remained (to break even) with these cost savings, this gap would need to be closed by expanding revenues
- to achieve this, the quality of service and standards generally at Champneys had to improve considerably – to the point where members felt a real difference and new members were brought in.

Although cost savings of half a million pounds per annum were achieved relatively quickly, it proved much slower to improve sales by improving customer confidence. However, within one year Champneys managed to break even. So, Lord Thurso was able to then put into effect his plan to obtain enough investment to reposition Champneys as an outstanding health resort.

The overseas investors were able to give Lord Thurso the vote of confidence he needed in order to move on to implementing Stage 2 of the turnaround – a major upgrading programme. So, at last, all the planks of Lord Thurso's future strategy were in place.

This is the story of Champneys' strategic turnaround, but told mainly from the point of view of the business. However, if we look at this situation from a more behavioural point of view, we find that this dimension has perhaps even more importance than more tangible areas of change.

The behavioural drivers

To begin with, if we look at the key forces enabling and constraining this change (see Figure 2.2), the most important forces are more behavioural in nature than anything else.

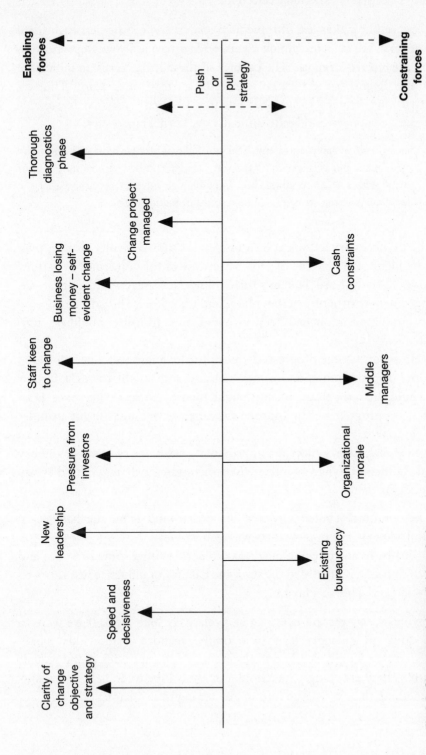

Fig 2.2 Champneys' force field analysis

Enabling forces

Constraining forces

Push or pull strategy

Thorough diagnostics phase

Change project managed

Cash constraints

Business losing money – self-evident change

Staff keen to change

Middle managers

Pressure from investors

Organizational morale

New leadership

Existing bureaucracy

Speed and decisiveness

Clarity of change objective and strategy

Figure 2.2 makes use of force field analysis, which depicts each force as an enabling or constraining arrow. Each arrow is drawn in proportion to its perceived strength. The balance of these forces gives an indication of the degree of difficulty involved. In this case, Lord Thurso's turnaround strategy turns what might have been a *Mission Impossible* project into one of moderate difficulty. As Lord Thurso says:

> You do have to have a strategy. You can fight battles without a strategy and have success, but it is a pretty haphazard thing. You have got to have a clear idea of where you are going, but, equally, you have to recognize that the achievement of the strategy will be a series of tactical steps.
>
> 1997 interview

It is also necessary to look at how implementation difficulty changes over time. Figure 2.3 gives an approximate view of this 'difficulty over time' curve. Initially, Lord Thurso's turnaround faced severe difficulties, but, once the new structure was in place, and once Lord Thurso's new vision for the organization had been unveiled, this difficulty would be mitigated.

However, as time progressed, this difficulty might well have increased as the organization found a new stability and sought to resist further changes. In turn, this difficulty might then begin to reduce once Lord Thurso's programmes to improve customer service and to shift attitudes begin to bite.

Next, Figure 2.4 plots the approximate positions of some of the key stakeholders who had an influence on this strategic change. This diagram highlights that:

- before Lord Thurso unveiled his turnaround plan, the balance of influence in the organization was against him
- equally, by introducing new stakeholders, exiting some old ones and by appealing directly to the staff, the balance of influence was reversed – in Lord Thurso's favour.

Obviously, this picture is drawn at a relatively high level. If we were to go down to a deeper level (that of the agendas of individual stakeholders) we would clearly find difference in the attitudes of individuals within these groupings. Stakeholder analysis (like force field analysis) is something that we will go into in greater depth in Chapter 7.

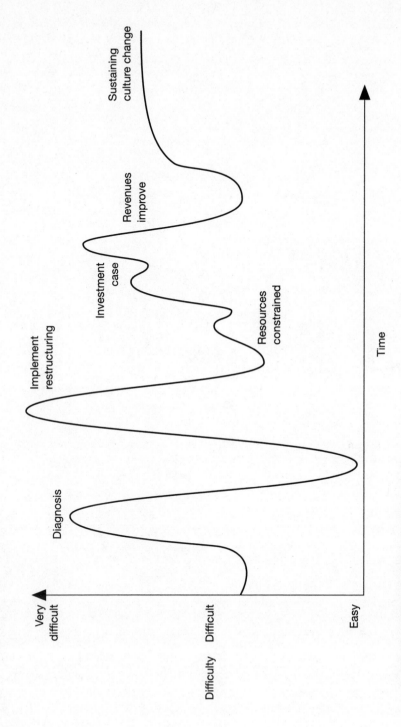

Fig 2.3 Champneys' 'difficulty over time' curve

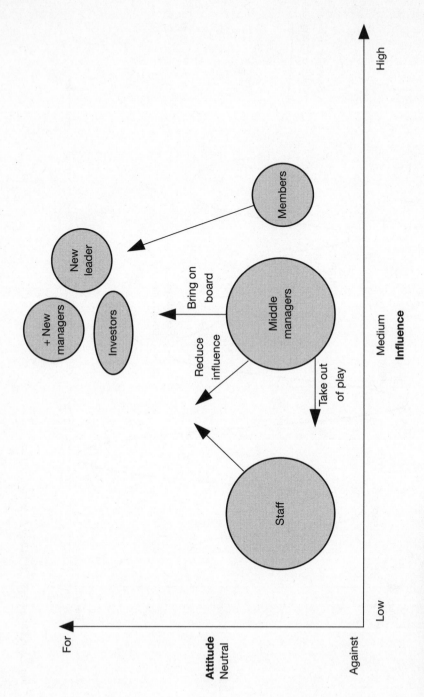

Fig 2.4 Champney's stakeholder analysis

To understand the influence patterns of these stakeholders, some additional factors need to be borne in mind.

- The agendas of stakeholders are not fixed, but will change over time as new issues arise and perceptions change within the organization.
- At any point in time, agendas may be fluid and ambiguous, particularly at the start of the turnaround. Key stakeholders, particularly middle managers, may not have any clear attitude at all. Although they may have some core agendas (such as 'I want to hang on to my job'), these might be very limited. Even here, core agendas might be conditional on Champneys being seen as a congenial atmosphere to work in, given its new leadership. Never assume, therefore, that attitudes and underlying agendas of stakeholders are always given.
- Individuals within one group will influence the agendas of others within the group. Via the informal network, opinion leaders will signal their approval or disapproval of particular actions.
- You may need to break down the change into a number of subchanges – as stakeholder positions will vary according to what is being implemented. For instance, a stakeholder may approve of Lord Thurso's plans to renovate the buildings, also approve of his plans to end the 'Health-For-Life' promotion, but be violently against running a smaller department.

Influencing stakeholders, equally, demands considerable leadership skills. Lord Thurso elaborates:

> You need a lot of managers in a business who don't necessarily have to be a leader themselves. But you damn well need one leader. You need a leader at each unit level. The leader doesn't have to do the things that a manager does that well. One of these things is asking people to execute the strategy. The first thing [for a leader] is the 'vision thing'. It is having a strategy, it is knowing how to think strategically or to have a process so that you can bring the organization to the point where it has a clear goal.   1997 interview

Lord Thurso's own vision for Champneys is profoundly simple. Lord Thurso prefers the idea of 'vision' to 'mission', principally because mission statements are harder to grasp onto, particularly in terms of the behaviours that are implied by them:

> If you cannot remember a mission statement (I cannot remember our old one), if you have to refer to something, that's wrong. To me, any mission

statement which is 'we will have care for our customers, be nice to our staff, be nice to grey squirrels on Sundays', you know, you have gone to sleep.

It has got to be something that encapsulates the spirit. 'Nowhere else makes you this good' (Champneys) – yes, it is a spirit statement. That's why, NASA's – 'To get a man on the moon' – makes sense. At Champneys it is 'Nowhere else makes you feel this good' – and that should apply to the staff as well.

1997 interview

Champneys Health Farm thus demonstrates how crucial the strategic behaviour is to managing strategic change. Here the rational side to 'analysis' and 'choice' models of strategy play more of a minor role compared with Lord Thurso's skill at manoeuvring through the interpersonal minefield. This minefield could easily have thwarted his strategic change ambitions.

KEY POINTERS FROM CHAMPNEYS

In summary, here are the key pointers for managing strategic behaviour.

- Stakeholder management is absolutely central to the strategy process. Accordingly, ample time should be devoted to analyzing the current and potentially future positions of stakeholders – and their driving agendas.
- Leadership is crucial in a situation where stakeholders are likely to actively resist implementation efforts. This leadership requires a degree of evangelical enthusiasm, a very explicit statement about the strategic vision and great practical tenacity in implementing that vision.
- Achieving headway depends not merely on forward progress, but on building a sufficient 'stakeholder platform' that can be used to achieve leverage from. This involved (at Champneys) key appointments of a new Finance Director and Property Manager – and winning over Champneys' front-line staff.
- The difficulty over time of a particular strategic programme will change. The shifts in difficulty need to be anticipated and managed rather than just coped with.

We can now see, graphically, how the themes that were distilled from Chapter 1 have been brought to life in the Champneys case. First, prior to Lord Thurso's arrival, managers were absorbed in short-term budgetary control and short-term projections. They did not seem to be able to think (or behave) outside the status quo.

Also, prior to the turnaround, Champneys' strategies appeared to have been developed in a relatively haphazard way. The most obvious example of this was the Health-For-Life (time-sharing) initiative. This strategic thrust was not well supported by the Champneys' resource base. It also seemed to conflict with Champneys' more up-market competitive positioning. The Health-For-Life project, although clearly not working effectively, had not generated any organizational learning or challenge – the Marketing Department was just intent on trying to make the formula work. More seriously, the deeper decisions that needed to be made to achieve a turnaround were not apparently in the frame on Lord Thurso's entry. Finally, Lord Thurso clearly needed to make a most direct challenge to the existing mindset. This meant that he had to shake the very foundations of the political boundaries.

Case postscript

After talking to Lord Thurso at length, the thought crossed my mind, 'Why shouldn't I repeat Lord Thurso's experience and stay at Champneys myself?' So, in December 1997, I visited Champneys myself for the day – with a friend.

We both found the experience like that of being carried along an hedonistic conveyor belt. At no time could we detect that morale suffered or was there the perception of an organizational change bomb having gone off.

The staff seemed to be genuinely excited about the developments at Champneys. They particularly mentioned the extensions to the range of treatments that were now possible given the expansion in treatment facilities.

The Champneys case thus highlights the need to accompany strategic thinking with a realignment of behaviour, not only at top team level, but throughout the organization. This need is equally applicable to behaviour associated with either strategic analysis or implementation.

There are some pointers that can be of major help in strategic facilitation, including:

● setting the behavioural climate
● monitoring non-verbal behaviour

- managing energy levels
- the out-of-body experience
- value and difficulty over time curves
- designing a strategic workshop.

Setting the behavioural climate

To help oil the strategic process a tool (developed jointly by myself and Dave King at Dowty Communications) is invaluable. This deals with the undesirable 'P' forms of strategic behaviour.

When beginning a strategy workshop or contentious meeting, you should ask all participants to brainstorm the 'P' behaviours that you want to avoid. To add some humour and reality, anyone caught using 'P' behaviour is asked to contribute £1 to the facilitator's or chairman's favourite charity. A list of possible 'P' behaviours is as follows:

- political
- parochial
- procrastinating
- posturing
- protectionism
- pretending
- pessimism
- pettiness
- preservation.

The real value of the 'P' process tool is that you rarely have to use it. However, if you are facing a 'P' behaviour event or meeting and you don't get the 'P' behaviours out up front, then invariably the event becomes a quagmire. For example, when facilitating the development of international strategy for a healthcare company some years ago, I used the 'P' behaviour technique to clear the air before we began. Potentially this could have been a very contentious session, particularly as there was some distrust between the British managers and those of another European country – which was the main business outside the UK and had been underperforming since its acquisition.

Remarkably, the 'P' behaviours only surfaced during this workshop on the second day and then just once. This really surprised me as I had expected a tough ride.

Monitoring non-verbal behaviour

It is often said that at least 80 per cent of human behaviour occurs at the non-verbal level. If you doubt this at all, imagine the last time that you had a conversation about some sensitive issues by telephone. It is very likely that you had to imagine (probably by visualization) the person you were talking to. Where you have not previously met that person, it may be particularly difficult to work out where they are coming from.

We do take for granted the influence of non-verbal behaviour, yet it can give us important clues as to what behavioural influences lie beneath the surface. Particular signs to look for are managers with their:

- arms (and/or legs) crossed – this is a sign of defensiveness
- bodies squirming in their chairs – signifying acute discomfort with where the discussion appears to be leading
- bodies slumped in their chairs – indicating withdrawal or disinterest
- faces taught, looking wracked with tension
- voices faltering, with little strength – signifying acute nervousness.

A facilitator who does not invest a significant proportion of their attention in monitoring non-verbal behaviour may well fall foul of a serious behavioural breakdown. Further, this non-verbal behaviour should not just be observed, but can also be questioned by the facilitator. For example, one might say 'Joe, you look a bit worried about that issue, do you have any big concerns about how difficult it will be to implement this area of change?'

Managing energy levels

Energy levels of a team will fluctuate considerably during any kind of strategic event. These energy levels depend on:

- **personal energy states**   the time of day, the duration of the event, the amount of work done previously, the degree of frustration already experienced with previous issues
- **interactive energy generated**   the degree to which a team gels together, generating energy via the interchange of ideas, interpersonal challenges and, frequently, the humour injected into the process
- **interactive energy dissipated via interpersonal clashes**   a feeling of 'getting stuck' on issues, that there is no way forward, or of individuals being cynical, protective or defensive

- **the team process**   including the clarity of the strategic event's objectives, the appropriateness of any analysis tools used, whether or not the key questions for the event are well defined and whether or not participants are very clear about what the level of outputs is going to be.

The out-of-body experience

The 'out-of-body experience' involves seeing the world through the eyes, thoughts and feelings of:

- all key stakeholders attending the event
- individual stakeholders.

This gives managers a first cut of stakeholder positions. Where a number of issues are likely to be discussed, then this analysis can be done quite distinctively for each issue. Obviously this opens up quite a considerable area for potential thinking. Here it is appropriate to identify those issues that are likely to be particularly sensitive – the 'hot' issues.

Further, it may be useful to look at how individuals may interact (given their agendas) on a specific issue. This can be used to draw out behavioural scenarios of how the debate will actually run. Here it may be fruitful to do some 'story telling'. For example:

> On the diversification issue, Peter will begin by highlighting concerns about the proposition 'If we don't do it, we will be vulnerable to reduced turnover in our car business', while Sandra will express her fears about whether or not we have the competences to diversify effectively, particularly as in her last role this kind of strategy was attempted but proved to be a disaster.

To construct a behavioural scenario, first identify what is likely to be on the agendas of each and every stakeholder. Then imagine how the issues will come up in the workshop or meeting and tell yourself stories about how the key players will interact, with what outcomes. For example, imagine you are about to facilitate a strategy workshop with the top team of a major communications business. The team has a new Chief Executive (who, although promoted internally, is anxious to make a real impact in moving the business forward over the next few years). His predecessor moved on to become Group Chief Executive and is a hard act to follow.

The team falls into two main camps. There is a new Finance Director and a new Technology Director (both appointed from outside) and a newly promoted Commercial Director (Europe). The Administration

Director, Services Director and Commercial Director (Far East) were on the old team, and are long-standing appointments.

Two of the long-standing appointments are still sceptical of the value of having a strategic plan anyway, feeling it will become bureaucratic and unwieldly. The new appointees are more obviously enthusiastic for a fresh sense of direction and, possibly, even for change. The old appointees (rightly) wanted to preserve those things that had made the core business so successful in the past. However, these differences in views could be more apparent than real.

In my behavioural Scenario 1 – 'muddling through' – the more sceptical directors feel threatened by the sense of challenge to what has worked in the past and begin to pick away at attempts to generate some genuinely new strategic thinking and breakthroughs.

In this scenario, frustration mounts as the team are unable to progress through the agenda. The Chief Executive tries to intervene to state that he really does believe the discussions have merit. I, as facilitator, end up having to go for a much more modest outcome: resolution of three major strategic dilemmas and action planning for how another four areas will be dealt with subsequently. However, we fall short of a strategic plan framework and the workshop is rated as 'Overall, good – better than past meetings'.

In Scenario 2 – 'Golden breakthrough' – the pre-interviews that I conducted pay off. There is, quite surprisingly, uniformly high buy-in to the process. Some discussions have to be tightly facilitated (as all members of the team are particularly bright, articulate and want to have their full say), but we do cover 80 per cent of the key issues and dilemmas.

In this scenario, during the two-day workshop, a couple of key challenges dawn on the team. Not only do they believe it was fruitful, but, even before the workshop closes, they have ordered a second one to deal with implementation analysis.

Having done this (high-level) behavioural scenario analysis, I would then begin to think about how I could leverage Scenario 2 into Scenario 1. I would also go through each one of the key strategic questions, imagining where the most sensitivities would arise and from where. This highlights just how much thinking is required to design (and run) a strategic workshop in a particularly challenging situation.

Value and 'difficulty over time' curves

It is also wise to anticipate the likely value that will be added over time during the strategic event. This might be added principally during the 'analysis' part of the workshop or the generating new 'options' phase or in making strategic choices or in discussing the implementation issues (and plans).

Equally, at what point in the day will the greatest difficulties be encountered? How does this relate to the running order of the issues, the stakeholder positions and agendas, and the behavioural scenarios imagined in the previous section? In the earlier illustration of the communications business, I imagined that the greatest difficulty would occur when debating where future resources should be prioritized both in external development (late in Day 1) and in developing internal capability (early in Day 2). This can be represented pictorially as a curve plotting the 'difficulty over time'.

DESIGNING A STRATEGIC WORKSHOP

There now follows some very practical advice on designing, running and getting maximum value from strategy workshops.

Although workshops can generate disproportionate value (and vision), this can be diluted considerably where:

- there is inadequate pre-planning regarding issues, the process and outputs
- there is no facilitation or where this is ineffective
- there are no plans in place to deal with the outputs and to move it on to the next phase
- there are no tools to help managers make progress (use the tools and checklists contained in this book).

Twelve key questions to answer, when you are planning to run a workshop

1　What is the objective of the workshop?

2　How does it relate to other initiatives?

3　What are the key outputs (learning, problem definition, action plans, behavioural shift and so on) and how will these be documented and communicated, and to whom?

4　Who needs to be involved?

5　How will it be positioned in the organization and by whom?

6　Who will facilitate and are they seen as competent and impartial?

7　Where should it be held and what facilities are required?

8　What are the next steps following the workshop likely to be?

9　What key barriers and blockages may arise and how will these be dealt with and by whom?

10　What specific activities will be undertaken and what will this input require?

11　How will these be broken down into discussion groups and who will be in each one?

12　How long will the workshop need to be to make substantial progress on each issue and what happens if tasks are incomplete?

Experience shows that it is essential to consider all these questions at length, rather than rushing into a workshop on a particular issue with merely a broad agenda. The questions emphasize both content and process, and involve thinking through how these interrelate. They also involve analyzing both current and future context. This process provides high-quality data and also helps thinking regarding how the outputs from the workshop will feed back into the management process, in detail and in advance.

It is vital to structure the content of each workshop so that it focuses on key questions. For example, for a fashion retailer a workshop could be set out as follows.

Morning

- What is our current position in both womenswear and menswear markets?

- What options exist for us to develop new products for new or existing markets?

- What competitive advantage would we be able to achieve and sustain, and how?

Afternoon

- What would the implementation implications be, and what would the direct and indirect costs be?

- Broadly speaking, what are the likely financial implications (and risks) of any new developments?

- What are our next steps?

Where you are dealing with particularly important or sensitive issues (or both) it may be advisable to use an external facilitator. There are situations in which having an external rather than an internal facilitator can help, not merely in terms of objectivity, but also because they can orchestrate the process so that it is genuinely a politically level playing field (otherwise you may be attempting the equivalent of do-it-yourself brain surgery).

The benefits of using an external facilitator (over an internal one or not having one at all) are:

- **speed** the team should make progress much faster
- **outputs** these should be more thorough, well-tested and complete
- **insights** a skilled external facilitator should be able to oil the flow of ideas, identify blind spots and provide ideas of their own
- **openness** an external facilitator should be able to elicit doubts that may have been exposed and generate a balanced, but incisive, discussion
- **implementation** an external facilitator should be capable of anticipating ahead what the key implementation requirements feel like relative to capability.

The costs and risks of using an external facilitator are:

- **search costs** of finding someone with the necessary skills and whose style fits with that of the management team
- **actual costs** these can vary dramatically from the small independent to the large consulting firm
- **risks** of the facilitator not being as good as their marketing presentation suggested
- **overdependency** the facilitator is relied on to the extent that the team becomes dependent on them, in order to make progress
- **the Holy Grail** by hiring a facilitator, management see them as being the primary agent of progress to use another analogy, as being not merely the conductor of the orchestra, but also the first, second and third violin).

CONCLUSION

Strategic behaviour involves a seamless interplay between managers of cognitive, emotional and territorial variables, both at visible and less visible levels.

The Champneys case study illustrated how this interplay should not be allowed to drift into formlessness, but can actually be managed deliberately. However, to achieve this, highly honed leadership skills are required – skills that will later on be subsumed into the category of 'meta-behaviours'.

Managing strategic behaviour requires astute analytical skills combined with a deep sensitivity to managers' emotional states. It also requires being able to manipulate organizational politics so that traditional territorial expectations and ambitions are continually challenged, especially by facilitating strategic behaviour.

SUMMARY

At Champneys Health Farm, we saw how strategic behaviour can become increasingly introverted and removed from the real world. The injection of a new catalyst – in the form of Lord Thurso – was needed to break up the old way of behaving and thinking. This intervention was able to put Champneys on a new organizational track – back to strategic health.

The Champneys case also highlighted the need for great tenacity in order to achieve a fundamentally new set of behaviours – even within a new structure and a new set of business imperatives.

For many organizations lacking a Lord Thurso figure, it may be helpful to use either internal or external facilitation. Facilitation can draw from a wealth of approaches and tools to oil the wheels of strategic behaviour.

Part II

STRATEGIC BEHAVIOUR IN ACTION

DIAGNOSING STRATEGIC BEHAVIOUR

Those who know when to fight and when not to fight are victorious. Those who discern when to use many or few traps are victorious. Those who face the unprepared with preparation are victorious.

Sun Tzu, *The Art of War*

INTRODUCTION

In this chapter, the factors at work in strategic behaviour in a real management team are explored, as well as how it can start to be managed. This is achieved by using a model of strategic behaviour developed in the course of the case study of British Telecom. Senior BT managers were observed in everyday strategic interaction. The team was then helped towards behaving more strategically. This action research involved studying the team's behaviours in a natural state, by means of interviews and a number of strategy workshops (for the full process, see Figure 3.1).

In Chapters 3 to 6, you will see how strategic behaviour has several dimensions. The forces that are uppermost in driving strategic behaviour are identified and then the question of how it might be managed more effectively is examined. At the end of each main section, the wider implications for behaving strategically are highlighted.

STRATEGIC BEHAVIOUR AT BT

Introduction to the BT team

British Telecom (BT) is a major player in today's global telecommunications industry. Although its traditional base is in the UK, it also has operations in Europe and elsewhere.

BT invests considerable amounts of money in technology development and its communications network. This investment totals several billions of pounds per annum – a considerable commitment, occurring at a time of considerable change and upheaval in the industry, both nationally and internationally. BT needs to anticipate technological changes, pre-empt them and track them, which is a tough challenge considering the number and diversity of competitive, technological and market issues that face BT at any one point in time.

71

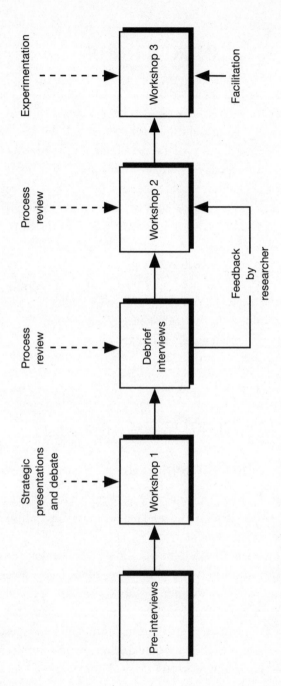

Fig 3.1 Strategic behaviour – the action research process

A number of areas in BT scan for external changes from a number of points of view. The remit of the department that will be studied here is 'technical strategy'. Thus, this department will be called the Technological Strategy Department, or TSD.

TSD consists of a significant number of staff whose activities are steered by a continually changing team of senior managers, headed by a very experienced BT manager, Andy. Andy has the task of prioritizing the work of this key department internally, aligning its results with the expectations of a number of internal stakeholders. These stakeholders embrace a number of senior managers, both at the centre of the group and also senior managers spread throughout BT's UK business and its international businesses.

The senior team within TSD is, typically, seven strong. These managers come from a multitude of backgrounds – economics, engineering and marketing. Besides differences in professional disciplines, there are also, inevitably, differences in personalities. These personality differences make the team environment a challenging place to be. This is particularly true if we overlay this fact with three layers of further complexity, which are technical, strategic and organizational.

The key members of the team at the start of the research study at TSD were:

Andy
David
Bonnie
Keith(A)
Keith(B)
Tim
John

John moved on three months after the start of the study, followed soon afterwards by Tim and Bonnie – the team is continually adjusting.

With the exception of David, Bonnie and John, all managers have had strong technical careers within BT. David and Bonnie both have marketing backgrounds, with David being trained in economics and Bonnie having a flair for creative thinking (following her earlier training, which, interestingly, was in English literature). John has, in the past, been both a psychologist and an architect.

Beneath the management team is a significant number of staff, all working on technical strategy projects. These projects have a considerable influence ultimately on BT's worldwide investment programme in technology (around £2.0 billion annually in the UK alone).

Natural state strategic behaviour of the BT team

The TSD team, like many others elsewhere, meets intermittently. Aside from a weekly (and more tactical) management meeting, its main meetings are:

- occasional away-days
- its annual strategic review, which occurs over February to June of each year.

During its meetings, the team members discuss at considerable length the technical and market-related issues of a more strategic nature facing BT. Before becoming immersed in these debates, let us first reflect on what the psychologists say is likely to go on during such sessions.

For instance, as Milliken and Vollrath (1991) have written:

> Whilst growing numbers of strategy researchers have recognized the importance of groups in strategic decision making, most research has treated strategic decision making as though it was a unitary task with a single outcome.
>
> Research on the performance of small groups with decision-making or problem-solving tasks showed that group effectiveness depends, to a great extent, on the specific nature of the group's task, as well as on the type of decision-making processes used, and on the nature of the group composition.

This rationalist bias is a characteristic of the wider literatures in psychology generally. As Boland and Schultze (1995) argue:

> This image of cognition is overwhelming, saturating not only the cognitive sciences but extending through other social sciences and our everyday understanding of cognition itself ... . Cognition's dominance has suppressed recognition and study of ... the narrative mode [how we talk to each other] where we selectively isolate events in our experience, populate the events with actors which have particular histories, motivations and intentions, and tell stories by setting the events and actors in a meaningful sequence.

Talk itself is thus at best partly rational – often being more emotional in its significance. This manner of talking by managers has its own role to play in manifesting the strategic behaviour of a management team. Boland and Schultze continue:

> Talking can have a haphazard quality if it is the expression of the speaker – the making of noise whilst putting a statement out into the world – irrespective of content or context.

So, talking is often thinking out loud, and often these thoughts are only semi-formed. This puts a different complexion on our views of how cognition works within strategic behaviour. In reality, it is infused with other more emotional (affective) elements and influenced by what appears to just come out randomly.

This randomness needs to be borne in mind when we examine what is said in the 'talk' of the TSD team. Much management discussion, particularly at a strategic level, appears to serve the purpose of manifesting fragmentary ideas, impressions, feelings and judgements. To one unfamiliar with the rich context of a management team, this talk may seem to be a sort of 'strategic soup' that seems inherently unmanageable. Over the course of this case study, it will be seen that the interactions of strategic behaviour – perhaps the main ingredient of this soup – can, in fact, be guided, albeit in a fluid way.

Overview of the model of strategic behaviour

Having introduced the TSD team, it is now appropriate to examine the model for managing strategic behaviour shown in Figure 3.2. This model was created by putting BT managers' observed behaviours into natural categories, and then mapping how these categories were interrelated. The model itself comes from clusters of grounded categories (ie categories generated directly from like groupings of data).

The lower-level categories are gathered together in a number of broader groupings, including:

- strategic tasks
- analytical processes
- individual characteristics
- interpersonal processes
- dynamic processes
- team interaction
- meta-behaviour
- organizational context
- outputs.

75

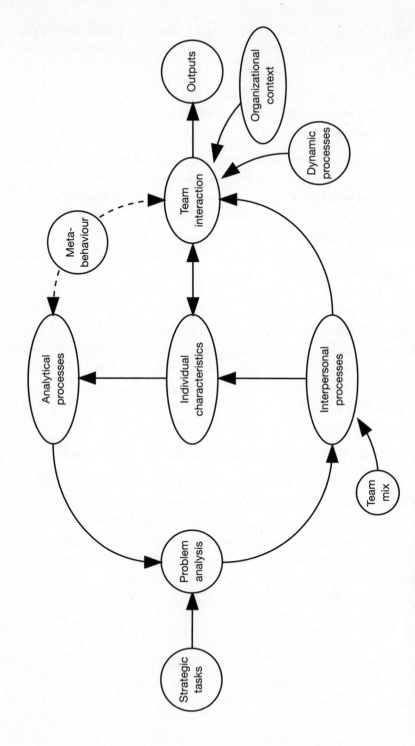

Fig 3.2 Managing strategic behaviour – the big picture

By strategic tasks, is meant, essentially, problem analysis, which splits into the following categories:

- constraints
- evidence
- impossibility
- interlinkage
- non-linearity
- problem architecture
- uncertainty
- the unthinkable.

'Analytical processes' breaks down into:

- anticipating
- brainstorming
- clarifying
- consolidation
- creative thinking
- criticizing
- expanding
- judging
- justifying
- picking apart
- probing
- questioning
- scene-setting
- scoping
- synthesis.

Some of the above categories require interpretation. For instance, you might categorize an utterance as 'picking apart' because it is going into detail about a particular topic. However, equally it might contain an element of 'expanding' on existing ideas. Where more than one category applies, the more prominent one is listed first.

'Individual characteristics' breaks down into, first, cognitive ones, then behavioural. Cognitive categories include:

- behavioural style
- cognitive style
- memory
- personal background
- personal careers
- personal strategic agenda
- personal traits
- team roles.

Behavioural categories include:

- anxiety
- comfort level
- frustration
- sensitivity
- seriousness
- vulnerability
- worry.

Next, 'interpersonal processes' (the processes concerned with personal interplay) comprise:

- agreeing
- challenging
- championing
- compromising
- consensus-building
- disagreeing
- ignoring
- influencing
- interrupting
- listening
- peer pressure
- sounding out
- summarizing
- tolerating
- winning over.

'Team interaction' (or patterns of behaviour between individuals) is again quite complicated, made up of subcategories:

- behavioural turbulence
- breakdown
- conflict
- excitement
- exposing findings
- hostility
- dominating conversation
- personality clash
- withdrawal.

'Dynamic processes' (the behaviours that affect a team's ability to cover the desired ground) comprise:

- diving in
- rushing
- setting time frames
- shunting
- slippage.

'Diving in' is concerned with getting rapidly into a debate without thinking about both process and content issues very deeply, while 'rushing' is trying to force the pace once the debate has begun. 'Shunting' is behaviour that reprogrammes tasks into future activities (due to time constraints). 'Slippage' is activity that has taken longer than anticipated, but which has not been accompanied by rescheduling.

Categories of 'meta-behaviour' (that which helps to steer other behaviours) include:

- breaking off
- facilitation
- feedback
- helicoptering up
- humour
- management tools (using them)
- monitoring value (of outputs)
- prioritizing
- reflecting.

Meta-behaviour here comprises a number of behavioural categories (including, for instance, leadership) which focus on coordinating the team's overall behaviour and process. Interpersonal processes concern the routines of interacting (including making presentations, for instance), whilst 'team interaction' covers some of the actual visible behaviours between individuals – which are not part of a set of routines.

'Organizational context' covers:

- bossiness
- distractions
- inaction
- inertia
- political recipes
- role climate
- stakeholders
- status
- strategic process
- structure
- symbols.

'Bossiness' here means a behavioural style where one person seeks to influence another primarily by use of power of their position. 'Political recipes' means individual's habitual ways of dealing with issues of power or influence.

Finally, 'outputs' includes a number of disparate categories, among them:

- broadcasting (the strategic message)
- change
- commitment.

Clearly, there is a very large number of behavioural categories at work in strategic behaviour. This generates considerable complexity in live inter-action.

Thinking about strategic behaviour

For one of the categories of strategic behaviour (interpersonal processes, meta-behaviour or another), which of the lower-level categories apply most to your team? What does this tell you about the climate of strategic behaviour in your team?

_____

_____

_____

_____

_____

_____

Questions to ask

- How complicated, uncertain and constrained are the strategic tasks that face your senior team?

_____

_____

_____

- What analytical process does your team rely on most heavily to deal with strategic issues?

_____

_____

_____

- How do different members in the team tend to think (their cognitive style) about issues, and how do their styles differ from each other?

_____

_____

_____

- What feelings are invisibly shaping surface behaviours, and how do these manifest themselves?

_____

_____

_____

- How does the team 'move around' the strategic issues, responding to each other interactively?

_____

_____

_____

- How does the team overall deal with conflicts, imbalances and dysfunctional behaviour?

_____

_____

_____

- How does the team move forward over the desired ground dynamically?

_____

_____

_____

- Does the team employ meta-behaviours to coordinate itself effectively?

_____

_____

_____

- How does the organizational context influence and possibly distort team behaviours?

_____

_____

_____

Now, let us analyze managers' perspectives on their strategic behaviour by taking each one of the category groupings in turn, beginning with 'strategic tasks'. At the end of each section, any patterns and themes are collected together as they develop. As each piece of data is examined, the relevant lower-level categories of strategic behaviour that occur are given in brackets or without, set in italics.

Strategic tasks

Besides TSD, BT also has a number of other parts of its organization working on strategic issues. Each of the main BT businesses has its own business strategy unit. In addition, the BT Group has a Corporate Strategy Department, and a small unit focusing on organization and people strategy. Network and Systems also has a substantial department called Evolution Planning which is concerned with the short-/medium-term migration of the network. There are necessarily slightly fuzzy 'Who does what?' boundaries between all of these groups when it comes to formulating BT's strategy.

TSD is charged with the longer-term strategic thinking underpinning BT's network development worldwide. Its task is to develop the technical strategy that supports the business strategy. It may also actually help to initiate the development of novel business strategies.

John describes the department's role (and the kind of thinking style that this role entails) as follows:

> Strategy is about taking a broad view of a problem. My background is architecture, and people talk about air sickness. People who do a successful job [in architecture] are the ones who can stand air sickness for longer. They can see enough of the ground. On the other hand, people who can't stay up for as long and who aren't as good at design … . They look down, and they see only the place that they understand, and they go directly into designing it. And they can design you only that piece, and it is rubbish, they are not logical about it.

(synthesis, problem architecture, helicoptering up)

John here is implying that only a minority of individuals are naturally comfortable with strategic thinking. This is not so much because of complexity, but because of the need to master feelings of strategic dizziness – and fear of falling (making strategic errors). This echoes the thinking in Chapter 1 on strategic mountaineering.

John also highlights a major challenge that you will see the team wrestling with later – namely, how it should tackle the sheer complexity of BT's strategic issues, and at what level, with what degree of systematic process:

> Obviously there are different levels of the strategy. Some of the debate is about what we should do as a company – our real interest here is technical. The kinds of debate that go on fly from the level of 'If we do this we make loads of money', down to 'We need this kind of technology', discussing detailed technologies, and so the arguments flow around like that … . Now the problem is, it depends on what category of debate or category of strategy, level of strategy, you are talking about.
>
> *(interlinkages, problem architecture)*

In Chapters 4–6, you will see that the TSD does experience some difficulty in anchoring its level and scope of strategic debate. As free-flowing thinkers the members of the team sometimes fall into the trap of being too wide-ranging in their debate.

David highlights the tension between having a core market in an area closer to pure technical strategy development on the one hand and the interfaces between business and technical strategy on the other:

> As a strategy unit, there has been a big debate between people who are broadly in favour of it [the department] being focused more towards business strategy issues and those who think the focus should be more towards technology strategy issues, and there is a tension [here].

Key behavioural pointers for strategic tasks

➡ Recognize that not all managers will be equally at home with strategic thinking.

➡ Support those who develop 'strategic air sickness' – helping them to come to grips with their fear of strategic heights (rather than just assuming 'that they can't do it').

➡ Be very clear and specific about what level of strategy you are dealing with on a particular topic.

➡ Tolerate ambiguity of strategic task, but only up to a point. Make clear statements about what you should be doing and then be tough on yourselves to keep the focus.

Summary

The department's overall role (and underlying strategic tasks) are in a state of ambiguity and flux, both at this juncture and, to an inevitable degree, in the future as well. Later on in this chapter (particularly under the heading Team interaction) you will see that the team has sometimes found it difficult to establish a process of coping with complicated issues when its own tasks and overall role have still been emerging.

Analytical processes

Analytical processes are defined as the 'individual and group's cognitive recipes for problem solving'.

Interviews with the individual managers in the TSD suggest that the team defaults to a small number of regular routines during its team gatherings. These include scene setting, brainstorming and creative thinking. All management teams have their recipes for analyzing problems – what is interesting here is that a relatively small number of these recipes occupy nearly all the activity.

These habitual routines are supplemented by a wider range of more behavioural recipes, such as *questioning, judging, justifying criticizing, clarifying, expanding, and picking apart.*

Andy, the Team Leader, describes how team meetings are run. Typically, they begin with an individual(s) making a presentation, which is followed by group discussion. The point of the presentation is to inject some structure into the process so that the more creative thinking tasks can follow.

> Time is spent on setting the scene, so we tend to have three or four, or whatever it takes, people giving their perspectives on what the scene is.
>
> After the presentation, there tends to be a lot of skirting around the subject – we are quite good at coming to conclusions, the strategic themes that we want to follow, the imperatives, out of a very complex subject. And what we tend to do – a lot of my group, including myself, tend to be very pictorial, and we tend to plot the problem in problem space, and then begin to say, begin to cluster the important things, and put things in useful clusters.
>
> *(brainstorming, picking apart, synthesis, cognitive style)*

Tim also describes their brainstorming process:

> Most of our sessions are very receptive. If it is a workshop, then we typically start off with a brainstorm. We have very commonly used the approach of the

yellow stickies, putting down the concern or the idea … the top things, discussing them, grouping them in some sensible way.

(brainstorming, prioritization)

The team appears satisfied with its ideas generation process and has established workable recipes for stimulating this. To make the process more effective, a suitable mix of people skills and knowledge base is deployed for each strategic event. Andy continues:

> This sort of prioritizing and pictorially clustering things seems to work quite well. But if you don't have the right mix of indicators clustering and getting sense out of the shambles and chaos it doesn't work. And when it hasn't worked very well I think it is because I haven't had the right people in meetings with the right kinds of skills.

(brainstorming, personal backgrounds)

However, the result of the actual mix of individuals within the team has sometimes been to generate more ideas than were capable of being easily digested, according to Tim:

> There have been several such sessions where there has been a braindump – lots of flip charts all around the walls. Someone types it up afterwards – a 1001 issues come out, roughly grouped, and very little action. I always feel when I see a typed-up list of issues, you know, why have we got 100 issues – we can't possibly address all those issues. I can only … why aren't we picking the top, critical ones? Why are we not doing something with them, why isn't someone actioning them?

(brainstorming, prioritizing, implementation)

Further symptoms of creative overload occur when key ideas are generated, but then they are not captured well. For instance, Bonnie reflects on one particular breakthrough in strategic thinking that was almost forgotten:

> People don't always realize what they have said. David might not have realized what he had said. We were with Anthony over lunch, and I suddenly said 'He has got it'. It was around Christmas. And do you know, after Christmas I couldn't remember it. I know I had been very excited when he had said it, but it hadn't clicked that it had been seminal. We were then sitting down, looking at his notes and then we found it, and I said 'That's it'.

(brainstorming, synthesis, rushing, insights)

This highlights a common problem of strategic meetings: the creative flow becomes so fast and strong that the most important function of recording the strategic ideas generated is neglected. Paradoxically, the more productive a strategic session is, the greater the need to capture the detailed outputs systematically becomes – without inhibiting the flow of ideas.

Tim identifies ownership and time and resource constraints as being central reasons for the difficulty of ensuring that all the key ideas generated are subsequently followed up:

> When the [strategic] event is over, we tend to assume that the person who owned the workshop is the person who primarily owns the issues and actions, and you know it would be their job if they wanted you to follow something up, to push it forward. It goes back to another angle, that we have all got other pressures on us. If we are just called into a session for our brains for the duration of a day, if we haven't been properly resourced, if we haven't properly factored our time in to support that activity, then it is not as effective as it might have been.
>
> *(prioritization, insights, ownership, implementation)*

The team's ability to capture the various insights generated during a strategic session together thus plays an important role in harvesting the value of strategic thinking. This capability in turn depends on carrying out important routines, particularly those of sorting out, directing responsibility and taking ownership of outputs. (How many of you recognize this phenomenon – of doing a strategic workshop and then waiting weeks for the documented output, let alone what the next steps in the process should be? Remember what Lord Thurso of Champneys said.)

Key behavioural pointers for analytical processes

➡ When using strategic presentations, avoid long and lengthy inputs and, at all costs, end them with some key questions for discussion.

➡ Do not confuse brainstorming with strategic thinking. Strategic thinking involves much more than just the generation ideas: it involves challenging, testing, reshaping and linking ideas together.

> ➡ Do not create so many ideas that you cannot really deal with them effectively – tease out the best, most useful ones, prioritize.
>
> ➡ Always decide in advance who is going to do what with the outputs of any strategic session – and what the value of the session will be, and how long it is likely to take.
>
> ➡ Consider who will own the outputs – this is never self-evident.

Summary

The BT team invests considerable effort in its creative thinking, but could fruitfully spend more time on capturing and distilling the value of this thinking.

Individual characteristics

A number of major areas of difference between individuals (or 'individual differentiation') exist in the TSD team. These differences are quite separate from the differences in professional/management training previously outlined. These differences include:

- preferred team roles (Belbin)
- attitudes towards process (in meetings)
- cognitive speeds
- personal strategic agendas
- preferred behavioural styles
- personal vulnerabilities.

Figure 3.3 maps the interdependencies between individual characteristics. Notice how attitudes towards the process in meetings (formal or informal and so on) are shaped by Belbin roles and preferred behavioural style. Also, a high cognitive speed might tend towards aversion to a more structured process. Equally, entrenched personal and strategic agendas might resist a process that is threatening to dislodge these.

Preferred team roles (Belbin)

In the past year or so, all members of the TSD's management team had used a Belbin team role questionnaire. The questionnaire highlights the primary and secondary roles of an individual within a team. By

87

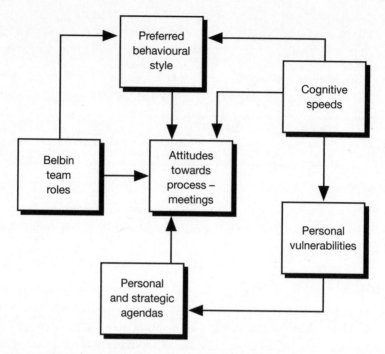

Fig 3.3 Individual characteristics – some interdependencies

comparing the roles of the team members, a good feel for the overall balance in team styles is highlighted.

Some of the Belbin team roles include, for example:

- **chairman** – team co-ordinator
- **plant** – ideas person
- **shaper** – ideas developer and prioritization
- **teamworker** – generator of team spirit
- **resource investigator** – fact finder
- **completer-finisher** – results person.

The main idea behind Belbin team roles is that if there is a predominance of a particular style within a team, then team behaviour will become unbalanced. For instance, when facilitating some strategic change projects with the Prudential several years ago, I observed that three out of four of the team members were all standing up. They appeared to be issuing directives to each other but were not listening to each other. (The fourth team member seemed, frankly, to be out of it.) So, I said, in a deliberately naive manner, 'Could I ask, by the way, what your Belbin team styles are?' Immediately, the three standing up all disclosed that they were out-and-out chairmen.

I suggested that at the next meeting the recluse manager became the chairman, and the other team members adopted their secondary team roles – of plant, shaper and finisher. Their next team meeting was revolutionary in its effectiveness.

Returning now to BT's managers, besides feedback on a one-to-one basis from a BT facilitator, they had also discussed their balance (or imbalance) of team styles openly as a team. When I interviewed them, the managers were acutely aware of major differences in their styles. For instance, David reflects:

> Nearly everyone in the team is a plant, and some are strong plants, and of course you are not supposed to have teams with more than one plant! We are always trying to get our ideas out on the table, but none of us is a completer-finisher, so any issue we can care to mention we can kick around and debate it until we are blue in the face. Getting nowhere when we need to get something done is an issue. It can be very frustrating at times.

> *(team mix, personal traits, creative thinking,*
> *personal strategic agendas, frustration)*

Interestingly, in the past, the department has put particular effort into recruiting 'plant-like' individuals (plants typically growing many, many ideas). Tim reflects:

> As a proportion [of the team], we have a very high proportion of plants. We have probably more than we actually need. It is interesting because when we actually advertise for people, we actively seek people of that persuasion.

> *(creative thinking, cognitive style)*

This predominance of plants (almost a 'jungle') clearly makes it harder for the team to process ideas effectively, but, on the other hand, produces a fertile, creative environment.

Despite the imbalance created by the number of plants, the team nevertheless has some very significant strengths. According to David:

> Keith[B] is a very strong change agent, a very good person to work with, actually. He will go out and talk to everybody. He has a very clear view of what

he is trying to achieve – this kind of dedication to the cause is really a good attribute … . Keith [B] is a wonderful politician, he is kind of, a very able committee person, and we have got Tim who will get on with almost anyone … . And you know Bonnie is a kind of ideas person. Loads of ideas. She wanders around with all these wonderful ideas blossoming in her trail.

(team mix, personal traits, influencing, creative thinking)

However, the team acknowledges gaps in its team styles. According to Andy:

Only two of us had any teamworking skills, myself and Tim.

(team mix, personal traits)

Danuta, the team's facilitator from within BT (up to the start of our study), says:

As a team profile as a whole, they should avoid completer-finisher, they should avoid implementation.

(team mix, personal traits, implementation)

The thing about Belbin is, with two or more plants in a group, you have got chaos. Well, basically, [here] you have got three people who are plants, you have got a whole group of plants to manage. This is [supposed to be] absolute chaos. It is extraordinary to have that intensity of plant together in one management team.

(team mix, personal traits, implementation, behavioural turbulence)

Fortunately for the team, this imbalance of styles is partly compensated for by its leader. Danuta continues:

Andy's natural role is teamworker, and monitor and evaluator. Most of these people have got about three natural roles, and they have got a couple, about three, to avoid. Andy is not someone necessarily with the ideas, what his skills are to say 'OK, let's break off' and 'This is my summary'.

(breaking off, summarizing)

So, although the team exhibits significant imbalances, there are balancing styles to put it on an even keel – although these are probably insufficient.

Attitudes towards process

Besides these team role differences, there also seem to be further differences in cognitive style (and in their attitude towards the management process) within the team. Bonnie elaborates:

> David and Tim are much more analytical, I think. David is always drawing mind maps but he, he is often the source of other people's big ideas. He has this thing about disruptive technologies and that came about because David had just circulated bits out of the *Harvard Business Review*. So he is often the source of other people's 'big moments of truth'. But he tends to, he will kind of see a new and interesting idea, but he will pull back from it and be more measured. And Tim's approach is much more measured like that as well. And Tim is much better at process. Keith[B] and I are appalling at process.

> *(creative thinking, probing)*

The result of these differing orientations is evident in Danuta's (the facilitator's) observations:

> There was quite a lot of frustration with everyone throwing in their ideas, and you would have a mixture of content and 'How do we structure the next steps and process?' and therefore different people, and at the same time in a meeting, you had the people who wanted to be planning the next steps, and you had the people who wanted to be having the ideas, and a mix of that.

> *(brainstorming, cognitive style, frustration, strategic process)*

These frustrations manifest themselves later on, particularly in the next chapter.

Cognitive speeds

There is another way in which individuals differ – in their cognitive speeds. These differences may be due to not merely sheer speed, but to variations in the thoroughness of cognitive processing going on. For example, Keith(A) says, of David:

> David does virtually slow things down quite a lot, but the effect of that – making sure that we are on absolutely secure foundations – has its positive side.

> *(picking apart)*

Here, the effect of being a particularly deep thinker is both positive and negative. It is positive in so far as it anchors the team in reality and

91

ensures that team members think about the detailed evidence. Equally, however, if carried to an extreme, it can act as too much of a handbrake – a major frustration when the team is in motion.

Personal strategic agendas

A further source of variation between the individuals in the TSD team is the rather different personal strategic agendas of some of the key individuals (who hold strong views), particularly David, Bonnie and Keith(B). David reflects that, for example:

> Some things people believe here very strongly and have been trying to get the business to change for a number of years. Keith[B] is very, very keen on BT getting fibre, becoming committed to a particular technical route. He's a very strong change agent. The difference then is that people actually get very hooked on their ideas. Their ideas become a kind of power thing.
>
> *(personal strategic agendas)*

There is also a strong personal attachment to particular ideas exhibited by individuals (establishing a kind of 'cognitive territory'), as David explains:

> They are their ideas, different flavours of their ideas, and you can be talking about a subject and everybody has to put their particular spin on it to develop it. If you put up an idea, there will be four or five particular alternatives which you have to consider.
>
> *(personal strategic agendas)*

Like many teams elsewhere, there are taken-for-granted points of reference that naturally attract attention, channelling strategic behaviour in particular directions.

Preferred behavioural style

Individuals also differ in terms of the behavioural climate and style that individuals prefer to have in a team. According to one member of the TSD team, there seem to be times when the healthy behaviour of team contention can look as if it is in danger of turning into the unhealthy behaviour of conflict. Contention is seen by at least some members of the team as being helpful in challenging the mindset. One team member reflects, vividly:

I am a bit of an integrity freak and I tend to think that the persuaders are selling us down the river. They must think that I am being Moluk-like and unreasonable. I think that they are Mammon and they think that I am Moluk – it's *Paradise Lost*. Moluk is an odd-style general-type – 'My council is for war' – whereas Mammon (the opposite of Moluk) would say, to pacify things, 'Why don't we just put a few flowers about in hell? I am sure that we could make this quite a comfortable place, but, no, I am not Mammon, I am Moluk.

(behavioural style)

Personal vulnerabilities

Individuals differ from each other in terms of their personal vulnerability. They also differ in their levels of underlying anxiety and feelings of vulnerability. One team member confesses:

Danuta (our facilitator) encouraged Andy (the team leader) to make us listen more and, er, have not so much conflict. But it caused me personally a lot of trouble, because I normally have a feeling, an anxiety, that no one is listening to me anyway. I think it is an in-built thing. I've had it for years.

This anxiety can feed into all kinds of behaviours, not only subtly affecting a particular individual, but also spilling over to influence the behaviours of others around them.

Under the heading Team interaction, later in this chapter, some of the consequences of all these differences in preferred behaviours are explored.

Key behavioural pointers for individual characteristics

➡ An imbalance of team styles in a senior team may make it very hard for it to reach its full potential.

➡ Try not to recruit into the team people who have similar team styles to one another.

➡ Differences in speed and depth of thinking can put further stresses on strategic behaviour that need to be managed well.

➡ The team should reach a consensus on the extent to which it needs a firm or more flexible process of working.

> ➡ Personal agendas need to be made explicit rather than left hidden, so that they can be tested.
>
> ➡ Personal anxieties need to be teased out and dealt with, otherwise they will distort strategic behaviour and throw the team off course.

Summary

The BT team faced (prior to the fuller intervention to help the team behave more strategically):

- a phenomenally complicated set of strategic issues that it needed to address
- the difficulty of deciding what level to address these at, how to limit the scope of their work and where to direct their attention
- the problem of transforming a multitude of creative ideas from very individualistic people into projects and programmes that BT could implement
- the challenge of managing cognitive differences between individuals and their varying attitudes, how to process the thinking and also underlying agendas.

Interpersonal processes

Turning next to its interpersonal processes, the team's sessions together frequently begin with a formal presentation. When I am facilitating any strategy workshop, I invariably use an illustration showing the well-known British weatherman Michael Fish set against a weather map. You will no doubt recall that Michael Fish told the British people 'not to worry' just a few hours before the great storm of 1987, which decimated forests across the South of England. The point of showing the Michael Fish picture, however, is to encourage managers to be extremely succinct when presenting their own weather forecasts. Invariably, the really big strategic issues can be presented in around three minutes, set against a brief storyline. As for the rest of the clouds, well, you can read them for yourself on the detailed flip charts.

In common with many managers elsewhere, BT managers tend to do fairly lengthy presentations. Tim describes the downsides of these substantial presentations:

I, whilst I like presentations [of diagrams and illustrations] – they are very important for imparting information – they, by and large, are not a very interactive medium. Somebody is setting out their stall, they have thought about it and probably know more about that aspect than anybody else in that room, which really only allows other people to challenge around the periphery, to gain points of clarification. It rarely challenges the fundamental tenet of what is being said. It is really imparting information. It is not a way of building consensus.

(scene setting, personal strategic agendas, tenets, consensus building)

He then describes how presentations are progressed:

Almost immediately, there would be interruptions or disagreement on points, on rather nitty-gritty points. That, I recall, rather quickly led to, a sort of well 'Why are we here?' sort of thing. You know, 'This whole thing is not going at all well'.

(interruptions, picking apart, helicoptering up, monitoring value)

Tim then suggests that this can result in slippage. On one particular occasion:

The next consequence of that was that the discussion dragged on. The agenda slipped disastrously, and in the day we just reviewed half the policy statements. The consequence was that a lot of things didn't get addressed.

(rushing, slippage)

Further difficulties emerge as a result of the interaction between individuals. As David explains:

You haven't got the behaviour [in the team] of 'Oh, this is what I think, what do you think?' It is what I call 'people throwing out their world views', and then I would say that there are two very strong characters on this and they say 'This is my world view, and I am just going to give you my world view. I will give you my world view. I will give you my world view'.

(questioning, personality clash)

Inadvertently, then, presentations give a particular individual almost too much control, resulting in colleagues taking opposing stances – sometimes artificially. This links back to the extent to which individuals within the team share (or do not share) common mental maps of the key strategic issues under discussion. Later it will be seen (particularly in Chapter 4) that the team iself views this as a major gap that it has not addressed effectively in the past.

Coupled with the perception that there is inadequate sharing of mental maps within the team, it is felt that individuals could practise more 'active listening'. Keith(A) puts this problem particularly powerfully:

> That has been blatantly obvious. People just don't listen to other people's ideas. One of the reasons is that you find that somebody is talking and you don't agree with one item. And if you don't interrupt then you never get heard.
>
> *(disagrees, personal strategic agendas, interruptions)*

The consequence of these interruptions is that, at least for Keith(A):

> I could sit back all day and there would be no gaps in the conversation. There have been times when I have been very quiet because I have been fed-up with this battle to get a word in edgeways.
>
> *(frustration)*

Key behavioural pointers for interpersonal processes

➡ Without an adequate sharing of mental maps (and assumptions), a team will run into counterproductive debate – and rapidly.

➡ While putting a particular point of view, team members must be engaged simultaneously in listening – continually eliciting the agendas of other individuals.

Summary

Interpersonal processes are perceived by the team to be a major constraint on its ability to debate strategic issues in a constructive and effective manner. The actual (negative) results of this are amplified in the next section.

Team interaction

Keith(B) explains how the underlying values of the team put a premium on creativity, and on being creative in an individualistic sense:

> So there is a tension between everyone wanting to, being creative people, and wanting to cut it into their own version of the way forward and, you know [on the other hand], we have got to get an output here, guys. I mean, none of these folks around here would be the kind of people who are happy in a straight production line role.

(creative thinking, personal strategic agendas)

In a more measured way than his colleagues, Keith(B) describes the intensity of team interaction as follows:

> And as such there's always a fierce discussion. I wouldn't say it was heated or feeling like anybody stuck a knife in me type of discussion, antagonistic, and I think it was a good, honest discussion.

(challenging)

Keith (B) also reflects:

> I mean, some individuals have strong views and tend to articulate it very strongly. There is nothing wrong in that ... . You know, the whole strength of this team – and I think it is a very good team – is that each brings a very different perspective into the picture ... .

(challenging, team mix)

Andy (Team Leader) also shares Keith(B)'s view that the polarity between views (and approaches of specific team members) can be both positive and productive:

> I have one or two people who always come in orthogonally on a discussion. And at first I used to find it incredibly irritating, but it was quite powerful. It does lend itself to, well, I wouldn't say 'chaotic', not chaotic, unruly, unruly meetings sometimes.

(diving in, behavioural turbulence)

However this polarity of views can also be counter-productive. On one isolated occasion a particularly difficult situation developed when a number of things conspired behaviourally, unexpectedly, to go wrong at the same time. Andy recalls:

> We had, the year before last, a top team meeting – on what we should be doing as a team. It was about how we worked as a team, as well as what we

should be looking at ... . It almost broke down towards, towards, about half-way through. One guy said, 'I don't want to be at this meeting. I don't think I like this at all'. He felt, and I agree with him, that a number of things were happening. One, there were a lot of interruptions, people were getting hostile to each other. The discussion wasn't converging, er, and before people had got their ideas out, people were jumping in and tearing it to pieces, and so on.

(priorities, interruptions, picking apart, behavioural turbulence, conflict, breakdown)

Andy's dilemma here was to create a balance between giving the team sufficient steer to avoid such situations and the need to avoid stifling creativity and debate. Andy says:

It is sometimes thought that we are too eager to get a consensus, and that we don't allocate either the time or the energy to take, to really see, the issues through in the debate. What I am doing – trying to pull it together and trying to get consensus, 'Well, we will do this then' – is thought to occur too soon. And I am missing a key point by doing that, and by cutting serious debate short, we never go the whole hog.

(setting time frames, strategic process, consensus-building, breaking off)

Interestingly, the team members who were able to reflect on the team's interactive style had clear and largely consistent cognitive maps of what had gone on behaviourally, and why, on specific occasions, things had got a bit out of hand even though it was not easy to discuss it as a team.

Key behavioural pointers for team interaction

➡ Avoid creating an unnecessary polarity of views – this can produce great difficulties in team behaviour unless there is a reciprocal sharing of mental maps.

➡ Contention needs to be skilfully channelled, and is not of value in itself.

Dynamic processes

'Dynamic processes' are defined as those team processes concerned with making progress in analyzing and evaluating strategic issues – 'covering the ground'. This time John describes how the team tries to move forward:

> There are certainly disagreements … . People throw ideas about, and kick them around. They disagree with each other. It does get quite heated at times. The other thing that stands out, in the kind of discussion which I have seen, is digression and not much focus. So a lot of the discussion starts, and it just moves sideways, and sideways, and sideways. It drifts away from the point.

(creative ideas, challenging, behavioural turbulence, picking apart)

Danuta reveals that the team perpetually seems to struggle in defining a process:

> One of them will come up with a better process suggestion, and they will dive off and will keep on adding to the problem. One thing that I pointed out at their last team meeting was that they would set themselves a task to do and prepare how to do it, and then they interrupt it and do it some other way. They never go and complete it – 'What can we learn from it?', 'What can we draw from it?' – and then take up the next ideas about a process improvement or a process suggestion.

(strategic process, interruptions, reflection)

The difficulty of getting the team to orchestrate their interactions and be able to control their behaviours is reinforced by Andy:

> They are not very good at that [process]. We tend to dive in – you know, we do the first bits and then we get to the point where we are not quite sure how to finish this, but I am sure that it will become clear as we get to the discussion.

(diving in, rushing, strategic process)

Some of the confusion in the team's debate appears to stem from a differing understanding of certain complicated strategic issues and dilemmas facing BT among the team members. Tim reflects:

> The reason why we did not achieve was that there was not a common understanding of either the problems faced or of the objectives of the meeting.

(judging)

There are also some basic issues regarding how the team programmes its work. Tim reflects:

> There were occasions where we were trying to achieve too much. It was as if we were running on borrowed time. We would get together for half a day and expect to achieve what in reality would have been several days' thrashing about. We were just pushing it too hard.

(setting time scales)

This is true of many, many group situations in companies elsewhere. From my consulting experience, managers underestimate the amount of time required to do justice to a strategic issue by between a factor of three to even nine times.

Key behavioural pointers for dynamic processes

➥ Unless the team has some process, then frustration will inevitably mount, demoralizing individuals, so put some process into the workshop.

➥ Do not try to achieve too much in any particular session, and what you do try to achieve, achieve by means of a fairly well-structured process.

Summary

The team has its fair share of disagreements, some of which produce genuinely creative thinking. However, at times, these disagreements seem to become intractable, making it very difficult for progress to be made.

Meta-behaviour

This is the group of higher-order behaviours that help to coordinate the lower-order behaviours. Meta-behaviour covers behaviours such as facilitation, feedback, humour, and also the use of management tools. While the team members describe some meta-behaviours that are in use, their application appears limited, making it hard to channel the team's more creative and divergent debates. Possibly more attention to meta-behaviours might help the team to focus to achieve its objectives more quickly.

One aspect of meta-behaviour – facilitation – stands out as having been particularly helpful to the team. Certainly all the members of the team expressed their appreciation for their facilitator, Danuta, and also of the value of the Belbin team role framework.

However, as Tim says:

> Certainly, if Danuta is with us we will do a sort of a workshop review of what was good and what was bad. And it is all positive in that sense.
>
> *(facilitation, reflection, feedback)*

> Somehow or other, we just find it hard to apply those lessons for the next time around. I don't know why, to be honest. We get perhaps more excited about the technicalities of the issues, more excited about the strategies which we are developing than the methodologies.
>
> *(implementation, change, inertia)*

This suggests that the team is likely to find it difficult to make sustainable changes in its strategic behaviour as it is currently constituted. This also implies that some change in the team is needed to secure a better team balance.

Apart from the 'ideas clustering' techniques used for brainstorming, the team employed relatively few strategic analysis tools at the time of the study. When asked what factors might inhibit the team from experimenting with new techniques, Tim responded:

> So used are we in our engineering world to tight disciplines, to support, to give us answers, then we move through that door [into strategy] then we come with our minds, hopefully full of bright ideas, we know that the area is fuzzy, it has uncertainty, er, we are presented with some management tools which we are told don't answer the question precisely. So, do we need to use the tools, aren't we bright enough to think it through on our own? I guess that's something of the process that we are going through.
>
> *(management tools)*

However, the very absence of management tools could have made it very hard to unravel BT's strategic complexity (subsequently the team came to use a number of these tools).

Tim also reveals an aversion to using these kinds of tools (this might go back to his own professional training):

When one does a scientific experiment it is quite clear, it is quite sound, and the answer is quite unambiguous in context. The natural scepticism, the desire for accuracy from anyone with an engineering background in applying it to a management problem, using tools that have been developed. They aren't really very robust, the [management] tools, they have a softness to them. They help, rather than provide the answer.

(management tools)

In Chapter 7 the various analysis tools that can be used to improve managers' cognitive maps of strategic issues are described. This might reduce some of the drivers of unnecessary behavioural stress.

Finally, humour does seem to play a role within the team, although it could perhaps play even more of a role. Danuta suggests that if one or more individuals are unduly serious, then this can set the climate for the rest of the team. Absence of humour can be a hidden constraint on a team. Although humour takes up some time, it provides an opportunity to re-energize and to refocus: it provides a 'break without a break'. Danuta tells us:

It is just something that comes out naturally, because one of the people with the dog with a bone behaviour is humorous. So they don't have the light touch. Everything is very intense when they are in that forum.

(humour)

In Chapters 4, 5 and 6 the individuals who are more prone to humour are seen to be Keith(A), Bonnie and Tim, with Andy being more reserved and David relatively serious.

Key behavioural pointers for meta-behaviour

➡ Plan explicitly which mix of meta-behaviours you are going to use.

➡ Try this mix out – be prepared to tailor and adapt it to a specific team until you have found what works really well.

➡ Do not be shy about using a selected number of strategic analysis tools to facilitate strategic thinking – and calm strategic behaviour.

> ➡ A team without humour will quickly run out of energy, and find it harder to actually analyze the issues at a cognitive level.

Summary

There seems to be some (limited) use of meta-behaviours to help the team. However, development of meta-behaviours should help significantly to orchestrate the team's processes and behaviours more effectively.

Outputs and organizational context

Once the TSD team has formulated its own strategic ideas, it then has to sell them to the rest of BT. This highlights another key domain of strategic behaviour – influencing strategies elsewhere.

The influencing process in BT is relevant because of the difficulties of implementing technology changes downstream in BT's Networks business. These blockages occur because the strategy team may become locked into a loop of strategic thinking that does not embrace implementation difficulty to the full. Because the team has a low level of influence on implementation, it can be excused for under-emphasizing implementation difficulty.

David explores this challenge of strategy implementation:

> There is a distinction between getting the strategy endorsed and actually getting the money to implement the strategy in such a large organization. I mean, you can always get the Board to say yes to it, but to actually make it happen you have to have very widespread buy-in.

Ultimately, implementation constraints may have major implications for the behaviour of individual team members, and also for their ability to present a common front outside their department. These implications may concern their influencing skills and style, and the extent to which they see their roles as being involved in the early stages of implementation. This raises issues about specific behaviours relevant to strategic implementation, which, we saw from the Belbin analysis, are not prevalent within the team. Even where team members' roles provide merely a catalyst-role in implementation teams outside the department, this is in conflict with their natural styles in several areas. Tim highlights the effects of having a pronounced style of 'plant-like' creativity:

… behaviours which have worked well have been where there have been 'plant' individuals, where, at the end of the day, there was a sufficient weight of opinion there to not only like what the plant said but be willing to take it, and action it. That's a typical converse to what has been unsuccessful, where the team has simply taken ideas, tossed them around and not then actioned them. Perhaps there has not been the ownership – or the assignment of ownership.

(creative thinking, competitive style, ownership)

Implementation poses significant dilemmas for the team. For instance, should the team focus only on those things that BT – within its current mindset – is prepared to implement within a particular time horizon? Should it instead focus on trying to change the mindset (or wait for it to change) and being ready with the appropriate strategic recipes as the right time occurs?

Andy's view on this is that:

Our first task is to be quite clear about what we are aiming for, what the target is and what we are trying to achieve. And we should be quite clear about that – we shouldn't compromise that by way of what the current implementation plans are or what the business is currently expecting to do.

(compromising, influencing)

Key behavioural pointers for outputs and organizational context

➡ Do not neglect the implementation skills needed to turn strategic ideas into business value, including skills in project management and influencing.

➡ A strategic idea will only ever add value when it is being implemented. Therefore, a strategy department, such as TSD, must always remember its implementation skills.

Summary

Delivering outputs to BT seems to imply not just handing over strategic ideas from the department, but, increasingly, handing over implementable ideas. This change may imply a further shift in behaviour within the team – from analytical to practical – which may not be easy to achieve with the current team mix and styles of behaving.

Summary and overview

The TSD team is, in some ways, an unusual team in behavioural terms (possibly it is an 'extreme team'), in the sense of being sometimes hard to manage, but nevertheless able to deliver some powerful new thinking when it is firing on all cylinders. However, this very extreme nature makes it of particular interest as patterns in strategic behaviour in other organizations, which might not be easy to discern, would be found here in an exaggerated form. The team's task is one of dealing with complicated strategic issues that are likely to have a major impact on BT's future, so its behavioural interactions are of some considerable importance.

Other major factors that seem to have constrained the team are its mix and its diverse personalities, its concentration of behavioural and cognitive styles (especially of 'plants') and its differing personal agendas.

A particularly important area for the team to address is the problem of getting the team to do a fuller sharing of its mental maps of strategic issues. Differences in these mental maps appear to have generated unconstructive contention at times. This area looks like being an obvious one for the team to work on.

CONCLUSION

There are several important implications to be gleaned from the BT team's behaviours so far for managers elsewhere.

- **Strategic tasks and cognitive overload** Limit the intellectual task being undertaken at any one time to something attainable, otherwise members of the team will be engaged on multiple tasks that only partially overlap or relate to each other.
- **Deploying strategic intelligence** Intelligence alone is frequently not sufficient to solve strategic problems. What is also needed are some analytical processes and tools to break down the cognitive task into manageable chunks. The management tools then deal with some of the more mechanical aspects of the thinking and provide a channel for testing out judgement and intuition.
- **Individual characteristics of the team** A particular team chemistry can be inherently unstable. Although it is still possible to achieve good –

indeed, excellent – results from an unstable system, it requires immense coordination effort. (This situation is like a Eurofighter – an inherently unstable jet fighter that can only fly with the aid of powerful computers.)

- **Interpersonal processes** Over-reliance on a single medium of interpersonal processes (such as making formal presentations, brainstorming or simply informal discussions) will unbalance the team interaction. What is needed is a combination of structured and less-structured debates, and a mix and balance of discussion formats.

- **Team interaction** This needs to avoid being either too 'nice' or too directly contentious. Individuals can still have strong agendas and be able to put down powerful challenges to the mindsets of others and themselves and, at the same time engage in each other's agendas.

- **Meta-behaviour** The more complicated and ambiguous the debate, the more evident meta-behaviour to steer the team should be, otherwise debate will ramble or become a free-for-all.

- **Outputs** Unless a team is really clear about what its goalposts really are – what value it is hoped will come out of its debates – again, it will tend to diverge in its discussions without much converging.

Key questions for your senior team

- How would you describe your own team's strategic behaviour? Is it particularly ordered (possibly too much so) or is it very fluid (and perhaps too unstructured)?

  _____

  _____

  _____

  _____

- What are its key strategic tasks and how are these prioritized?

  _____

  _____

  _____

  _____

- What is the team mix and does this work well?

  _____

  _____

  _____

  _____

- Where it doesn't work so well (and where you are looking for improvement), where should it seek help?

  _____

  _____

  _____

  _____

- Does your team apply sufficient management processes and meta-behaviours to become really effective?

  _____

  _____

  _____

  _____

- Is your team really clear about what its key outputs should be and what value these outputs should have?

  _____

  _____

  _____

  _____

SUMMARY

Strategic behaviour involves a complicated flow of behaviours that occur in debates on strategic issues. Already patterns and processes in strategic behaviour are discernible. Each process (and subprocess) has its own role to play in delivering the almost music-like flows of debate – whether these are harmonious or in discord.

The BT team seems to be grappling, with varying degrees of success, with complicated strategic issues in a rapidly changing environment. Following on from the TSD's reflections on past strategic behaviour, the next chapter shows how the team's members progress while being observed as a team in the action research process.

SHAPING
STRATEGIC
BEHAVIOUR

> *Good generals are not committed to death but do not expect to live. When they see possibility they are like tigers, otherwise they shut their doors.*
>
> Sun Tzu, *The Art of War*

INTRODUCTION

In this chapter you will see how the TSD team actually managed itself immediately before it sought to behave more strategically. The team's first workshop followed a similar pattern to previous workshops, beginning with strategic presentations, followed by discussion. In the second part of the chapter, the team's reflections on this first workshop (in the second workshop) are examined.

All managers will, I think, recognize the problem of sustaining thinking and debate at a genuinely strategic level. It is always tempting to follow the flow of talk to wherever other managers take it, regardless of whether or not it adds value. There is a kind of unquestioning respect for the idea 'If he said that, then I should say something that now relates to that'.

The problem is that the 'that' can be relatively detailed or trivial. It could be important, but often it can make the discussion swerve in a quite separate direction, and the cost is that the 'talk' becomes more and more cloudy, confusing and potentially exhausting. Thus, not only is it crucial to track the strategic level of debate, but to steer it – proactively.

The workshop was attended by team members from the department and elsewhere. The members of the team involved were:

David
Keith(A)
Bonnie
Tim
Andy (present at the very beginning and at the very end)
Ross (invited)
Jonathan (invited)
Adrian (invited).

The first part of the workshop involved three presentations, followed by a debate on the strategic issues coming out of these. Just one presentation is examined to get a flavour of the team's habitual behaviour. Before beginning, however, let us just reflect on what typically happens in our organizations on an everyday basis.

111

In this chapter, the debate is categorized at periodic intervals as being at a 'high' (*H*), 'medium' (*M*) or 'low' (*L*) level of input.

'High' was defined as being a discussion of the bigger picture, 'medium' as discussion of a sub-issue (but one that was still related to the high-level issue). 'Low' took the form of discussion of something that was a very specific part of that sub-issue (often at a microscopic level).

For a quick illustration of what the levels mean in practice, later on in this chapter, David introduces the question 'What is BT's strategy?' ('high'). Keith(A) then talks about a sub-issue – 'To what extent does a summation of people's work constitute a strategy?' ('medium'). Bonnie then describes how uncertainties underneath a strategy can be addressed by building specific scenarios ('low'). This highlights the tendency of the team to burrow down to lower and lower levels of detail. Such increasingly detailed analysis can frustrate 'bigger picture' thinking and can make it more difficult to cover strategic ground. However, what may be called 'rabbit hole management') is by no means a characteristic that is unique to the BT team. Rather, it is very common, if not endemic, elsewhere in other organizations. (See also Chapter 7, especially Figure 7.1, for more on this idea.)

To make it easier to follow the sometimes zig-zag nature of the debate, 'strategic issue maps' depict the flow in the content of the discussion. Later, fluid debate on further strategic issues that emerge out of the discussion following the strategic presentations is examined.

However, before beginning, a very important point needs to be made. The debates that the BT team generate at this stage may seem to be somewhat haphazard and not always productive. Lengthy extracts are presented so as to highlight what may be going wrong in the behavioural process so it is possible to understand what could go better. I therefore ask that you bear with me so that we can unravel exactly why the team finds it hard to behave strategically.

The two key presentations that are gone into in depth in the first workshop are:

- downstreaming technical strategy – that is, influencing the organization to 'get on and do it'
- the planning process – old and new styles.

THE BT CASE STUDY
(Continued)

THE FIRST WORKSHOP
DOWNSTREAMING TECHNICAL STRATEGY

Following David's presentation of the various problems involved in ensuring that technical strategy is implemented, Andy reflects on which forms of strategy are most appropriate within the BT planning process:

> It is the classic Mintzberg stuff. It is going to be chaotic by the nature of the work, the changing objectives.
>
> And taking Adrian's point a stage further, you might well start off with the chaotic and, when the time is right, when you are into volume deployment, you are into the well-oiled [operations], and you know, it's getting the balance right.
>
> *(expanding)*

Jonathan then interjects 'This was supposed to be a presentation, so please could we not interrupt'. David then picks up his presentation, but after several minutes, group debate breaks out again. Bonnie then challenges David as follows:

> *Keith(A)*: Can I just say, Dave, that I felt that you presented two models – the X model and the Y model [of technical strategy]. Actually, I think we have a hybrid somewhere between. (*picking apart*)
> *David*: Well, I think that ...
> *Bonnie*: I think that they are the same model ... there is lots of bifurcating [going on] and the concurrent one you can't cope with. (*expanding*)
> *Bonnie*: I think it is the same model. (*judging*)

Bonnie then provides an example to illustrate how many strategy ideas never fully develop and mature:

> *Bonnie*: But it is like the hornbills – did you see the hornbills on TV? It is about when animals get to be grown up, you have to have so many eggs that don't hatch, you have so many chicks that don't get down on to the ground, and so many ... [David tries to interrupt] that get down on to the ground but don't breathe. (*creative thinking*)

However, before there is chance to develop this interesting and fruitful idea, another quite separate idea is put into the discussion stream by Jonathan:

> *Jonathan*: From the perspective of having now seen the other side of the gate in department Z of BT, they are first of all a pretty large organization with their own set of problems, and they are very, very focused on today's issues. The way in which the senior managers in the outfit work is to say 'Give me your top three problems, give me your top ten issues'. And the problem is, the strategy issues are nearly always not going to be the top issues. They don't get looked at. And there are some things ... (*presentation*)

This interaction is darting about, making it hard to build up a more coherent picture of what the group thinks. In fact, it is hard to discern at this point much group purpose in the discussions. If there is any purpose to the discussion, it appears to be 'emergent' with the team members hoping that something valuable will come out in a serendipitous way. It should be remembered that at this point the team leader, Andy, has had to go to a pressing meeting, leaving at least a partial vacuum of direction in the team. Nevertheless, no one in the team has taken up Andy's steering role.

A more concrete dilemma is now identified. Jonathan starts off the discussion in a focused way, but the discussion then rapidly diverges.

> *Jonathan*: The other issue which I will just finish off on, and I apologize for dragging this in again ... there is a significant difference between technical changes and business-driven changes [he elaborates]. If they are technically-driven changes, they will pick them up. If they are business-driven changes, they will only pick these up when they become really, really serious. And I think that's when somebody at the top of the company says, 'Well, I think that it is time you set up an outfit to handle Technology Q'. (*strategic tasks*)
> *Bonnie*: Well, it is too late ... (*judging*)
> *Jonathan*: Of course it is. (*agreeing*)
> *Bonnie*: And by that time you have lost a lot of leeway and competitive advantage. (*expanding*)
> (Lots of people are now talking simultaneously.)

David tries to get the discussion back on track – to the theme of 'down-streaming technical strategy', or, in simpler terms, making people actually implement it:

> *David*: That's exactly the mode which we are in – the change agent mode. That is the political domain, what it is all about, mobilizing people, the people who are actually going to do the work [elaborates]. This is a really big issue. And unless we are good at doing that, we aren't going to get the change to happen. (*judging, expanding, influencing*)

Jonathan now moves on to a related, but separate, issue, thus moving the debate sideways:

> *Jonathan*: Unless we do it another way, as we were discussing last week, by spinning off a separate, independent, small outfit, and feeding resources into it, and saying here you are, get on with this. (*expanding*)
> *Bonnie*: That's a piece of our strategy. (*picking apart*)
> *David*: That's concurrent engineering. (*picking apart*)
> (Lots of joking now ensues, presumably reflecting an in joke.)

This discussion has been unpredictable and divergent, zig-zagging over a range of slightly connected issues. Also, the level changed during the course of the debate in the following ways:

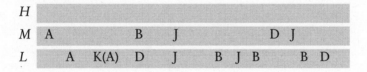

but, as you can see, stayed mostly at a lower level. So, not only has it moved, at times, almost randomly over the issues, it has also been primarily focused at a detailed level with little notion of BT's overall strategic architecture.

David's presentation (and debate) having ended, it is now Tim's turn to input. Tim simply begins just after David has finished. Note that the team omitted to summarize or reflect on the value added at this point. This may be partly the result of Andy's absence, having left the workshop at the very start of the presentation. However, it is also likely to be due to the team's tendency to enjoy the stimulus of debate without being equally concerned to harvest its value in the most tangible terms.

The examples so far are by no means unique or unusual. Elsewhere, in other organizations, having a 'strategic debate' seems to produce an attitude in managers of 'Maybe something useful will come out of it' rather than 'We must definitely have something of significant value from it'. Although there is some logic, some flow in Figure 4.1, it is easy to feel that there are many other issues that this topic could have surfaced.

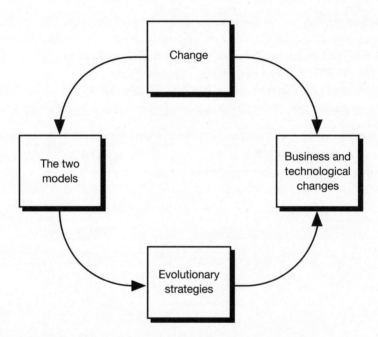

Fig 4.1 Strategic issues map – downstreaming technical strategy

The planning process – old and new styles

Tim's presentation on the department's planning process attempts to define the concept 'strategy'. Tim's view is that strategy is about positioning, and being able to respond flexibly to unpredictable change. He then moves on to describe more specifically the process and outputs of planning, trying to relate technical strategy, business strategy and corporate strategy. Immediately, the question 'Is this too big and wide-ranging a set of topics?' comes to mind.

The first phase of interactive discussion is then triggered by a debate about the architecture of strategy. Of particular importance here is knowing the level of strategy being talked about. For example, is it at corporate, business or programme level? You will recall from the beginning of Chapter 3 that John highlighted the ambiguity resulting from uneven understanding within the group about the architecture of strategy.

In the following discussion you will see that corporate-, business- and programme-level strategy (and forms of strategy) are all covered in a single debate. Ross begins:

Ross: But we need to avoid getting into too much detail. Just thinking a bit more radically, it is quite reasonable to think of a model where you don't have a deliberate strategy, where the group-level strategy is simply the summation of the trading unit's strategies. (*expanding*)

Tim: No, I think not. (*disagreeing*)

Ross: I am not suggesting that, I am saying that ... (*clarifying*)

Tim: There are major things which perhaps at group level, the radical things ... (*expanding*)

David: Can I just say something there, if you actually look at the enterprise model ... where you are actively operating a set of separate bits of businesses, then the main role is actually deciding what type of businesses we want to develop, and investment planning, rather than a true strategy. (*expanding*)

Tim: Ah ... (*interrupting*)

(Lots of interruptions ensue.)

Bonnie: I don't agree.

David: We are in this line of business, but now 'this is how we do it'. (*expanding*)

Bonnie: I don't agree.[*disagreeing*] The last thing that we have got to decide is what lines of business we are going to be in. But what I think it should be about is things like principles [*expanding*], like 'Which business should optimize its own results without regard to the others, or not?'

The level of debate thus ran as follows:

H									
M	R								
L		T	R	T	D	T	B	D	B

which, again, quickly descended to a lower level of discussion, with no real looping back to higher-level issues that might have generated a greater sense of vision.

Examining the content and dynamic of this debate, a number of processes are at work. First of all, Ross sets out to expand on earlier ideas of deliberate versus emergent strategy (building on what has already been discussed). However, he does not develop his ideas sufficiently to show clearly what he does (or does not) mean. This produces some unfinished business. Tim then quickly whips in and disagrees with him, but without saying why. Bonnie also disagrees, putting more of a feeling of struggle into the debate. Tim neither probes nor questions Ross to expose his assumptions and, thus, try to uncover his mental map. Although Ross then tries to clarify what he said, Tim gives him insufficient time and space to develop his ideas. Tim exposes (one might even say imposes) his own mental map rather than trying to surface Ross's understanding.

It is quite possible that these two managers are entirely in agreement about what should go on here, but, because of their interactive style, end up disagreeing with each other.

Before this debate can be taken further, David then pours another theme into the arena. This input is partially helpful as the 'enterprise model' he describes helps to define a model of BT's strategy, structure and corporate style. However, in process terms, David's new addition to the debate brings in more complexity on top of the previously discussed issues, which have only been dealt with in part (adding to the number of unfinished sessions). This new input also serves to distract the team from its earlier unfinished tasks.

At this point, it would have been most helpful for someone to display some kind of meta-behaviour, to intervene to steer the debate, but this does not happen (perhaps because the team leader, Andy, had to go to another meeting).

There are then so many interruptions that clear transcription of how the debate continues becomes impossible. Bonnie disagrees (but she does not say why she disagrees). For a second time there is a pause when Bonnie tries to tackle the idea of 'strategic principles', but this discussion is then cut short by Tim who closes down the debate by restarting his presentation.

So, once again, there has been energetic discussion, a considerable divergence of debate, but little discernible output that you might say the group has agreed or disagreed with. Perhaps the individuals themselves have added to their own mental maps marginally, but it is hard to see how the group as a whole has extended its common view of the strategic issues. Further, there has been no direct linkage in the discussion with how the department itself could influence the conduct of strategy in BT.

All of this underlines the need for continuously monitoring the value of any strategic debate. It embraces the value of the strategic debate to date, the value of what is currently coming out, and also the probable value of where current lines of enquiry are leading to.

The notion of 'lines of enquiry' is a most useful one. Strategic enquiry is very much a process of conjecturing, collecting evidence and exploring possible solutions, ruling these 'out' or 'in' as the enquiry develops. This often reminds me of the American TV detective Columbo, who painstakingly pursues his suspects. The BT team might do well to follow this model, to provide more structure and direction to their debate. Simultaneously, it might have the effect of curbing their excitement and feelings, which very quickly run hot.

Key points
··············

➡ Avoid using lengthy presentations as the major primer or driver of a strategic debate.

➡ Where you do use strategic presentations, focus these by posing between one and three key strategic questions.

➡ Keep the primary strategic agenda tightly focused.

➡ Monitor the flow of issues (even if they are emergent). Ask: 'Is there a pattern?', 'Where is this leading to?', rather than just

▶

> allowing a random flow. Use a strategic issue map either for-
> mally or in your head to keep track of the flow.
>
> ➡ Be clear what level of strategy you are actually considering – to
> avoid inappropriate generalizations.
>
> ➡ Be genuinely proactive in steering behaviours (using meta-
> behaviours).
>
> ➡ Develop and pursue interesting lines of enquiry (the 'Columbo
> approach').

The next phase of discussion, following Tim's continuing presentation,
focuses on the structure and content of plans, with a number of questions
aimed at clarifying these aspects. There is a gradual return to Tim's
original input on 'deliberate' planning. Tim now picks up the debate:

> *Tim*: ... if you can capture the uncertainty. It is there to start, to position some
> of the programme managers as to what their next area of activity will be.
> (*clarifying, judging*)
>
> *Keith(A)*: OK, at one time we used evolution plans in such a way that we
> focused people's views. Picking up on what Jonathan was saying, we
> encourage them to develop extra functionality in this area, and perhaps
> wither and die this piece here. So ... I think that ... evolutionary planning
> shouldn't do that, but, rather, be a pure and simple reflection of what the
> reality is at that time. (*creative thinking, expanding*)
>
> (Various interruptions break out.)
>
> *Tim*: Well, I think that the plan itself will be ...
>
> *Keith(A)*: It needs some thinking through. (*probing*)
>
> *Tim*: That question – what convergence might you have? – is something that
> comes out of evolution planning activity. [Tim elaborates, continuing his
> presentation.] (*scene setting*)
>
> *Keith(A)*: I feel, I know that we could spend quite a lot of time on this, that we
> are in danger of wandering about in a significant area. It is just simply an
> audit, and actually taking on board some of the strategic ideas. It is not clear,
> between these two extremes, where we are. (*setting time frames, picking
> apart, meta-behaviour*)

This short burst is again at a lower level, making it hard to get a coherent view of where it is heading, and why:

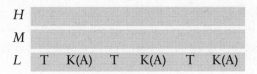

Although once more there has been a burst of interruptions, the discussion seemed to have gained slightly more focus, at least staying on one issue rather than roving over terrain at random.

Keith(A) has then intervened to suggest that some kind of steer on discussion is needed, but this helpful meta-behaviour is not picked up on by the others. After a long and philosophical input on change (that change is not a 'constant') from Bonnie, Tim once again resumes his formal presentation. Again, there is no summary of the output (nor of its meaning or its value to the team) before Bonnie is then invited to begin her presentation. Figure 4.2 summarizes pictorially the flow of debate.

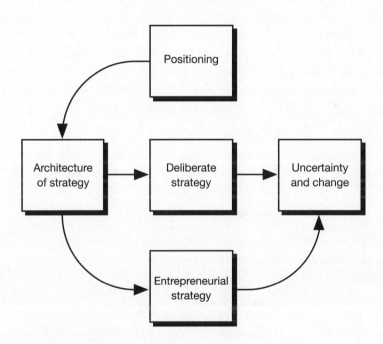

Fig 4.2 Strategic issues map – the planning process

121

In summary, there is the contrast between a formal, set piece presentation and the extremely fluid and fragmented debate that then occurs. The two discussion styles vary between 'extremely tight, no room for fluid debate' and 'extremely loose, with no time for structure and process'. Team members seem to respond to the unstructured debate by 'throwing more and more in' to the discussion, perhaps in the hope that something will ultimately come out. (In terms of Bonnie's earlier example, the team hopes that at least one hornbill idea will survive.) What might have been helpful to the team is for it to have resisted the level of complexity in the debate by insisting that each major issue arising was dealt with reasonably thoroughly before moving on.

Why, though, is the team apparently so prone to diverge rather than to converge in its debating? Is it because team members are unaware that the level of cognitive difficulty they have created for themselves is so high? This is certainly very possible. Are they aware what influence the role they are playing as individuals has on the pattern of interaction? Possibly not. And even if they were aware of how their pattern of interacting is making them less efficient and effective, do they know how they could behave differently to make it more cohesive and productive? Perhaps certain team members are aware that they are not managing their interaction effectively, and at times strive to do things differently, but their recipes for behaving in habitual patterns seem to be very strong. The behavioural recipes might therefore be difficult to alter, even if the team members wished to change their style of interaction.

Key points

➡ Try to focus on just one issue at a time.

➡ Never state disagreements without, in the same breath, saying precisely why you disagree.

➡ Allow other managers to develop their thoughts rather than butt in prematurely with your own orthogonal ideas.

➡ Do not dash off sideways into your pet issues – even if they are important, log them for later debate.

> ➡ Monitor the level of complexity the debate is building up to.
>
> ➡ Where the debate has been divergent, periodically summarize and then distil the essence of the value (if any) that has been added.
>
> ➡ Try to deliver some clear outputs so that business can be finished off rather than just added to the 'unfinished' pile.

Let us now look at the team's 'free-style' debate that followed on from the more formal presentations.

Debate on emergent strategic issues

The first issue to emerge is culture change. After Keith(A) kicks off, Bonnie introduces a wonderfully creative example, which – at least for a time – focuses the group's thinking. Sometimes creativity gives the team a much clearer focus (particularly where it holds the team's strategic attention for a while). At other times, the continual stream of more isolated creative ideas actually dilutes it.

Culture

> *Bonnie*: ... I thought of a culture change, one of the faster culture changes I remember – when they changed cultures on the drain [the underground train line between Waterloo and Bank] so that the doors were not lined up against the little lines where people used to queue. The next week, people stopped queuing by the doors because the train didn't stop at the marks. And within a week it was mass riot, with the children and widows to the back. The entire culture of the drain changed from the 'well-behaved, furled umbrella culture' to a 'savage hooligan-ridden culture' with the same people using the facility – within the week. Now, all you have got to do to change the culture is to change the environment. The change in culture will change very fast if you make the right change in the environment. We can spend some time on the one thing or two things or three things we could imagine that would really change BT's culture. (*creative thinking*)
>
> *Keith(A)*: Good point. (*agreeing*)

This metaphor potentially gives the department some powerful clues on how and where to introduce change in thinking to BT. This was built on,

123

however, as further metaphors were then discussed in a divergent fashion. (It is as if the other individuals feel a need to compete with Bonnie by offering different metaphors rather than collaborating with her to build on and refine what she has put forward. This suggests a kind of 'cognitive rivalry' within the team.)

Keith(A) then introduces an even bigger and broader issue – that of a strategy for culture change at BT. This is also an issue that may be beyond the department's immediate scope of influence (*expanding*).

> *Keith(A)*: Can we just sit back and ask ourselves the question 'How much of BT's culture do we need to change?' Is not the process culture absolutely right, even in the information age, for delivery or not? (*questioning*)

By introducing the issue of process, this takes the team down a level (within the strategic architecture), to examining the pros and cons of process.

> *Bonnie*: But it [process] is not what the guys who are successful in information services do.
> (Several interruptions occur.)
> *Keith(A)*: But you know that's only one layer …
> *Jonathan*: I think that the process approach does have great value in a steady state situation. (*judging*)
> *Keith(A)*: I agree, you are absolutely right. (*agreeing*)
> *Bonnie*: Have you actually got any evidence of that, of people actually keeping to the process when things work? (*questioning, probing*)
> *Jonathan*: Well, I mean, the arch-advocate of process is manager F who is very strongly driving that. He can achieve mega changes, positive changes, by doing it. (*expanding*)
> *Bonnie*: OK, if you have got evidence for it. (*probing*)
> *Ross*: We have also got people like manager H who have a view of the future based heavily on process. With more planning than ever before, but with plans which have new forms of processes which are more responsive, and cope with a number of scenarios, but heavily plan-based … . These are exceedingly interesting models. (*expanding*)

By now, there is very little sense of where the discussion is heading. Perhaps this is inevitable, given that the issue of 'culture' is clearly very big and complicated. Also, the team did not begin by posing some specific questions in advance of their debate, which seems to take the form of 'strategic roaming'. While this interaction may seem to be at one end of the spectrum, you will no doubt identify quite a number of situations in your own organization where a 'hot issue' like culture change is thrown into a debate. While generating strategic energy, sadly this is almost impossible to focus because the issue is simply too big and complicated to deal with just like that. Indeed, it is a composite of many issues and, thus, generates multiple discussions rather than a single discussion. But because managers have these discussions in the same place and time, this creates an illusion of one discussion, even though there are actually many going on.

The debate on culture now moves to more tangible and relevant ground. Ross flags up some major concerns stemming from the impact of organizational change on the planning process.

> *Ross*: I know from the little probes I have inserted outside that we are approaching the reorganization on 1 April like the *Titanic* going into an iceberg. It will make a lovely noise, and then we will wonder why we are sinking. There is a lot of doubt and uncertainty about what these roles are, even in the existing stuff. And if you ever wanted a harder time to do a platform review, this is it because, you know, like the supertanker, they are hard enough to change at the best of times. When they get dozens of conflicting orders, the chap in charge of the boiler room will go in the direction which he thinks best. It is a very convoluted metaphor creeping in there. (*expanding, uncertainty, structure*)

He continues (following an attempted interruption by Bonnie):

> *Ross*: But what I am saying, then, is that it is really going to be hard out there, and it may be that we have to be more compliant in having to tailor your, how can I put it, tailoring your conversion process more according to the market that you are trying to meet. There may be people in Bonnie's area who really have got to do an organic thing [in dealing with more emergent rather than deliberate strategies] and produce all these ideas – they are not in the supertanker, they are in the little speedboat, bouncing around in the bow waves, and other chaps have got to, you know, er ... (*strategic process, anxiety*)
>
> *Bonnie*: We will get sunk all the time. (*humour*)

However, instead of addressing the implications of these issues for the team (and its role and priorities), which would have been very useful and thought-provoking, then David says (perhaps at this point overly concerned about time pressures):

David: We are running out of time, so let's move on ... (*setting time frames*)

Tim now attempts to go back to Bonnie's metaphor:

> *Tim*: One point from Bonnie – when she said if you want to change the culture, you change the environment. Can that, is that process, does that process naturally lead, initially, to a very chaotic situation – like you said with the drain? (*expanding*)

Tim's intervention thus leads to further divergence in the debate, with an increasingly microscopic discussion and no *helicoptering up*.

> *Bonnie*: It is much easier to do a backward culture change than a forward, a nice culture change.
>
> *Ross*: Bonnie, did chaos rule forever or did order resume after some time?' (*expanding*)
>
> *Bonnie*: No, no, it gets worse all the time, it is terrible, absolutely appalling. (*questioning, judging*)
>
> *Keith(A)*: [You] keep reorganizing, keep changing the bosses and then you all change the culture. (*expanding*)

Some limited value is then drawn out of the debate by Keith(A), which reflects on the new political climate that will form the backdrop to the next planning review.

> *Keith(A)*: It is very obvious that you guys have noticed that, from what you have said. And that should tell you that manager D's empire is likely to be much more chaotic than manager E's empire. (*structure*)

The profile of this debate is as follows:

H			D	
M	B K(A) K(A)		R B T	
L	J	B K(A) J K(A) B J B R		B R B K(A) K(A)

Figure 4.3 gives us a feeling of the direction of debate.

Fig 4.3 Strategic issues map – emergent strategic issues

Refreshingly, Keith(A) and David now lead the level of debate upwards, but this is offset by Bonnie's inputs, which are pitched primarily at a lower level.

At this point in the workshop, the team leader, Andy, returns. Keith(A) then asks whether or not the team feels that it has behaved differently from normal in this particular workshop:

Keith(A): … people have been exceptionally well-behaved this morning, and that includes me as well. We normally have a fairly rough and tumble punch-up, you know, and it is often difficult to get a word in edgeways. That wasn't terribly evident this morning, was it Dave? (*questioning, probing*)

David: I agree. [Laughter ensues.] (*agreeing*)

Andy: It was probably because I wasn't here that you behaved better. (*humour*)

David: There is a lot of that [behaviour going on], well. (*humour*)

Bonnie: Well, we were going to be on a tape recorder, for crying out loud. (*reflecting*)

Tim: Well, we were a much smaller gathering than we were last week, with Keith(A) and John. (*reflecting*)

Keith(A)'s comments may seem to be somewhat surprising, given the rather divergent nature of the debate, frequently punctuated by disagreement. This suggests that, without an observer present, their behaviour could become somewhat difficult to steer.

Andy then decides to come in:

127

Andy: On the other hand, I think – we discussed this with Tony – the sort of interactions which do go on, and some of the tensions there – that clearly didn't come out this morning – some of these tensions are healthy, the net result of which is quite good, but quite what route is best I don't know. Did we get as good a level of debate as a result? (*questioning*)

Finally, David explores whether or not the debate was relatively calm because some of the more contentious issues were left untouched.

David: I think it was also, there were other tensions in the session which we have just had, that are there, they are just under the surface, but we covered them. What we didn't really cover was the difference between the technology and the business. (*reflecting*)

Generally, the team seems to have enjoyed, or found useful, being, as it were, 'observed'. The members of the team reflect:

Bonnie: I think it would be a good idea to tape-record ourselves in every meeting if it makes us behave better. (*reflecting*)
Andy: Even if there is no tape in the box? (*humour*)
Bonnie: Yes – no, no, no, you can't do that. (*humour*)

Key points

➡ Do invoke a picture or metaphor to act as the centrepiece of the strategic debate (as in Bonnie's hornbills story).

➡ When discussing something abstract and ambiguous, such as 'process', begin with a clear definition of what it means and also explore the kind of context in which it is being used. Without this you will invariably generate much unnecessary heat.

➡ Do not continue discussion if there is literally no idea at all where it is heading – or whether or not you might ever exert a significant influence over it.

➡ If a subset of the team is, in effect, pulling down the team to a purely microscopic area of debate, stop working and reflect on what level of debate you really need to have.

Review and conclusions

The first team workshop has put flesh on its members' earlier accounts of the team's behaviour in Chapter 3. Clearly, the team's habitual behaviours (especially in their leader's absence) tend towards generating a proliferation of ideas and then picking them apart in a generally informal and unsteered way. This gives rise to a rush of disparate behaviours, often centred on agreeing or disagreeing with one another. This is interspersed with moments of clarity, when the group sometimes reaches some valuable insights and conclusions.

Perhaps because the team's official task is 'strategic thinking', its members appear to be comfortable with the more discursive nature of their output. In Chapter 6, it will be seen that even with their team leader, Andy, there (and with more active facilitation), they still find it hard to converge in their discussions. However, before leaving this first workshop, let us examine some of the managers' own reflections on the workshop. The quotes come from interviews with the team members individually the day after the first workshop.

The debrief interviews

The size of the agenda

First of all, Tim suggests that the team's agenda was a very ambitious one indeed:

> Yes, it was large, it was large, and I don't think we really, we listed concerns and issues, but we didn't really … . Sometimes there were nods around the table and we would say 'Yes, we agree that is an issue, we agree that we need to do more of that'. We have those kinds of nods. But it didn't result in a plan of action.

This suggests that much of the time was spent skimming the issues and actually staying away from harder debate, dilemmas and actual decisions. Again, this might have been amplified by Andy's unavoidable absence.

In Tim's view:

> More time is needed to really develop a way in which we can behave differently. We can approach the strategy actually differently … . I think, on our own, we would just chew over the same old ground again and again and again. Much of the stuff that we heard this morning, to be honest, we have heard in

various guises over a long period of time. I think there is a lot of – Dave has tried to interject a slightly different kind of thinking.

(more strategy recycling)

Tim also reveals the significance of absent players, which appears to generate a kind of shadow behaviour (which can be defined as behaviour generated by individuals who are actually not present).

It was good. First of all, it was good. I enjoyed it … . It was a shame … . We were missing Keith(B). Because, although you – I don't know how much you detected – I think that a number of my comments were actually, in a kind of way, directed at Keith. Comments with respect to pitching our, our output, our strategies, at the right level. I had that notion of levels of strategy. It is appropriate to what we are doing within the group function.

(problem architecture)

This extract also highlights the influence of the personal strategic agendas of specific individuals on other members of the group. Keith(B) has some strong views about part of BT's technical strategy, and this appears to result in the other team members having to take this into account in their discussions. At times, personal strategic agendas were thus, as it were, 'strategic baggage' that the rest of the team have to carry throughout their discussions. This is not to imply that this is good or bad baggage, simply that it was there. However, this said, strategic baggage might itself reduce the flexibility of the mindset and behaviours of the group to less than it would otherwise have been.

The architecture of the presentations

David describes the design of the workshop as revolving around creating a number of presentations underpinned by a common theme:

Well, I suggested this idea – to actually have this meeting – and said, we have talked about how we would do it. I suggested that a sensible thing to do would be to get two or three of us to do presentations. And we said, 'Who is interested in doing what?' and Tim said, 'Oh, I would like to do one', and Bonnie said she would like to do one, and I said I would do one – giving us three, which was enough to work on. These were presentations on downstream strategy.

The architecture of these presentations thus appears to have been an important factor in shaping both workshop debate and behaviour of the individuals. The three presentations do not seem to have been particularly well targeted in relation to the higher-level issues facing the department (including its role). The answers to the various questions raised in the presentations impacted inevitably on the resolution of this role ambiguity. Hence, by framing the presentations in the way that it was done, there would be some problems in resolving the issues.

Further, as the presentations were both detailed and prepared independently, it is not surprising that they were orthogonal and did not really mesh together. Discussion of strategic content then merged together with discussion of the planning process, making it hard for team members to unravel what was going on.

David is relatively self-critical of his own facilitation role. He appears to have been aware (at the time) of the gaps in facilitation that existed, but felt unable to deal with them then and there:

> Well, one of the things that I was unhappy with all the way through was that we weren't, we weren't addressing things which we could influence, particularly when we got to the point of what we were going to do as a result of it.

When probed about whether or not it would have been useful to make more linkages back to what had gone before, he reflects:

> Well, it wasn't one of the options, given our timetable. That is something which I am vulnerable to doing. I will come to a conclusion on what needs to be done, and go down that route, come what may.

He now turns to the process of the meeting:

> Er [sighing], I suppose that what I would say is that I would like us to be far more aware of the processes that we are using. And think more about the structure of the meeting and the goals … . Behaviour, I think, and one of the reasons why we need to do that is because we don't have terribly positive … I think you intervened at one point and said that we were all talking at the meeting but not really building at the meeting, which was very, very true.

He then reflects on the team's ability to gain a common focus – and to hold to it:

> I suppose each time when we do something like this, I have a vision that we do end up with a shared, mental map. We actually agree the areas where we agree – and agree the areas where we disagree. We must realize that we actu-

ally have different positions. I think, you know, we are a long way from doing that.'

In summary, David is concerned that the team's process could be sharpened up to give a clearer focus for debate.

Collective team behaviour

Unpeeling 'what is really going on' and now looking a layer deeper, David now surfaces questions about whether the team is really a team anyway or merely a collection of individuals who come together for periodic discussions:

> Well, I think that we do see it as a part of our role to actually become more effective at what we do. And that's really why we are there. Er, I guess I am less clear as to the extent to which we believe it is possible to operate as a team, and actually improve effectiveness because, in a way, it is a lot of individual operators doing their own thing.

David's reflections thus closely mirror Tim's, that 'the team' is highly individualistic. The lack of cohesion within the team appears to be an important constraint on moving towards a decision to do anything. Equally, the perception that 'action is unlikely to come out of debate' may itself encourage the tendency to roam around the strategic issues without particularly stopping to really deal with any one issue firmly. (It is almost as if the individuals are acting like 'tourists', except, of course, when they are dealing with matters central to their own, personal strategic agendas.)

> *Myself*: It didn't feel like we were looking at anything particularly close up.
> *David*: [chuckling] I think that any one of those issues – if pushed to a conclusion – would have generated a lot of tension.

Once again, the picture emerges of a team trying hard to tackle a number of overlapping, complicated and very large issues. The tackling is done, essentially, by means of the brainpower of themselves individually, rather than by harnessing their behaviour with a clear focus of attention and process.

Next, Bonnie (like David) shows an eagerness to develop ways of focusing the debate:

> What we need is some shorthand for places which we have already been, but, the trouble is, it takes – it is taking – too long to get them. For example, I do

think now that we can take the fact that modern, information-based organizations are more likely to be chaotic and less likely to be hierarchical as a given, and not have to revisit it all the time.

Bonnie thus gives us some important clues as to how the team can move forward more effectively in future. By establishing quite clearly and firmly areas of common agreement, it will be better able to isolate areas of disagreement and areas that are simply underexplored.

Key points
················

➡ Discuss *before* starting how absent players are going to be represented – or simply kept in tune with things – rather than simply trying to manage around the problem.

➡ Always define very clearly the role of the facilitator. Who is going to do it? How should they separate this role from their own personal and strategic agendas?

➡ Do try explicitly to build shared mental maps that can then act as guides to 'places where we have been'.

➡ Define what role 'the team' has anyway. To what extent is it an ongoing team or simply a group of managers who occasionally collaborate to debate strategic issues?

Key themes from the interviews

A number of significant issues regarding the group's ways of working came out of (or were amplified by) the debrief interviews. These naturally cluster into:

● process issues
● cognitive issues
● behavioural issues.

Process issues

Taking process issues first, the unavoidable absence of the team leader, Andy, probably did not help in focusing the team interaction. The style of facilitation also played a key role in determining the shape of discussion – especially in the absence of the team leader. David took upon himself the task of facilitation, but felt somewhat constrained. This was partly because of ambiguity over who should be steering the workshop. David also seemed to be constrained by his notion of what being a facilitator meant, and, particularly, that he could do more than he did to steer the team.

Also, the degree of thoroughness of preparation prior to the workshop also appears to play a major role in shaping an ordered debate. Although much work went into preparing content, less work went into the process. This might include setting a targeted agenda, thinking through the various stages of discussion and the specific outputs the workshop has in mind. At least two players in the team – David and Bonnie – would like to see the team have an agreed process. The workshop process highlighted the strong interdependency between all the different ingredients. Process thus provides a key role within the overall behavioural mix.

The existence of absent players is a further influence – the absent player exercising almost a 'shadow' or ghost role. Here, the other team members feel impelled to almost enact the absent member in order to give due weighting to all the personal strategic agendas of the players (present or absent).

Finally, the team process seemed to follow a highly divergent trajectory. There seemed to have been very little convergence within the debate (or much synthesis of outputs). This may have been due to not merely the natural style of the individuals present, but also due to the absence of Andy. It may also have been due, once again, to the lack of a commonly agreed team process and to the team seeking to cover a very wide agenda. Just one of these factors in isolation could produce an unstructured and less than focused interaction; when combined, they result in a cumulative, disruptive effect.

Cognitive issues

Turning now to cognitive issues, both Bonnie and David wanted to expose their mental maps (on key strategic issues), far more explicitly than perhaps they have done in the past. Also, interviews with Tim, Bonnie and David revealed an apparently greater degree of cognitive clarity on certain issues (within their individual mental map) than perhaps was expressed at the time of the meeting.

It was also noticeable that the event itself seemed to generate almost an excess of interpersonal energy, especially among some individuals. By creating a 'hothouse' environment, the team unwittingly produced a large quantity of mainly disconnected ideas. Some of these ideas might be of longer-term interest, but some less so. Even those of interest might not be so well thought through or be underexploited subsequently.

The result of this informal, ideas-driven process was that the individuals may have tired themselves out, both cognitively and emotionally. An alternative approach might be to have set a tighter agenda, targeted at achieving fewer outputs of higher quality.

Further, ambiguous terms, such as 'technical strategy', or particular words used on flip chart outputs can also generate loosely focused debate. Also, such terms can be potentially highly charged emotionally. Here, meanings of specific terms and shorthand ideas have just as much of an affective content as they do a cognitive content.

Behavioural issues

Finally, certain members of the team appeared to operate according to a set of behavioural recipes that had a considerable momentum of their own. For example, their habitual behavioural style might mean that any efforts that were made to listen more actively or avoid making premature interruption would be virtually impossible to sustain.

Key points

➡ Prepare well for any strategic meeting – not only defining inputs, but also the process. This involves splitting up the tasks into manageable chunks and posing specific questions to focus the work at each stage. Allocate at least 50 per cent of the workshop effort for preparation time.

➡ Also, provide sufficient time to digest and distil outputs following the workshop. Again, allow at least 50 per cent of the workshop time, pro rata, for a review of outputs.

➡ Ruthlessly prune back the agenda to a reasonably small number of issues. To focus managers' behaviour, show what these issues are (and how they interrelate) on either a white board or flip charts. This enables managers to keep track of where they are within the strategic architecture, thus channelling strategic roaming.

➡ Ensure that there is ample facilitation to keep up the momentum of the meeting, deal with any blockages and direct the focus of strategic attention.

➡ Set expectations that the meeting will be very much about 'helicopter thinking', so that managers avoid going down too many rabbit holes and getting lost.

➡ Seek to build on and synthesize what has gone on previously, rather than always be engaged in 'picking apart' behaviour.

➡ Where there is evident disagreement, you must always accompany this with a precise statement of exactly what it is you disagree about and why.

➡ When managers do get their teeth into a really meaty issue, avoid just rushing on to other topics purely because of time considerations.

➡ Equally, avoid giving little time to issues that are less immediate or over which there is (unavoidably) less influence (like that of culture change at BT).

➡ Even where the team leader is absent, do not neglect to use sufficient meta-behaviours to steer the interaction of the meeting forward.

Finally, if I were to choose a single thing that would be most likely to help the BT team, it would be for them to continually monitor the value added (or destroyed or diluted) over time.

A useful picture to reflect on here is the 'value over time curve'. Originally invented as a means of understanding customer value (Grundy, 1998), the value over time curve plots how value is added (for a customer) by a product or service over time. In the case of the BT team, for 'product or service' read 'the meeting', and for 'customers' read 'managers – here and elsewhere'.

Figure 4.4 is an approximate representation of value being added or diluted or destroyed during the first BT workshop. Managers should carry this model in their heads so that when value is not being added, they then pause and decide whether or not they should be behaving differently or should refocus their behaviour on a different target.

A most fruitful, everyday way of remembering this is to imagine that you have a set of traffic lights on your forehead. 'Green' means 'value being added – without a doubt'. 'Yellow' means 'unsure as to whether or not much value is being added'. 'Red' means 'value definitely being diluted or destroyed'. This gives managers a really sharp focus on value, helping them avoid being swept along in the drift of meetings.

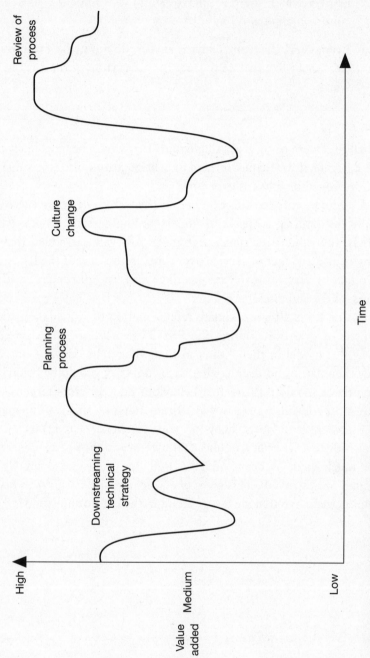

Fig 4.4 Value added over time – first BT workshop

Appreciating value

- What value is added by particular kinds of meeting that deal with strategic issues?

  _____

  _____

  _____

  _____

- For one particular meeting recently, draw a 'value over time' curve. Why were there times when value was diluted or destroyed? What could be done (see the key points above) to enhance the value that was diluted?

  _____

  _____

  _____

  _____

- Identify a number of situations when the coloured lights on your forehead turned red. Why did this occur and what could you have done to avoid this?

  _____

  _____

  _____

  _____

THE SECOND WORKSHOP
WHAT IS OUR PROCESS?

In the second workshop, the team deals with:

- strategic assumptions and mental maps
- strategic agendas and the strategy process
- strategy, power and personal agendas
- active listening.

Strategic assumptions and mental maps

In this session, the team reflect on whether or not their debates are made more difficult because they have not always shared their strategic assumptions and mental maps in the past.

David begins the debate as follows:

> *David*: It goes back to the common assumptions of the business. Because, actually, those words are actually used in a way that is kind of – we assume that they are pulled together by some kind of common assumption, but I suspect they are not. (*mental maps*)

Keith also highlights the need to expose assumptions:

> *Keith(A)*: We often listen to our, to each other's views, and then say, 'No, I don't agree with that', but without asking why we think that. What is behind it? And it often removes 90 per cent of the tension. (*reflection*)

Unless strategic assumptions and mental maps are well shared, this may give rise to:

- premature interruptions and unnecessary disagreement, resulting in zig-zag discussion, frustration, loss of time and lack of team focus
- relatively little building on what has already been said, so that continuity is lost, ideas are not fully developed and radically new ways of looking at things occur less frequently
- over a period of time, individuals may build up personal strategic agendas that then become hard for the rest of the team to own.

Next, a short side-debate on strategy, measures and outputs.

140

Strategic agendas and the strategy process

First of all, the team reflects on the amount of presentation material that was input within the team workshop. As their facilitator (my role at this stage), I then likened it to the feeling of being overwhelmed when looking at a menu in a Chinese restaurant:

> *Keith(A)*: You pick at random, don't you, from the issues. I think that that is the answer. (*picking apart, prioritization*)

Bonnie draws out from the discussion some points of practical significance for those managing the workshop process and in relation to how individuals develop their own mental maps.

> *Bonnie*: Where we have got stuff that has been in circulation before, what we need is a quicker way of saying 'Now, er, would you all put on the mental hat of Module A. Remember, Module A, and let's go on from there ...', but we don't, we don't start from the beginning of Module A. We say instead, very slowly, 'Once upon a time ...', thus we always begin afresh. (*expanding*)

Keith(A), David and Andy all agree that a different approach to their existing one needs to be adopted:

> *Keith(A)*: I agree we go back to the beginning, but we don't start slowly – that's not one of our characteristics. (*reflecting, rushing*)
>
> *David*: But, you know, we need those mental models, we need to understand what they are. (*reflecting, mental maps*)
>
> *Andy*: Some pre-digestion might help. (*expanding*)
>
> *Keith(A)*: We should start from here, don't we chaps, sort of thing. (*expanding*)

While this is a most laudable discussion, what the team does not flag up is how they will put this in place or how (and when) they will discuss this further – the discussion thus just hangs.

Bonnie reveals a wider fear, which she also shares with Keith(A), about making the debating process too rigid and unwieldy:

> *Bonnie*: Wherever we have process – and I understand the need for process, a certain orderliness, because otherwise nothing ever comes clearer. But, for example, the strategic review ... always feels mechanical. It never feels as though it is doing anything more except that to ensure that you get whatever it is that you are going to get at the right time. It doesn't help you get the right theory at all, in my view. I am not saying that it

can't. I am just asking everybody who hasn't felt this. (*strategic process, judging*)

Keith(A) then echoes Bonnie's concerns:

> *Keith(A)*: I think we define process in this company as a very mechanistic thing. I mean, you are absolutely right to put your finger on that ... I am kind of anti-process because my thinking has been totally tramlined in the past. And I do object to that. (*agreeing, reflecting, behavioural recipes, strategic process*)

Once again, although there has been a relatively fruitful and structured debate, it is hard to discern any really specific outputs from it. For instance, what is the team actually going to do new or differently as a result of this discussion? How will it reconcile the need for some process alongside continuing flexibility?

We now turn to some key linkages between strategy, power and the agendas of particular individuals.

Strategy, power and personal agendas

Bonnie now reaffirms her preference for contention as a way of teasing out new ideas:

> *Bonnie*: I mean, I believe in dialectic. I don't believe that something really worth while will come out without some kind of argument ... (*reflection, behavioural recipes*)

She then describes how the interplay between individuals can become territorial.

> *Bonnie*: I mean, it [territory] is almost prehistoric isn't it? (*questioning, anxiety*)

She now appears to think out loud about how she (and others) deal with perceived attacks on their own ideas territory:

> *Bonnie*: How do you say, either, 'I think that you are not understanding me because you are coming at it in a different, cognitive way to me' without being rude? How do you say, 'Stop attacking the top of my hill' without being rude? You know, 'Because you are getting really close to me and I don't know what to do with this'? (*questioning*)
>
> *Bonnie*: Supposing you know where they are coming from, and they are attempting to get your hill? (*questioning, politics*)

The way Bonnie describes personal ideas as being 'territory' suggests the idea of 'power contours'. Here we see that where an individual has, over a period of time, become deeply committed to a certain set of ideas, then these become their 'ideas territory'. Around this ideas territory, newcomers will find that as they encroach on the territory, they feel increasing resistance. As they get to the heart of the ideas territory, they are strongly resisted – where the power contours are at their highest point.

David takes this opportunity to signal to Bonnie how he feels she can respond when she feels threatened:

> *David*: I think that there is something else you can say. I think that you can say that you feel threatened. And by doing that you are actually showing a bit more of the mental map. If people say that, you can understand that, you can understand why people feel threatened. (*expanding, anxiety*)

Bonnie continues her reflections:

> *Bonnie*: It is all about personal power. It is all about personal views as to what constitutes my personal success and those have an enormous effect on what … I suppose they do on any team but they have an enormous effect. (*judging, personal success*)

Bonnie amplifies this further – obviously feeling strongly about the interplay between work, power and personal recognition, possibly alluding to others in the team.

> *Bonnie*: But there are people who see personal success in a different way. There are some people who feel that, you know, only particular pieces of information – particularly if it is very private information – is power. There are some people who feel that having a large area of work that nobody else is allowed to do is power, right. And those things affect how we do things. And you know what the results are. (*expanding, personal success, political recipes*)

Strategic agendas and personal ideas are thus very much bound up in the political manoeuvres of individuals – both in this and in other teams. Here we see certain ideas themselves taking on the nature of personal territory, bounded by power contours. These power contours are very tangible indeed when someone deliberately occupies ideas territory or even strays inadvertently on to protected ground.

Active listening

Andy is particularly keen on exploring the idea of active listening. This borrows from my own earlier analogy of debating strategic issues being akin to the challenge of being an air traffic controller at Heathrow:

> *Andy*: I like the idea of the active listening. Er, where people should be aware of who is queuing up to land. (*listening*)

Keith(A) supports Andy very strongly at this juncture:

> *Keith(A)*: I think that you are absolutely right. Most of us, sitting around the table, are keen to put our own points of view. And we are queuing up to land, and we don't notice those other people, you know, trying to land also. And to a greater or lesser extent, most of us are guilty of that. That is the kind of people that we are. And we ought to be more aware of that issue. (*listening*)

But David is sceptical that individuals are capable of changing these behaviours:

> *David*: And we need to find ways of managing it, too. I think it is all right to put 'active listening' on the chart. And it is all right that we all try to do active listening a lot more than we do at the moment, but, to be honest, I suspect that, a week down the track, we will be back to our old habits again. (*listening*)

Andy, not surprisingly, picks up the idea of 'active listening' as a way of harnessing the team's strategic behaviour. However, this is only one of many techniques the team can use to adapt its behaviour.

> **Key pointers**
> ·················
>
> ➡ A team without a process will find it extraordinarily difficult to tackle complicated, strategic issues, however bright its members are.
>
> ➡ Power is not something that is unspeakable: all teams should identify the really 'hot' spots that cause interpersonal contention. It should also expose, explicitly, the person who has the most intense power contours on those issues – in a zero embarrassment environment (drawing on meta-behaviour).
>
> ➡ Active listening requires at least as much energy and attention as does providing strategic input.
>
> ➡ When making an input, always think about whether or not an assertion or judgement can be turned around into a strategic question. The strategic question, ideally, may suggest a line of enquiry, but, hopefully, will also trigger thinking on new lines of enquiry.

CONCLUSION AND SUMMARY

There are several things that are impeding a more stable climate for debate within the TSD team. Some of these reside in the team's own context – its strategic tasks and role in the organization – but some are internal. For instance, the lack of explicit sharing of strategic assumptions and mental maps causes problems. Also, personal strategic agendas appear to impede the team's fluidity of strategic debate and its behaviour generally.

The TSD team is now becoming more aware of the limitations in how its members interact to create strategy. Soon it will be seen what happens when the team tackles some particularly tricky issues with renewed vigour.

REFOCUSING STRATEGIC BEHAVIOUR

> *Disputation is a proof of not seeing clearly*
> *Bhagavadgita*

INTRODUCTION

Before resuming the story of the TSD team at BT, I would like you to imagine that you have a dream (hopefully not a nightmare!) In the dream, you have been appointed the new Chief Executive of a subsidiary of a major car company. The subsidiary was acquired four years ago from a conglomerate that divested itself of its motor operations in order to strengthen its financial base and refocus its corporate strategy.

Its new owner is a very successful motor company, renowned throughout the world for its technological prowess, prestigious models and the durability of its cars. The subsidiary has, however, a more diverse mixture of vehicles. Its products range from distinctively unsporty small cars (which appeal to those over 50 or to the young with lower incomes) to executive cars aimed at the fleet market and also include off-road and other niche vehicles.

The subsidiary has been struggling to support this wide range and is being helped by its new owners to gradually reposition itself – hopefully up market. Since its acquisition, the subsidiary was initially managed essentially by its original team, but, two years ago, its Chief Executive and several other senior executives were moved on. The team now has a mix of local managers and managers from the rest of the group.

You, as Chief Executive, are now returning to the parent company for a well-earned rest after beginning the first phase of the turnaround plan.

You are told that the changing team has been under intense pressure for the past three years, but that the new blood has managed to steer it through tricky times. You are also told that the team members tend to become engulfed by very detailed issues when they meet, and find it hard to really address some of the bigger dilemmas and choices that they will face over the coming three to five years.

How would you prepare for a workshop?

You plan to run a two-day workshop off site to review the key strategic issues facing the business. Based on what you have learnt from the book so far, how would you prepare for the workshop? What behaviours would you wish to avoid and how would you attempt to head these off?

_____

_____

_____

_____

Would you choose to simply chair it yourself or make use of a facilitator? What other process arrangements would you put in place? Would you consider using some psychometric analysis of team styles and, if so, how would you persuade the managers that this was an opportunity and not a threat (that is, ensure that they do not think 'Am I being lined up for yet another redundancy?')

Having spent five or ten minutes thinking about this (hopefully some of which was not spent choosing which model to have as your company car), I will now return you to the BT team. As in the car company example, periodically we all need to refocus our strategic behaviour (not just our strategic thinking).

In the third workshop (which was a facilitated session), the team initially finds itself getting bogged down but is then able to structure debate more effectively. This highlights that although it is difficult to achieve, strategic behaviour can be refocused successfully.

THE BT CASE STUDY
(Continued)

THE THIRD WORKSHOP
WHERE DO WE GO FROM HERE?

The third team workshop was run very soon after the second. During the first part of this third workshop, I took on the role of a more active facilitator (as was pre-planned). My interventions took a number of forms:

- providing ideas for the team to converge on
- giving feedback when more disruptive patterns of behaviour emerged
- using a number of management tools to provide a clearer focus to the debate.

In the second part of the workshop, the team worked without any facilitation, so that the team could try out new ways of interacting. By this stage the team began to align their behaviours quite well.

In order to track the dynamics of the debate, the same coding system – of 'high', 'medium' or 'low' level – as was used in the last chapter is used here. However, this time, the code is given at the end of each statement as well as being summarized at the end of a section. This is because the debate was, as before, somewhat jumpy and a degree of concentration is required in order to make sense of what is going on.

The first part of the workshop

The topics covered in the third workshop were:

- strategic roles
- what business we are in?
- what value we add (and to whom)
- the role of the department
- key priorities – importance and influence
- process review.

Strategic roles

First of all, the team discusses the overall strategic role of the department.

151

Keith(A) begins by questioning the team's assumption that the department is there to create 'all of the strategy' itself:

> *Keith(A)*: I think that the message, for me, seems to be that we, in the past, we have tried to do it all ourselves. And, because there is insufficient resource, what we ought to be considering ourselves is as sort of 'strategy facilitators'. (*expanding, strategic roles*) (*H*)

Andy amplifies this before I then support this line of thinking:

> *Andy*: I think that that is the new point that is coming out. We don't have to do it all ourselves, or own it ourselves necessarily. (*expanding, strategic roles, monitoring value*) (*H*)
>
> *Myself*: Isn't that about leveraging the strategic thinking elsewhere within BT? (*expanding, questioning*) (*H*)

Andy, Keith, Bonnie and David then reflect:

> *Andy*: Yes, we have been rather jealous of anyone else doing the thinking. (*agreeing, strategic roles*)
>
> *Keith(A)*: Yes, much too jealous. Sitting in a little castle. (*agreeing, strategic roles*) (*M*)
>
> *Bonnie*: You have got your own little castle. (*M*)
>
> *David*: One of the things that is also an issue here is the level of mature working – I think that if you really want to have an influence on corporate strategy, you really want to talk to people on the main Board. If you are going to have an influence on the main operating business strategy, you have got to have workshops, sessions with their Board. (*influencing*) (*M*)

David then relates this discussion of 'strategic roles' back to the discussion in the second workshop about the extent to which the department could really shape BT's overall strategy and, indeed, what forms that strategy would actually take (including deliberate strategy, emergent strategy and so on):

> *David*: They are the people who have to do it. [Naming one senior manager] – it is not us. You know. And that deliberate/emergent strategy distinction, I think, has got a lot to do with that – who has really got the ability to really create strategy for the business. And a department like ourselves does not really have the capability to produce the strategy, except for a few, small, technical areas. (*influencing, judging, strategic roles*) (*M*)

The need to narrow the focus of work performed by the team is a relatively new line of thinking. Initially, the department saw itself as being the core 'manufacturer' of technical strategy. This is a very common characteristic of strategic planning departments generally – they feel nervous unless it is they (and not line management) that are delivering the strategy. However, now the department is beginning to see itself creating strategy in certain technical areas while also playing the role of facilitating strategic thinking elsewhere in BT.

The pattern of interaction in the initial debate has been at a consistently high level, as follows:

H	K(A)	A	T					
M				A	K(A)	B	D	D
L								

Following this early consensus, the course of the debate now turns to what turns out to be much more difficult terrain – the question 'What business are we in?'

What business are we in?

This discussion was facilitated by myself. First, I introduced and explained a model for understanding 'What business we are in' from marketing theory. This model contains three main topics.

- Who are the customers?
- What are their specific needs?
- How are these needs met?

Clarifying your own mental maps

Invariably, the questions given in the model are testing and expose uncertainties about why a particular department exists. Ask yourself the questions 'Why does my department exist?', 'What value does it add and to whom?', 'Do they share the same perceptions as us as to what value we add and should add?'

Only when you have reflected on these questions yourself will it be fair for you to evaluate the BT department's clarity of thinking about how it generates value.

Bonnie begins the discussion that follows. The discussion is highly punctuated, with little opportunity created to develop ideas at length.

> *Bonnie*: What does 'What business we are in?' mean? (*clarifying*) (H)
> *Myself*: It means what business is the department in. And where could you add most value? (*expanding*) (H)
> *David*: The biggest impact would be on the customer group which we mentioned the other day. (*diving in*) (M)
> *Bonnie*: Like manager X, manager Y ... (*expanding*) (L)
> *David*: That's interesting, I would actually agree with that. (*agreeing*) (L)
> *Paul*: Who are the customers, first of all? (*questioning*) (M)
> *David*: I don't think everyone would ... (*picking apart*) (L)
> *Bonnie*: I think that it is everyone who ... (*picking apart*) (L)
> *Andy*: Sorry, for us? (*clarifying*) (L)
> *Myself*: Yes, for us. (L)
> *Keith(B)*: For us, the customer is the main operating business Board. (*picking apart*) (M)
> *David*: I don't think that's ... (*disagreeing*) (M)

At this point, the discussion seems to be zig-zagging without much feeling that anything clear has been established. I then try to intervene:

> *Myself*: Let's prioritize them. (*facilitating*) (M)

There is now a spontaneous attempt from a new source to steer the debate. Keith(A) now asks a broader question to try to clarify the discussion.

Keith(A): Can I just ask a question, rather than sort of comment specifically. And that is, one of the things, you know, we haven't actually decided was whether, as one group, we are really supporting main operating business or are we supporting BT as a whole? And I think that is a lack of focus across that dimension. And I think that the focus is on main operating business, but it is not solely main operating business, and that's the issue. (*questioning, judging, challenging*) (M)

This longer input might have provided a cognitive and behavioural anchor. However, Bonnie's fresh input effectively pre-empts the opportunity to set a clear direction for the debate:

Bonnie: There is no point in supporting main operating business except to support BT. And from where we are, we ought to function and to see BT's needs, and how main operating business has to function to support that. (*judging*) (M)

The trajectory of the above discussion looks like this:

H	B T			
M	D P		K(B) D T B A K(A) B	
L		B D D B A T		

I then tried to help the team get more of a focus to their discussions:

Myself: This is supposed to be a single task – asking who the customers are. You see you are doing another task, which is to prioritize them. (*facilitation*) (M)

Keith(A) reflects on why it is not that straightforward to define, in simple terms, what business they are in:

Keith(A): We are not trying to do that specifically. The trouble is that if you don't bound it when you comment, then you immediately jump in and say, 'Well it's so and ...' (*facilitation*) (M)

The discussion resumes with Keith(A) linking back to what has already been discussed:

Myself: Let's start again. (H)
Keith(A): I think that they [the main operating business Board] must come in. (*judging*) (M)

155

> *David B*: I have a problem with the main operating business Board. (*challenging*) (M)
>
> *Bonnie*: Put main operating business Board, and then put managers X, Y and Z separately, as well. (*expanding*) (L)
>
> *Andy*: I don't think we should put P and Q down. (*disagreeing*) (L)

The discussion thus becomes focused primarily on specific names of customers, rather than on generic types or generic needs. (Obviously the team could work from the specific back to the general, but the danger of a bottom-up approach is that it could fragment and, also, fail to identify all clusters of customers.)

> *David B*: Well, these individuals should not be put down because I don't think they would pay for us. (L)
>
> *Andy*: Oh, well, that's a different definition. (*challenging*) (M)
>
> *Myself*: Well there are some customers … (*facilitating*) (M)
>
> *Bonnie*: [Interrupting] We are also saying the BT Board. BT, you know BT? (*expanding*) (M)
>
> *David*: BT corporate. (*expanding*) (M)
>
> *Keith(A)*: Yes, BT Group. (*agreeing*) (M)

The team's debate produced the following profile for this sequence of interactions:

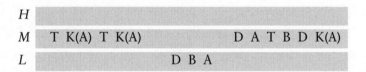

```
H
M     T K(A) T K(A)              D A T B D K(A)
L                      D B A
```

This shows that the debate is being pulled down to a more detailed level.

One of the major problems here is that the team has dived into the analysis without first examining what 'customer' means. Potentially this might have been headed off by more active facilitation, but the problem a facilitator often faces is that they cannot see ahead of time all the areas that may be ambiguous. What is perhaps more revealing is that, although the team is obviously struggling to get a hold on the debate, the discussion continues anyway. The debate has here its own 'strategic momentum'. It might have been more helpful to the team to have broken off at that point and reflected on the question, 'If we are having such a difficult time debating this, why is this?'

> **Key points**
> ················
>
> ➡ If you do not define 'the business that your department is in', then your team will invariably engage in behaviours that generate undue heat and tension when discussing strategy issues.
>
> ➡ You will need to examine, quite explicitly, who your customers actually are, and prioritize their relative importance. Also, you will need to look at all this against your value-creating activities.
>
> ➡ Before you enter this kind of debate, you need to look at 'point of entry' options. If, for instance, you enter the debate at one point (by asking 'Who are our customers?'), where will this lead to versus another point of entry (asking another question, such as 'What are our value-creating activities?') given the personal and strategic agendas of the key players?

What value do we add (and to whom?

The team members now turn to the equally difficult (and related) topic of what value the team's activities add. I start them off by suggesting that they should put their mindset in 'customer mode'. Rapidly, it is apparent that even the notion of 'value' is unclear and needs to be defined.

> *Myself*: What are the biggest areas of value you add? Try to have an 'out-of-body experience' – imagine you are actually the customer. (*H*)
> *Andy*: Well, I don't know. I am not sure which issue we are addressing. At this kind of level, that is the right level – to be against those customers [pointing to the flip chart]. (*clarifying, helicoptering up*) (*H*)
> *Bonnie*: Well, I think they need to be alerted, to what they haven't seen – to what they don't know yet. (*picking apart*) (*M*)
> *Andy*: Well, that is a subject in its own right. (*H*)

With hindsight, it is apparent that the department adds value in a diversity of ways (and these ways need to be unravelled). This diversity did not surface in any systematic way, perhaps because the team did not have more complete (and shared) mental maps of its own activities. I then continued:

Myself: So that is something about blind spots? (*clarifying*) (H)

Bonnie: Or simply something that is there, that they haven't taken account of, but you want them to, and you think that they should have been able to see. (*picking apart*) (M)

Myself: Whose mind are you now in? (*probing*) (H)

Bonnie: I am in manager X's mind. He can't see everything going on everywhere ... and something may be happening. (*picking apart*) (L)

Myself: Is this an intelligence map? (*probing*) (M)

Bonnie: Yes, yes. (*agreeing* (M)

David: I don't think that's an issue here ... (*judging*) (M)

Although the discussion has some focus (on what is on specific customers' minds, using the out-of-body experience technique), it has again become very specific and has thus lost its links to the bigger context. I then tried to move things on:

Myself: Let's carry the flow on. (H)

Keith(A): Yes, yeah. (H)

David: I think he has got a number of jobs that he has been given to do, which he needs to sort out. (*picking apart*) (L)

Myself: We seem to be up there and now we are back here. I know that there is no right process, but we have got one, so let us stay with it. (*reflecting, facilitation*) (H)

I again bring to their attention that the discussion is wandering around, hoping that the team can agree to talk about more specific things. This is echoed by Andy and seized upon by Bonnie.

Andy: I am a bit confused. We are assuming that we are manager X, and what is it that we need from us? (*clarifying, helicoptering up*) (M)

Bonnie: Yes, what does he need from us – a helicopter view? (*questioning, helicoptering up*) (M)

Andy now guides me:

Andy: I should just put them down, Tony, don't qualify them – the technology X problem [discussed earlier] stands. Bonnie's point is equally valid, so it doesn't negate it. Second operator in Europe. (*facilitating, anchoring*) (H)

Paul now exercises a useful check so that quality control is maintained on the team's debate:

Paul: My worry is that we have gone straight to the main operating business Board. And we have direct reporting to the BT Board. (*picking apart*) (M)

However, then, Bonnie dives down into some specifics, rapidly followed by David who also defaults to 'picking apart'. I was curious here about why the debate was so consistently disjointed, until the thought occurred to me that Bonnie might be working up her next thought rather than actively listening to Paul's contribution, hence leading to dislocation of ideas.

> *Bonnie*: What's going on? Dangers and opportunities are things which ... It is not just the general world around us looking, it is not just the world around us. The Internet is getting bigger ... (*picking apart*) (L)
>
> *David*: Infrastructure sharing. Working with other companies. (*picking apart*) (L)

The debate at this point contains an effervescence of ideas, reminiscent of a sprinkler system spurting water droplets over a lawn in summer. While the lawn does get gradually wetter, the effect is diffuse, takes a long time and leaves other parts of the strategic terrain arid.

The team members are then caught by Keith(A)'s timely intervention:

> *Keith(A)*: Gosh, aren't we getting rather specific? (*reflection*) (H)
>
> *David*: It is. (*agreeing*) (H)
>
> *Myself*: If I am in their heads ... (*facilitating*) (H)

To help give more sense of focus, I suggested the following line of enquiry:

> *Myself*: Are these sort of, it is like the distinction between features and benefits? Are they too specific? Are these rather like activities? What activities are you doing that will really help me? ... specific issues? The issues will change. (*facilitating*) (H)

This debate appears to have jumped from level to level (with Andy, Keith (A), Tim and myself operating primarily at the 'highest' level) as follows:

H	T K(A) A T T	T K(A) T A A	K(A) D T T
M	B B T B D		B P
L	B	D	B D

Here, it is conspicuous that Bonnie tends to worry about more detailed issues (possibly sometimes rightly) and does not seem to be drawn back upwards. Although this is not 'wrong' – as it is crucial in a strategic team that there is someone there to jump on very important details – too much attention to specifics can be counterproductive. The 'big picture' gets cloudier and cloudier.

David starts again, but once more picks up on a very specific activity rather than starting with the 'value to the business' statement. Maybe he sees this as an opportunity to input the idea of 'the business model', which might be a particularly important point of his mental map and play an important role in this personal strategic agenda.

> *David*: I would say more than that because it is actually called the business model. We need to understand the business model of global operations because this business doesn't understand that. (*justifying, mental maps*) (M)
>
> *Andy*: If we were only in the main operating business we would be purely acting out the role of supplier. We are no longer in that role of supplier. (*strategic role*) (M)
>
> *Keith*: I am surprised. I don't share your view. (*challenging*) (M)
>
> *Myself*: Are we getting confused here? (*questioning, feedback*) (H)

Here I want to check whether or not Andy and Keith are genuinely openly disagreeing with one another.

Andy, again, tries to grapple with the central issue of the role of the department, pulling back the group discussion into some kind of clearer focus.

> *Andy*: Well, this is the area we need to hammer around because ... I think we understand this. We could spend all morning arguing over the words, and we will do that, but we understand, more or less, what we were doing before. Right. The issue at stake for us at the moment, it seems to me, is coming back to what Paul was saying. Is, we know we need to make a significant change. It is either in addition to, or a replacement to, the things that we are doing. The organization ... the new remit ... to have 'global' in our title and in our job description. Now the issue is, what does that mean? Now we have already got a tension on the table as to whether it is just looking at the global or the technical perspective, all right, or whether we are part of the general thinking on where we are going. (*summarizing*) (H)

Andy is continually having to work really quite hard to give the debate some centre of gravity. It is now taking much input by both Andy and myself to give the team direction.

I then redoubled my efforts to focus the debate:

Myself: What is the product which is adding value to the main operating business? (*H*)

David: It is a model of how the global business operates. (*clarifying, mental maps*) (*M*)

Keith(A): We are setting direction – to use your analogy … (*M*)

Andy: You have moved up a layer, Tony. (*helicoptering up*) (*H*)

Myself: I am trying to get up to the level of, well, if someone says to you, 'Why do you exist?' (*helicoptering up*) (*H*)

Andy: Ah, well, that is a different matter. (*helicoptering up*) (*H*)

Although Andy appears to question my line of enquiry, he rapidly latches on to the high-level focus that I am trying to attain.

The dynamic thus follows this pattern:

H			T	A	T		A	T A
M	D	A	K(A)			D	K(A)	
L								

Once again, Andy and myself are trying to move the debate up to a higher level. This is with the intent of trying to map the 'bigger picture' issues first, before diving down to the detail.

Then, Bonnie drops down a level of thinking, putting a strain on our sense of continuity but not losing this entirely:

Bonnie: So that manager X can be successful, he can only be successful by understanding what the business needs to be to be global. Understanding his role in that – what is his role in that – and being able to do it. Now, if we come out with 'being able to do it', we come out with, might come out with, helping him to understand what he needs to do to enable BT to participate in global, both from a business point of view and a technical point of view. (*scoping, picking apart*) (*L*)

However, Andy – determined as ever – challenges the team to go up higher in their thinking on the scheme of things.

Andy: I would move up even a higher notch than that. (*H*)

Paul, however, is left with unresolved issues preoccupying him – highlighting the problems of coping with unfinished business.

> *Paul*: I am confused a bit. I am not too sure whether we are doing technical strategy from the point of view of a supplier or technical strategy from the point of view of a customer or internal customers or are we doing technical strategy for combining both? (*clarification*) (M)

Once again, Andy remains undiverted – he is insistent on getting to the bigger picture:

> *Andy*: I am going to go higher than that. I think that the question that Tony asked is right. We cost about £X million on pay – £X million. What value do we give for £X million per year? If you cut all our throats, what difference would they perceive? Because, Tony was asking, quite rightly, not about what we actually do but why are we actually here. (*helicoptering up*) (H)
>
> *Myself*: Even if we didn't have you, what would be the need, the latent need that isn't being addressed?' (H)
>
> *Andy*: Yes. (H)

Now he has them all together, to begin a proper debate:

> *Keith(A)*: Let's try and … (*facilitation*) (H)
>
> *Andy*: Let's try and answer that question. Then the next layer down. (*helicoptering down*) (H)
>
> *Myself*: Once we have got the highest level, then you can try and … [am cut off] (*facilitation*) (H)

Bonnie, however, is still circling at another (and lower) level of analysis within the problem architecture. Her thought stream appears to have its own flight path and is only gently pulled in a new or different direction. (This suggests that a particular thought stream typically has its own 'cognitive momentum'.)

> *Bonnie*: And it is kind of, what do you want to be successful globally? And we have asked questions like that in the past. We just said that. David said, I said [mentioning enterprise working], he said it probably, had in a way, OK, so its pointing out things with evidence that enabled BT to be successful in attempting to do what it is trying to do. (*synthesis*) (M & L)

Keith(A) feels impelled to follow Bonnie's course of thinking:

> *Keith(A)*: That's right, that's important. Championing change. (*agreeing*) (L)
>
> *Myself*: What kind? (L)
>
> *Bonnie*: It is technical. (L)

162

David: I am not even sure that it is technical. It is change that is to the overall benefit of the shareholders. I mean the enterprise stuff. (*challenging*) (*L*)

Now I try to refocus on the bigger, higher-level question:

Myself: You can still think about the £Xm or £Xm that you get paid to do this. (*H*)

Andy, forever patient, now reiterates where he would like to see the discussion going:

Andy: The discussion is wandering around the place. I am saying for starters that the main operating business Board is our customer, for starters. We can't actually get out a simple statement of why the business pays us £X million. (*facilitating*) (*H*)

This debate is thus profoundly sensitive to the pushes and pulls of key individuals – and, in this case, is often being pulled in habitually opposing and self-cancelling directions. One senses that, faced with this input, the team finds it necessary to fall back on habitual behaviours. What follows is their habitual recipe – brainstorming.

Keith(B): We need to save the company. (*picking apart*) (*M*)
Keith(A): Gosh, no, I don't think that it is as simple as that. (*disagreeing*) (*M*)
Bonnie: Our role is to save the company by championing business and technical change and by improving efficiency and there is also all those other things. (*picking apart*) (*L*)

I once again intervened, and Andy jumped back in to defend what the team had been doing.

Myself: Can I think aloud on this. What we are doing is keeping on throwing things in. No one has said 'What do you mean by … ?' We are fragmenting. (*facilitating*) (*H*)
Andy: Well, you told us Tony, you told us to brainstorm. (*H*)
Myself: We are coming off the brainstorming, and, secondly, we are going back to behaviour as normal. (*H*)
Keith(A): Yes, yes. (*agreeing*) (*H*)
Myself: But you are right, we are both right. (*H*)

This is interesting from the point of view of how a facilitator operates. At the time I remember thinking 'How can I help these people to gain a clearer focus and at a higher level of debate?' (My role at this point, as researcher, was to see if – with facilitation – the team could shift its behaviours, assuming it wanted to do so.) However, unwittingly, I may have suggested, by implying that they were getting into too much detail, that what I was looking for was a stream of brainstorming. Unless a facilitator can give simultaneously clear signals about not only what they expect to happen as well as not to happen, then they can generate unintended confusion.

The dynamic of this debate thus jumps levels suddenly, which is captured below:

H	A	A T A K(A) A T	T A	T A T K(A) T
M	P	B	K(B) K(A)	
L	B	B K(A) T B D	B	

This pattern of dislocation of levels is perhaps even more noticeable than the previous ones. Bonnie's cognitive style appears to attract her to a more detailed discussion than Andy, Keith(A) (and myself) are trying to attain. She does not seem to pick up the signals to 'move up' a level. At times, the others are forced to fly down two levels of analysis to maintain a thread of debate.

Andy next takes up the theme of 'saving the company', but assumes (apparently erroneously) that 'we all know what we mean here'. This underscores the importance – not just here but elsewhere – of always defining the meaning of terms, and doing so almost obsessively.

Andy: But let me say, Tony, that we know what Keith means by 'save the company'. (*questioning, probing*) (M)

Bonnie: But I want to ask what he meant. (*questioning*) (L)

Andy: But I honestly think ... (*judging*) (M)

Bonnie: I am not sure that we all do. I don't know, we do, but Paul ... (*disagreeing*) (M)

Keith(B): To ensure long-term financial viability of the network business. (*expanding*) (M)

Bonnie: Or BT as a group. (*expanding*) (L)

Keith(B): I am not sure I can do the latter bit. (*picking apart*) (L)

Myself: Currently we are focusing on the main operating Board. (*facilitation*) (M)

Bonnie: What the need is. (*expanding*) (L)

Myself: But suddenly, by talking about BT, we have widened the whole arena of debate. (*facilitating*)

Myself: You have got to have discipline in strategic thinking. (*facilitating*) (H)

Andy: Absolutely. (*agreeing*) (H)

The profile of this latter discussion looks like this:

H						T	A
M	A	A	B	K(B)		T	
L		B			B	K(B)	B

Once more, a similar pattern emerges, with discussion torn between Andy and myself attempting to debate at a higher level, and Bonnie at a lower level.

I was obviously taking some risks in potentially upsetting Bonnie. This risk-taking is intuitive and based on the perceived need at the time to get a grip on the debate. Paul now circles back to his earlier questioning:

Paul: That's why I came back to my question of whether we are acting from a supplier perspective or what. (*strategic role*) (M)

I tried once again to give the debate a direction, suggesting that the brainstorming is focused more specifically:

Myself: Can we go into a more deliberate process of brainstorming, please? (*facilitation*) (H)

Bonnie: Saving the alliance. (*interrupting*) (L)

Myself: You see how hard it is to do this, it is almost impossible. Imagine an invisible gag around your mouth and it is only in certain situations that you are allowed to take it off. (*facilitating*) (H)

This highlights how hard team members find it to adapt their behaviour. Again, I took some risks in my feedback, but I felt I had to gradually escalate my directness.

Now David puts the process into a new trajectory by reading out a policy document – Andy's – effectively cutting across Andy.

David reads out of the official document ...

Andy: Hang on, these are my words your reading out. David. (*challenging*) (H)

(Presumably David's focus at the time was on making an effective input, but he overlooked – from a process point of view – inputting the words of the team leader without attributing their source.)

Keith(A) now highlights some unfinished business by once again making a well-targeted, probing comment:

> *Keith(A)*: I find it difficult to progress without asking a question, but I think when Keith said 'saving the company', I think he meant from a financial point of view. I think that there are some very specific issues about saving the company from the regulator, the environment, whatever. (*probing, picking apart*) (H)

The final phase in this interaction looks as follows (again reaching a higher level):

H		T	T	A	K(A)
M	P				
L			B		

This important debate is obviously a sensitive issue for the team, and one it is hard to be objective about. Because of its emotiveness and because it clearly impinges on territorial perceptions of the team, discussions are relatively unstable and difficult to steer.

Key points
....

➡ When looking at the question 'What value do we add?', always have the 'out-of-body' experience of imagining that you literally are that customer or stakeholder. Get inside their thoughts, agendas, feelings – especially their hopes and fears – and their histories.

➡ When doing strategic brainstorming, at least set some focus for the brainstorming. Otherwise, it may come up with a real mishmash of ideas.

> ➡ Where the team has, at some stage in the past, hammered out some firm ideas on a particular topic, this must be your starting point. You do not always have to reinvent your thinking.
>
> ➡ Facilitators sometimes need to take risks – they are there to actually stick their necks out and managers ought to be tolerant of the occasional mini-blunders. A reasonably humble facilitator can bounce back from making a misjudgement.

At this point, it is worth while just pausing for a moment to retrace the strategic issue map (see Figure 5.1). Although the discussions might, again, have seemed somewhat erratic, there is quite a strong sense of order in the flow. The third workshop began with the TSD team understanding its scope and then trying to find out who it added value to. This was followed by a discussion (albeit in conclusion) of customer need, before returning to the theme of how value was added. Somewhat tangled up in these discussions were debates about both external (customer) issues and internal issues, and debates about who the TSD team reports to.

There now follows a useful discussion about the split between 'deliberate' strategy-type work and 'emergent' strategy-type work:

Keith(A): Could we get – in your terms, Andy – a split? (*probing*) (*M*)
Andy: Well, it will vary depending on the area you are in. (*expanding*) (*M*)
Keith(A): Across the piece. (*clarifying*) (*M*)
Andy: An 80:20 wouldn't be a bad split. (*strategic role, clarifying*) (*M*)
Keith(A): OK, fine. (*agreeing*) (*M*)
Bonnie: But there is a load of other people there to cope with it. (*strategic role*) (*L*)
Paul: To deliver the strategy component of that. (*strategic role*) (*L*)
Myself: Is Bonnie saying that we see ourselves as partly adding value through other people as well? (*strategic role*) (*M*)

This conversation leads to Bonnie drawing out some practical implications:

Bonnie: In other words, you could spend the 20 per cent and not do anything particularly useful and not deliver anything amazing which in the event is added to shareholder value. On the other hand, that 20 per cent could deliver far more than the 80 per cent. (*strategic role*) (*M*)

I then facilitated more actively:

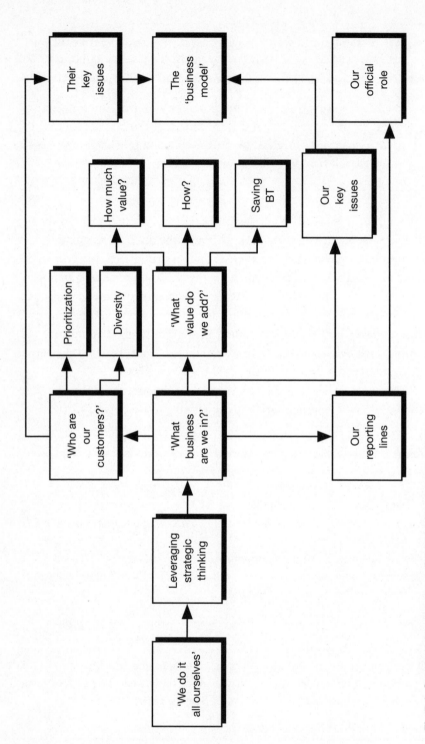

Fig 5.1 Strategic issues map – 'What business are we in?'

Myself: But if your mindset is the set piece battle, with the troops and the tanks there, you might forget the SAS mission where you wiped half their communications behind the lines and ... because you weren't in the business of that, you were in the business of fighting big wars – and being killed ... you are just shooting everyone. [Laughter erupts]. (*strategic role*) (M)

David immediately agrees with this perspective:

David: There is a lot of truth in that. Some of these things are big wars. (*agreeing*) (M)

The dynamics of the process look as follows:

H											
M	K(A)	A	K(A)	A	K(A)			T	B	T	D
L							B	P			

The continuity of this debate (at mainly the middle level) suggests that this has been a much more coherent debate than those typical of the earlier workshop.

The role of the department

Andy now takes up the theme of the role of the department, following on from reflections on recent policy statements on what this is.

Andy: I mean, I think we are just talking at different levels here, Tony, if I might say so. Let's go back, let's summarize. This one sentence still stands as far as I can see. A lot of what we are talking about, is the following. The prime role of the TSD is to develop, champion and communicate BT's global technical strategy, covering all BT and alliance networks and systems in the UK and overseas. (*summarizing*) (H)

David now amplifies Andy's view:

David: Well, you see, that role would actually cover those about saving the company, and it would also cover some of the other things on there. I couldn't even choose between the two. For example, and one of the issues facing us, is we have got to make a choice either between selecting areas to work in, specific areas, we are trying to cover the whole patch. Yes, it seems that both are covered by the role, but for 'save the company' I would argue, goes to the specific areas. (*strategic role, expanding*) (H)

And Andy now continues:

> *Andy*: I fully agree with you David, because I think what we do is ... The first sentence that I read out still stands. And the prosaic answer to 'Why?' is, well, we have been asked to do it, we are being paid to do it. Now, the point that you have just described is that, what you then have to apply is deciding that, I have only got so much resource. What is it that we really must do, and that's where the 'Why?' comes in there. (*agreeing, expanding, strategic role*) (H)

We now get the distinct feeling that the debate has moved to more solid ground – it has become anchored (but not rigidly fixed), it has a centre of gravity and it is building on what has gone before, creating a more solid, strategic architecture.

Bonnie and Keith(A) amplify on these themes:

> *Bonnie*: To make BT the best. (M)
> *Keith(A)*: Exactly, you know, saving the company brings us up to an average, and, if you like, I want to see us move up above the average. So ... (*expanding, picking apart*) (L)

The team maintains its strategic formation, with Bonnie complementing Andy's points:

> *Andy*: 'Save the company' actually speaks a mouthful, because it suggests that if we didn't do it, then we fall over a precipice, and that's the point. Doing nothing is not an option. (L)
> *Bonnie*: When you said 'we have only got so much resource, you do so much to save the company', you do *sufficient* to save the company, you do sufficient to make us believe that it will work. And those two 'sufficients' might be different things. (*picking apart*) (L)

And the flying formation continues:

> *Bonnie*: Could it be a useful thing for this company, this department, to be doing, to identify those areas of putting effort in which would do both. You know ... (*questioning, probing*) (M)
> *Andy*: A double whammy. (*clarifying*) (L)
> *Bonnie*: Where we could be saving the company and making it the best. (*expanding*) (L)
> *David*: I do think that there is a tension between these. (*judging*) (L)
> *Keith(A)*: I think that there might be some. (*judging*) (L)
> *Myself*: Can we list them out? (M)
> (*They then proceed to list the issues.*)

The whole sequence of the debate is interesting from the point of view of its harmony and sense of purpose. It is not suggested by this that contention is necessarily destructive – far from it. However, a team that spends 80 per cent of its time locked in intense and divergent contention may not prove to be a particularly productive one.

The behavioural sequence here is as follows:

H	A D A							
M		B			B		K(A)	T
L			K(A) A B		A B D			

So many of the difficulties and frustrations of the group seemed to arise because of undershared mental maps, the individualistic styles of the team members and because of some personal idiosyncrasies.

Andy now reflects on the level of clarity that has come out of the fog of the discussion, by bringing in the department's formal objectives:

> *Andy*: It seems to me, Tony, that we have got a very nice fit between, these are the objectives of the BT Board, and we have gone through and got a pretty good mapping of this, notwithstanding this ... there they are, a pretty good mapping of those objectives and the ones that we can see for the main operating business Board, and our role within that. So that has been very helpful in that respect. (*summarizing*) (*H*)

Bonnie amplifies Andy's point:

> *Bonnie*: There is an interesting dynamism issue that ... Most of those things are there partly because at an earlier point we said – in some document or another – that they were a good idea. Partly ... (*expanding*) (*H*)

Andy now latches on to Bonnie's input, incorporating it immediately into his own mental map of the department's emerging priorities:

> *Andy*: I think that Bonnie has actually put her finger on it, which I tried to say not so well a while ago, which is, most of our work is servicing this lot. But, *en passant*, and in addition, we also need to pull out the new strategic targets which will emerge over the year. (*expanding*) (*H*)
> *Keith(A)*: Yes, fine, fine. (*agreeing*) (*H*)

171

Andy now hungers for concrete value to come out of the totality of these discussions:

> *Andy*: But it is very important for us to agree that that is the kind of stance we take, because it then says we focus most of our energy on delivering a strategy there. And I feel we do. Because I feel that I want to get something out of the loop. [Attempted interruptions.] But we also have some of the energy spent on ... (Keith(*A*) again tries to interrupt 'could we'.) (*helicoptering up*) (*H*)

Andy next draws out some potential implications for how the department organizes itself:

> *Andy*: And if you look at the job descriptions, they were very carefully worded with that in mind. So, I think there is a difference between being involved and having the possibility for driving it. (*expanding, strategic role, structure*) (*M*)

This final sequence of behaviour in this part of the workshop runs at a consistently high level, as follows:

H	A	B	A	K(A)	A
M					A
L					

In summary, the team members initially wrestle to get to grips with the issues of their own role, and what value they add, and to whom. However, Andy then manages to give them sufficient behavioural anchors to conduct a more proactive debate.

Key points
················

➡ Sort your key strategic tasks into those that are intended and predictable ('deliberate') versus those that are more unpredictable ('emergent'). Think about the kind of team style that best fits your future stream of deliverable versus emergent strategic tasks. Does this shift in mix imply a different mindset and behaviours?

➡ Use Pareto thinking to prioritize not only strategic tasks but also issues for debate (20 per cent of the issues typically constituting 80 per cent of the total importance).

➡ Consider what you are currently not doing at all but should be doing – if you take a look at the overall business or group's strategic context.

The second part of the workshop

During this part of the workshop, I indicated that I would not actually be facilitating, other than to provide guidance on the use of a specific management tool – the importance and influence grid (see Figure 5.2), which was used to understand the priorities of the group. However, during the first phase of this second cycle of discussion, I was drawn back in to facilitate in order to establish at least some sense of order. In the second phase, though, the team was able to manage without further intervention.

Initially, discussions fragmented considerably as the team appeared to succumb to 'diving in' and 'picking apart' their priorities, but then the team got to work to break down the issues into manageable units for analysis – in terms of importance and urgency. Their methodical working sets the tone for around half an hour's discussion.

David: What we actually do have is a list of the priorities in the business that you can use. (*picking apart*) (M)

Keith(A): Could we ... (L)

Bonnie: [interrupting] We could have used that in the first place. That is rather circular. (L)

173

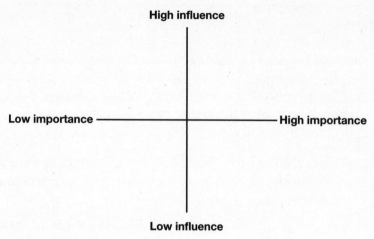

High influence

Low importance ──────────┼────────── High importance

Low influence

Fig 5.2 Importance and influence grid

Myself: Can we get down to this small number of things. (*facilitating*) (M)
Keith(A): Yes. It is no. 2, let us put that as the opposite. (*picking apart*) (L)
David: Issue 2 is very big, I would have grouped it with 'broad band.' (*picking apart*) (L)
Keith(A): No, I ... (*disagreeing*) (L)
Keith(B): Can we tie it into breaking into new revenues? (*probing*) (M)
Myself: If we can identify a grouping, then we can split it down later on. (*facilitating*) (M)
Andy: I am not sure. (*disagreeing*) (M)

Although the team members are methodical, they seem to lose sight of what they are trying to achieve. I facilitated:

Myself: Again, you see, we are doing it, aren't we, we are picking. Sometimes you have got to not pick to move on, you can always come back to that. (H)
Keith(A): This is not the final list. (H)
Myself: We have this mindset that we have got to bottom out everything. But if we can activate strategic patience, and get that into the process. (H)
Andy: We will never get ... (*disagreeing*) (H)
Keith(A): We need to cultivate strategic patience [chuckling]. (H)

The team then makes better progress for a while, until Bonnie jumps in to disagree – without being very clear why she is disagreeing:

Bonnie: But we just said, sorry David, we just said that the reason that Keith's thingy isn't in there is because ... (*disagreeing*) (L)
Andy: It is in there. (*arguing*) (L)

Paul: It is in there. (*arguing*) (L)

David: The benefits … (*arguing*) (L)

Myself: Just in terms of the style here, we seem to focus on areas for possible disagreement rather than hunting for areas where we do agree. (H)

This is followed by a discussion where Bonnie tries to defend her intervention by saying that she wanted to understand.

Bonnie: Yes, but I don't understand. (H)

Myself: Well, it is a style issue, it is to do with going for things rather than saying, 'Let's give someone the benefit of the doubt', maybe they are clear but they haven't expressed it or it is because of the language. Probably if you had had an hour outside then you wouldn't have had any disagreement at all. (H)

Bonnie: But you said, if we didn't get clarity, share mind maps. (*clarification*) (H)

Myself: True, but it is the way in which you set about that, it is kind of, too almost – er – adversarial. It can get to be counter-productive. (H)

Here, there seems to be a relatively slow process of understanding not only what in behavioural terms to do (sharing mental maps) but also how to share them.

The discussion so far has moved through the following levels:

H					T K(A) T A K(A)		T B T B T
M	D	T		K(B) TA			
L	K(A) B	K(A) D K(A)				B A P D	

This is a relatively smooth debate, with the 'low' level of debate being dictated by the team task – the prioritization of detailed issues. In the past, the team had not been as able to prioritize its issues effectively. Using a visual prioritization technique appeared to stabilize not merely the team's behaviour, but also its thinking.

Once the task of prioritizing the issues was virtually complete, the discussion then widens out to reflect on how these issues sit within the wider context:

David: If you are talking about the means and how to do it, then it is not that at all because I think that a lot of this analysis has already been done. We have a shopping list at corporate, which is generally agreed, which says 'These are the sorts of things that we ought to be doing, chaps' – most of which are on our list, right. There are 14 items, of which 4 or 5 are actually important. (*clarification*) (H)

After this point Bonnie was still present but was less active in the discussions.

Andy reinforces David's argument, suggesting that the team should sort out what they are not doing as well as what they are doing:

> *Andy*: I think that David has a point. There's a danger in fact. If we stand back a bit, and whilst it is right that we should question things, it is right that we should raise things totally out of court, and that's actually right, I think we should also try not to do the rest of BT's job for them. (*agreeing*) (*H*)

Andy moves on to more practical terrain by suggesting that their focus of attention could be narrowed down still further:

> *Andy*: And what you could do, for example, is to take the ten points from corporate strategy, which were part of the thinking. And say, 'Of the ten, we are going to address the following four'. Right, that's our agenda. Now that would be a logical way of doing things, it is not presumptuous on our part to be running the whole business. (*prioritization*) (*H*)

Andy now brings the discussion together as a grand summary, which finally anchors the debate with what has been achieved:

> *Andy*: I want that conversation to finish first, but there is a second question. It seems to me that we have got a close enough fit. We agreed, a few moments ago, that we didn't need to have a 100 per cent lock-in of all the things that we do. What we have got is a pretty good fit between the company's top objectives and what we think we should be trying to do. Right. There are some bits – the Venn diagram goes beyond what they have got there, which is what you would expect. You would expect us to be looking beyond what has been said explicitly. Now that, I would have thought that an 80:20 fit, is what we have got, is pretty good. (*summarizing, judging*) (*H*)
>
> *Keith(A)*: It is pretty good. (*agreement, judging*) (*H*)
>
> *Andy*: It is better than we would normally want. (*judging*) (*H*)
>
> *Keith(B)*: Absolutely. (*agreeing*) (*H*)
>
> *Andy*: I have never seen such a good fit before. (*judging*) (*H*)

The discussion has been maintained at a consistently high level:

H	D	A	A	A	K(A)	A	K(B)	A
M								
L								

Andy has steered the team in a real and direct way. They now have better shared mental maps of what the department is about and may now be less prone to unnecessary disagreement on this topic.

The team now prioritizes the issues in more detail, using the importance–influence grid. At this point, the team settles down into a much quieter, methodical routine. The downside to this is that they do not actually cross-challenge each other's assumptions on the positioning grid.

I then attempted to raise the level of debate, trying not to facilitate as I did so (as this was the team's opportunity for a 'freestyle' discussion):

> *Myself*: Can I just make a quick suggestion. What you could do is to say – to get people to position it in their minds, or on a bit of paper – what those were. And you take one of those Post-its, and you say, from someone, 'How do you position it?', and you say 'Why do you position it there?', and 'Why?'. But you first need to identify why the first person said that, so you start off and you say, 'Why did you position it there?', and then you can say, 'Why did you position it somewhere else?' And then someone – like Dave – another arbitrator – could say 'Let's move it around', and get a fair balance. (*facilitation*) (*H*)

So, although the team has taken positive steps to improve its process, there are further areas where they could sharpen it up so that it results in a richer and more questioning debate. Again, the BT team seems to view process as relatively simple and mechanical. Instead a 'process' can be fluid, organic and consist of a number of ingredients that become more and more effective with learning.

Key points
....

➡ **The team leader and/or facilitator can add considerable value by providing the occasional summary of:**

- **what has been said**

- **key points and insights that are emerging**

- **lines of enquiry that have opened up**

- **things that have crystallized for them – such as, decisions, judgements and so on.**

▶

> ➡ This should be done without distortion: you cannot claim that a group consensus has been achieved when it is just your particular view.
>
> ➡ Where you do want to stake out a decision that runs counter to the agendas of at least part of the group, then this has to be brought out explicitly with a signal, such as 'I am now taking the lead'.

Figure 5.3 depicts the final strategic issue map. This shows how the team moved towards a relatively effective way of prioritizing its issues.

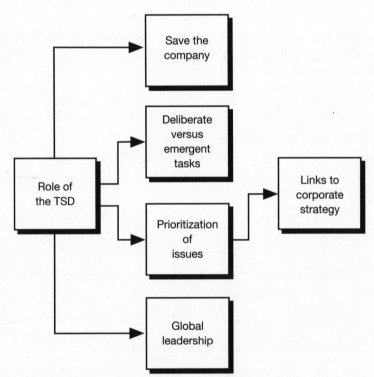

Fig 5.3 Strategic issues map – the TSD's future plans

178

PROCESS REVIEW

At the end of the workshop, the team members agree that they need more time to examine their prioritizations:

> *Keith(A)*: Do we all agree that, to come back to the question, that we ought to spend more time on this – to get the best clarity that we can. (*time frames*) (*H*)
>
> *David*: And how much time? (*questioning*) (*M*)
>
> *Keith(A)*: Well, I think as much as is reasonably necessary. I mean, I would be prepared to devote another day to actually looking at these specific issues. (*judging*) (*M*)
>
> *David*: We could probably even spend a day on each one of them. (*expanding*) (*L*)
>
> *Keith(A)*: No, I am not prepared to spend that long. (*disagreeing*) (*L*)

Andy now skilfully turns to dealing with the process issues – taking forward the prioritization into the department as a whole:

> *Andy*: We will get Mike up to speed as best we can, plus the new person. I think we should spend some time, take this a little bit further, because it does tease out a couple of points. One, it helps us with a common understanding, so half the team will be new, and half the team will be old strategists, as it were. And I think that the old and the new mix is a very important one. So I think that it does tease out some of the language issues. And the second thing is, I think that we do need to agree, on a cabinet basis, that these are the major issues that we are going to tackle over the following year. (*ownership*) (*H*)

Keith(A) agrees with Andy's proposal and expands some thoughts of his own:

> *Keith(A)*: I agree – that's right – but I would like to go on beyond that, Andy. It isn't about taking the department away at some time, and I would like to … having got our view as a management group, I would like to, if I could, put it sort of emotively, encourage them to come to a similar view. (*expanding*) (*H*)
>
> *Andy*: Oh, I am happy about that. (*agreeing*) (*H*)
>
> *Keith(A)*: Rather than present it on a plate. (*ownership*) (*H*)

The above debate has moved through the following levels:

H	K(A)				A	K(A)	A	K(A)
M		D	K(A)					
L				D	K(A)			

In this case, the dynamics of the debate look appropriate, given the content of discussion as the team genuinely had a need to debate the specifics of the topics being talked about.

In conclusion, the more structured approach used in the final workshop appears to have given the team at last the beginnings of a set of priorities. These priorities had eluded them previously. Indeed, this was the subject of a workshop held during the previous year, which left these issues substantially unresolved.

Certainly the result was not achieved easily, as it took considerable time – even with Andy present and steering the discussion to a substantial degree – to channel the debate in a meaningful way. These difficulties appear to have a number of causes, not least of these being the problems of defining the terms that the team members were using and the lack of clarity about which levels of analysis were needed. At times, it felt like a blindfolded person groping around a room to get a feel of its dimensions, and of the relationships of objects in the room to each other. There was an apparent absence of problem architecture and incomplete and differing mental maps within the minds of the individuals there.

Individual members of the team had a tendency to dart off in different directions – especially towards specific ideas that had either just occurred to them or were related to their personal strategic agendas. Andy's persistence (together with David's input on the technical strategy objectives – as set by corporate) helped to anchor the debate, along with the use of the importance–influence grid, which calmed individuals down and channelled the thought process.

In the final cycle of debate, the team now reflects on its workshop process:

> Keith(A): It was nowhere near as contentious as I have seen in the past. (reflecting) (H)

However, David points out that:

> David: The problem that we usually have is we go through this exercise, this

180

prioritization before, the real battles come through when you are actually going through 'Why?' ... It is only then that you are really challenging people. (*anticipating*) (*H*)

Andy confirms David's impression:

Andy: I think there is potential for a lot of conflict, but I think that the real conflict comes when you take the output out of this and use it to influence the allocation of resources in time or budgets. But when it applies to a budget or a departmental resource allocation, the pain comes on. (*control, anticipating, conflict*) (*H*)

Again, this highlights that beneath the surface of the behavioural pond there were some very important, if hidden, processes at work. There appears to be a mixture of personal strategic agendas, anxieties and political manoeuvring.

CONCLUSION

The third team workshop offers a further insight into how the team operates in strategy making (and also why it has the difficulties it has). The core topics for debate that surround the department's role, the value it adds to BT and its priorities are evidently complicated, sometimes not fully mapped out and frequently emotive.

It would be slightly surprising to see that this territory has been relatively ill mapped out if it were not for the fact that the department has an ambiguous, fluid and changing role. Also, this degree of ambiguity is by no means unknown elsewhere. Indeed, because of continual reorganization in some companies, it is almost the norm. In BT, this situation presents the team members with many fuzzy issues, which they seem to have great difficulty in grappling with.

Taking a bird's eye view of the whole debate, it looks as if the team is still working according to the mindset 'If we just discuss this enough then we will get the answers'. Yet, paradoxically, relatively little of the debate (save for Andy's summaries and the prioritization exercise in the second part) seems to deliver much concrete output. (The most helpful output seemed to be confirmation that BT's expectations of the department were 'appropriate', but this was based primarily on David's input, not on any other novel discussion.)

181

Interestingly, a focused and productive piece of work is achieved as the team members prioritize their issues using the importance–influence grid. However, the distinctive absence of more vigorous debate or contention gives the feel that the team may be avoiding the really important discussions on its future priorities. (The individuals' subsequent reflections on this team process bears out this impression.)

An additional problem for the team is that its members may face a high proportion of emergent strategy, dictating their work in the foreseeable future. This not only makes the team's role and priorities somewhat harder to tie down, but might also provide a shelter for Bonnie, Keith(B) and others to 'do the things we are most interested in or committed to'. Andy therefore has a tough job to reconcile those demands.

On several occasions, I attempted to flag up this issue of 'avoidance' of the more fundamental issues. David did not respond to this, perhaps because he was keen to get at least some output or because he wanted to avoid further bouts of erratic discussion or contention. Alternatively, he might simply have been concerned with time pressures. In any event, to have done a first-cut prioritization without significant exploration of why things were positioned how they were means that further rework is called for and might actually make further analysis harder. Having said that, using this kind of management tool was a new experience for the team members and so they may simply have been content to enjoy a welcome 20 minutes of working in what, to them at the time, seemed an effective manner (which it no doubt was compared to what had happened in the past). Certainly, this tool did seem to act as a profoundly calming influence on the hitherto more usual style of debate.

From a research point of view, it was very rewarding to experiment by collecting data using a strategic analysis tool/grid. Normally, such techniques are seen as merely management tools rather than as means of surfacing data.

A final issue is the team's tendency to diverge, not only in terms of actual content of discussion but also in level. Perhaps, with practice, they can fly more in formation.

Key points

➤ Where your department or company is being reorganized, invest considerable time defining what business it is in.

➤ Where boundaries of roles are unclear, iron these out.

➤ Avoid throwing discussion time at problems. Instead, employ some problem-solving techniques to bottom-out issues quickly and effectively.

➤ Recognize emergence in your workload, and avoid using coping strategies to deal with it.

➤ Create mini-scenarios to anticipate your workload as best you can – (tell stories about how it might develop.)

➤ Do not use excuses to avoid dealing with apparently intractable, 'hot' issues.

➤ Use prioritization techniques to sort out what you should focus on and in what order.

SUMMARY

One of the most valuable – yet underused – applications of strategy is to ask a department 'What business are we in?', 'Who are your customers?', 'What value do you add, and how?'

By applying a clearer process to the use of these questions (and some strategic analysis techniques), BT's TSD was able to inject more order (and productivity into its behaviour). This was achieved without any evident loss of creativity.

Part III

HARNESSING
STRATEGIC
BEHAVIOUR

THE KALEIDOSCOPE OF STRATEGIC BEHAVIOUR

So when the front is prepared, the rear is lacking, and when the rear is prepared the front is lacking. Preparedness on the left means lack on the right, preparedness on the right means lack on the left. Preparedness everywhere means lack everywhere.

Sun Tzu, *The Art of War*

INTRODUCTION

In this chapter the patterns of strategic behaviour emerging from the case study are examined and what implications these have for strategic management is discovered. These patterns are very much like a kaleidoscope. A few basic ingredients can be mixed together in different combinations to give a myriad of different patterns. However, in each particular instance, there are usually certain key variables that provide the clue to us being able to steer strategic behaviour a certain way. (By implication, as Sun Tzu describes opposite, in practice we focus on these at the expense of others.)

Before looking at practice, however, first it is necessary to explore how strategic behaviour impacts more generally on the management process. Then several separate, more specific dimensions are analyzed. The final section then examines how strategic behaviour might be controlled. The patience and concentration you have exercised in the last three chapters should now reap its reward.

WHAT IS STRATEGIC BEHAVIOUR?

In this section, the following key questions are addressed.

- How should 'strategic behaviour' now be defined?
- How does strategic behaviour drive the management process?

How should 'strategic behaviour' now be defined?

A working definition of 'strategic behaviour' could be said to be as follows:

> Strategic behaviour is the patterns of interaction by means of which senior managers set longer-term direction, manage change in the business as a whole, and in relation to external change, and add value for its key stakeholders.

Having now analyzed the BT case study, it is possible to refine this definition (from a principally theoretical definition to one that is more grounded):

The cognitive, emotional and territorial interplay of managers within or between groups when the agenda relates to strategic issues.

Here a 'group' is two or more managers. Also, this definition takes 'strategic issues' to be shorthand for the following part of the original definition:

... longer-term direction, manage change in the business as a whole, and in relation to external change, and to its key stakeholders.

The new definition highlights the blend or 'behavioural cocktail' of cognition, affective and politically inspired activity that is inextricably intermingled within strategic behaviour.

How does strategic behaviour drive the management process?

Strategic behaviour is also significant as it helps in understanding the behavioural process (and the forward momentum) of strategic debate (see Figure 6.1), which shows this process as a cycle), particularly the following aspects.

- **Initiating the debate**   This may be the result of a deliberate input or result from more emergent creative thinking. It can also be influenced by the pool of personal strategic agendas existing within the team.
- **Developing the debate**   This may occur in a convergent or divergent way (or both). The debate may be focused in scope or it may be rampant, straying over wider areas of the architecture of the strategy, at times apparently randomly. Alternatively, it may be focused on circling issues (becoming 'strategic roaming' – the expression 'roaming' here not suggesting that the activity is fruitless).
- **Steering the debate**   This not only involves steering the content of the debate, but also team behaviours. In particular, it may draw from the team's repertoire of meta-behaviour.
- **Completing the debate**   This may involve agreeing on a particular point or deciding how loose ends may be investigated or if something has been agreed, who is going to do it and how? Otherwise, it may simply be ending a particular debate without necessarily identifying how it might be moved on into the future.

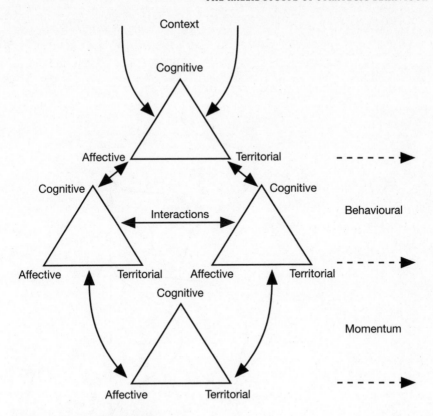

Fig 6.1 Strategic team behaviour

From the BT case study, it can be seen that the above four behavioural phases inevitably overlap. For instance, while the debate begins to develop, some active steering might occur early on, and 'steering' will occur in parallel with ongoing development. Indeed, there is every possibility of fresh inputs to the debate even as current themes are being developed or completed. Each phase is therefore wave-like, cascading onto the next phase, rather than being a mechanistic process. Figure 6.2 shows how these themes develop.

What is absent from team behaviour can sometimes be at least as important as what is there. For instance, if there are very few behaviours focusing on completion, then this may, in itself, encourage ill-directed strategic roaming and divergent debate with very little convergence.

This discussion of 'completing' is reminiscent of Belbin's 'completer-finisher' team role. However, I think that 'completing' is a more funda-

191

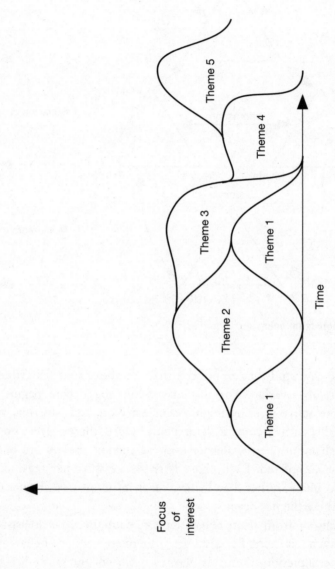

Fig 6.2 Themes of strategic debate

mental activity than Belbin suggests, one that all team members can be involved in rather than it being seen as a function of an individual in a team fulfilling such a role.

It is interesting to reflect here on the output of this research relative to a more traditional Belbin-type approach. With Belbin, the prime focus of team mix is team roles. The system of strategic behaviour set out in Figure 6.1, however, requires some other critical ingredients to be well aligned and operating, including:

- analytical processes
- interpersonal processes
- dynamic processes
- meta-behaviour (which goes beyond a Belbin 'chairperson' role).

While team mix is still important (and having a predominance of 'plants' evidently caused problems for the TSD team), these other processes seem to have a major influence on the shaping of strategic behaviour. For instance, in the second half of the third workshop (Chapter 5), injecting some improved analytical processes calmed down the more turbulent behaviours.

So, strategic behaviour is considerably more complicated than a Belbin perspective can readily cope with. Managers may be able to adapt to a variety of team mixes by adjusting other parts of their system of strategic behaviour.

WHAT FORMS DOES STRATEGIC BEHAVIOUR TAKE?

Having re-examined 'strategic behaviour', let us look now at how it manifests itself in practice. The forms it takes include:

- problem analysis
- analytical processes
- interpersonal processes
- dynamic processes
- meta-behaviour
- team interaction.

193

Only the top two categories – problem analysis and analytical processes – are primarily rational ones. The others are much more concerned with task-related and behavioural areas, and these are obviously key to moving – as much as possible – beyond organizational politics.

However, the rationalist viewpoint still provides a very forceful influence on how managers' (and other individuals') behaviour is interpreted. As Boland and Schultze (1995, pp10–11) argue:

> This image of cognition is overwhelming, saturating not only the cognitive sciences but also our everyday understanding of cognition itself … . Cognition's dominance has suppressed recognition of … the narrative mode. Here we selectively isolate events in our experience, populate the events with actors which have particular histories, motivations and intentions, and tell stories by setting the events and actors in a meaningful sequence.

Managers' own talk creates the drama of strategic behaviour, by externalizing the inner thoughts, feelings and territorial concerns of managers. Because the rational filter in managers' talk is frequently weak, the result can appear partly random and certainly disjointed. Boland and Schultze continue:

> Talking can have a haphazard quality if it is the expression of the speaker – the making of noise whilst putting a statement out into the world – irrespective of content or context.

The very same talk also creates political drama. Some of this political drama is clearly essential in order to oil the wheels of the organization. Other political drama seems to be created, perhaps to generate a sense of internal excitement and stimulus, but very soon this becomes distracting and costly.

The result of chaotic strategic talk is akin to the disorder created by a washing machine. However carefully the clothes are ordered as they are put into a washing machine, the end product is an entangled mess of clothes that are not in any kind of order. This example puts a rather different complexion on thoughts on how cognition works within strategic behaviour. In reality, it is infused with other more affective elements and is also influenced by what appears simply to just come out in talk, giving it a sometimes garbled character. Also, because managers' talk is overlayed on other talk, the end product of interaction is even more confusion. This is hardly a sharp, analytical tool, skilfully honed to analyze and resolve strategic issues. Not only is the 'washing machine effect' at work here, but results of numerous (often autonomous) machines are pooled – akin to a great strategic launderette.

Returning now to the categories listed above, these form part of a complicated system. This system is relatively sensitive to imbalances in a small number of behavioural hot spots. For instance, at BT these include:

- Bonnie's tendency to think out loud, while others are speaking, and to focus on primarily detailed issues
- David's facilitation style
- Keith(B)'s personal strategic agendas.

Thus, although a team may potentially have a very broad and rich agenda, its predominant patterns of behaviour occur in a relatively limited mode. In the BT team these were:

- creative thinking
- picking apart
- interrupting
- judging.

So interconnected were the various elements of the behavioural system in the case of BT that it was at times hard to untangle them. Frequently, there were several kinds of behaviour going on in the same individual, more or less at the same time. Besides these variants, behaviours would shift from individual to individual (and rarely remain consistent for any length of time). They would sometimes occur for long bursts, sometimes for short bursts. Sometimes there would be a clearly identifiable 'phase' when a particular theme would be engaged. At other times, there would be considerable competition regarding setting the theme.

As seen in Figure 6.2, interaction typically develops and is shaped in overlapping phases of debate that cascade into and over one another, sometimes moving forward, sometimes looping back. Although it is sometimes shaped deliberately, more often it emerges. Frequently it occurs as a result of essentially default behaviours. Its dynamics are thus fluid and not readily susceptible to being 'controlled', 'directed' or even 'managed' in the conventional sense. However, these dynamics may, nevertheless, be influenced more indirectly once 'what is going on' is better understood (which is what is discussed next).

WHAT ARE THE KEY DIMENSIONS OF STRATEGIC BEHAVIOUR?

Figure 6.3 explores some of the more important dimensions of strategic behaviour. Strategic behaviour is an amalgam of cognitive, affective and territorial elements, but, on top of these elements, behavioural momentum is a key variable of strategic behaviour.

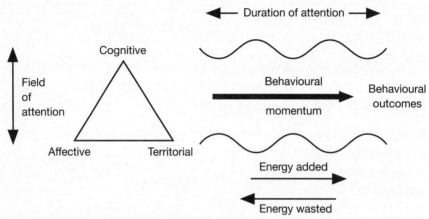

Fig 6.3 The key dimensions of strategic behaviour

Factors that add energy include, for example, creative thinking, leadership or simply a sense of urgency. Factors that dissipate energy include having too little process in debate or interactions, generating considerable strategic frustration (for example, where the quality of listening is poor). These 'energy-givers', or 'energizers', versus 'energy absorbers' can be explored by teams drawing up a force field analysis chart. Here, the relative length of the arrows signifies the relative strength of the force.

Figure 6.4 gives an example of energizers and energy absorbers that emerged in a workshop with a major retailer. This force field pattern is particularly interesting. Overall, there is a very good dominance of energizers. However, this is marred mainly by the lack of buy-in and involvement of one manager who could not seem to change his mindset. Eventually, he decided to leave of his own volition as he was obviously not getting what he wanted out of the session (a functional strategy). Given the workshop's objectives and agenda, there was no way these expectations could ever have been met.

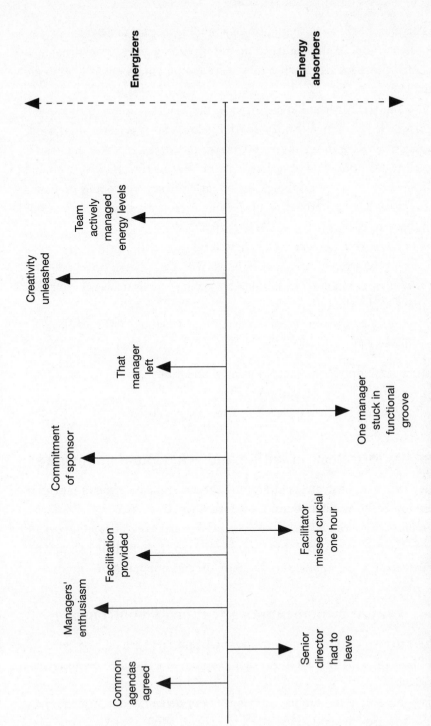

Fig 6.4 Energizers and energy absorbers in a retail strategy workshop

This particular workshop was outstanding as the managers spontaneously monitored and managed their own energy levels, rather than just accepted these for being what they were (employing a kind of 'strategic tonic').

Coming back to the BT experience, the field of attention of the BT team was a key dimension. In the BT team, this was generally broad, leading to a loss of momentum and diffuse outcomes. Another dimension was clearly the duration of strategic attention – was it sufficient to enable managers to move on thinking, feeling, and territorial agendas on issues in the way they had hoped or not? (This notion of 'strategic attention' links back to earlier work by Chilingerian, 1994.)

Finally, as we have seen, the behavioural outcomes that can accrue as a result of the strategic debate can be very diverse. These could take the form of greater alignment of mindsets, feelings about team cohesiveness or about each other.

A number of patterns can be seen in the BT study. The first three of these deal with:

- strategic attention and behavioural momentum
- momentum, attention and outcomes
- affective and territorial elements and energy wasted.

Pattern 1: strategic attention and behavioural momentum

Where the field of strategic attention is broad and where the duration of attention is short, behavioural momentum will be reduced.

In most cases, the BT team's debate was spread over a large number of issues, but for relatively short durations, even though their complexity level was high. This tended to dissipate the behavioural momentum.

Pattern 2: momentum, attention and outcomes

Where the behavioural momentum is high and there is a narrow focus of attention for a longer duration, there should be richer behavioural outcomes.

Possibly the best example of this was the debate about strategic priorities towards the end of the third workshop at BT.

Pattern 3: affective and territorial elements and energy wasted

Where affective and territorial elements are dominant and where behavioural outcomes are diffuse, the greater the amount of energy wasted becomes and the less momentum the team has.

Again, the affective and territorial elements will impact on the degree to which the meaning or debate is transparent, opaque or a mixture of the two. Certainly, some of these elements were detected around the issue of prioritizing strategic tasks at BT.

Pattern 4: diversity of mental maps and behavioural control

The more diverse the mental maps of the team are and the less these mental maps are revealed, then the more difficult strategic behaviour will be to control.

Here, the issue of 'control' raises questions as to why there is a need for control and who should be doing it. Control might be needed simply to gain valuable output from a strategic debate or, as in the case of BT, in order to avoid interpersonal damage occurring or to provide some cognitive and emotional stability for the individuals involved (one manager at BT complained of 'getting the heebie-jeebies' after a previous session).

Pattern 4 does not mean that mental maps must be aligned in order to be productive in a strategic sense. Indeed, one might well expect non-aligned mental maps to generate some fruitful creative thinking.

Throughout the case study there were various influences that appeared to be inseparable in the reality of management. This gave rise to the next pattern, which highlights an important characteristic of strategic behaviour – intermingling.

Pattern 5: intermingling

Cognitive, affective and territorial elements are frequently so inseparable in strategic behaviour that managers become unaware of what is actually driving their behaviour.

Pattern 5 makes a very big difference to strategy making. A single expression or behavioural act may contain (either explicitly or implicitly) a variety of complicated meanings and signals. This package of meanings, or 'behavioural package', might thus be profoundly ambiguous, even within a team where individuals know each other very well. It is perhaps therefore less than surprising to find in debates over strategy that the behavioural system is relatively sensitive and volatile.

The idea of a 'behavioural package' is very interesting, particularly in its role in organizational politics. A 'behavioural package' is a behavioural act that is presented as if it were one but which is actually several or many acts. As participants may present not just one behavioural act at a time but several in a strategic debate, this means that 'unfinished business' inevitably mounts up. For instance, a casual comment by one manager may be underpinned by nuances that may start off a series of thoughts and feelings – at a variety of levels – among the others. Managers might be consciously aware of parts of the behavioural package, but only partially aware of, or even unconscious, of others. This behavioural indigestion frequently manifests itself under that catch-all label of 'organizational politics'. For instance, looking at one thing Bonnie said, there is we see a variety of possible interpretations:

> How do you say either, 'I think that you are not understanding me because you are coming at it in a different, cognitive way to me' without being rude? How do you say, 'Stop attacking the top of my hill' without being rude? You know, because you are getting really close to me and I don't know what to do with this?
>
> But supposing you know where they are coming from, and they are attempting to get your hill?

This behavioural package could be interpreted as being any of the following:

- a comment on the group's general behavioural process
- an expression of a personal feeling of discomfort in dealing with emotional issues
- an olive branch to David Brown – and confession that she may have overreacted
- a subtle prod to David that he was seeking to enter her territory
- a semi-conscious reflection on the assumption that individuals need to have a staked-out territory.

A key pointer from this for managers generally here is that you need to identify where these political hills are, understand why they are there and then identify options for either:

- going around the hill
- going under the hill
- dissolving or dismantling the hill.

Pattern 6: cognitive and territorial ambiguity, emotions and control

The more ambiguous the level of cognitive understanding, the greater the emotions and the territorial uncertainty around an issue, the harder the strategic behaviour will be to influence.

This pattern shows how cognitive, affective and territorial outputs are linked in shaping strategic behaviour.

Having explored the dimensions of strategic behaviour, and how they might interact with one another, it is now possible to explore the opportunities for shaping strategic behaviour more actively, either deliberately or via emergence. Here the wider bundle of territorial and emotional variables are perhaps harder to influence, at least in the short to medium term. However, from a team process point of view, the focus of strategic attention and the strategic momentum of the team offers at least two relatively immediate (and important) targets for influencing. Both of these flow on from Pattern 1 – focusing strategic attention and strategic momentum.

Focusing strategic attention

Attention is a separate (although related) thing from strategic thinking, which implies a cognitive process. 'Attention' concerns the way in which a team (and individuals) decide whether or not something is worth thinking about, worrying about or doing something about.

The pattern of interplay of cognitive, emotional and territorial interaction within a management team on strategic issues inevitably plays a big role in directing attention. For instance, at BT, the sheer fluidity of team behaviour meant that issues such as the threat of an operating company in the UK and the high percentage of the world population without telephones, were able to float into the debate without being rejected as 'outside our interest'. However, in this case, the duration of strategic attention was short-lived.

Strategic momentum thus plays an ongoing role in shaping strategic behaviour, operating at a micro level.

Strategic momentum

The team's extremely fluid way of extending or condensing its focus of strategic attention clearly enabled it to scan a diverse range of issues. This made it possible to cover considerable ground, but at the expense of depth of analysis. However, perhaps, more importantly, might this fluidity have dissipated its momentum and absorbed large quantities of its energy? (This is not, of course, to argue that general debate does not have value, but it can come to dominate, with the result that it becomes highly diffuse.)

If this is linked to the content analysis given during the course of the descriptions of the workshops earlier, you might recall that the team frequently analyzed a number of issues at a number of levels at the same time. This meant that it was very hard to create and sustain a sense of strategic momentum. The one exception is perhaps the final discussion of the department's priorities, but at this point momentum (of a kind) was achieved only at the expense of depth of thinking and exposure of feelings.

Having now dealt at length with the question 'What is strategic behaviour?' (including its dimensions) the next question is about its overall significance within the management process.

WHY AND HOW IS STRATEGIC BEHAVIOUR IMPORTANT?

While some of the BT team's interactions did seem chaotic – both to the observer, initially, and the participants – in fact, it was possible to uncover quite a significant degree of order at a lower level (for instance, within an individual's personal and strategic agendas). Equally, had it been possible to explore strategic behaviour at a BT-wide, organizational level, it is possible that further orderly patterns might have been discerned.

Nevertheless, the potential effects of these behaviours can be mapped out and thus some idea of their potential significance can be achieved. A key feature, however, to remember in this section is that what is being judged here is how salient particular patterns of behaviour are to producing strategic outcomes.

In Chapter 1, you will recall, the existing literature (particularly that which takes more of a strategic decision line) has a primarily process-related or cognitive perspective on strategy making. The decision-making literature highlights the 'messiness' of strategic decisions, which has been very much a characteristic of the discussions of the TSD team. However, it is also true that this 'messiness' may be compounded to such an extent that progress (from a manager's perspective) becomes virtually impossible.

It is now possible to explore the more specific reasons for strategic behaviour's importance from managers' own perspectives – especially in terms of how it might add to or detract from value. Based on the BT case study, these value drivers or destroyers break down into a number of headings (which have been distilled from themes emerging in Chapters 4–5) as follows:

- quality of strategic thinking
- sharing of mindsets
- creating an imperative to act
- territorial barriers may be changed
- building a platform for influencing
- time expended
- timeliness and utility of outcomes
- cognitive and emotional energy expended.

Quality of strategic thinking

In the BT case study, the strategic thinking undertaken by the team was relatively divergent. While this may have been an extreme situation, it is possible that strategic thinking elsewhere is similarly impaired by weak control over strategic behaviour.

Where strategic behaviour is not particularly well shaped, then management debate can, as a result, be too narrowly confined in scope, or too superficial (lacking depth) or fragmented (missing key interconnections). It might also fail to identify strategic blind spots or it may identify them as vague, possible opportunities and threats, but not have diagnosed those sufficiently in order to add value.

Sharing of mindsets

Linked to both 'quality of strategic thinking' and 'refocusing of attention', the commonality of mindsets also plays a major role in determining strategic outputs.

In the BT case study, managers expressed concerns that they lacked sufficient understanding of each other's mindsets, or 'mental maps'. For instance, David says:

> I suppose each time when we do something like this, I have a vision that we do end up with a shared mental map. We actually agree the areas where we agree and agree the areas where we disagree. We must realize that we actually have different positions. I think, you know, we are a long way from doing that.

Strategic behaviour that is not underpinned by a continual sharing of mindsets may thus inhibit a healthy degree of challenge and testing during strategic debate. Poorly shared mindsets can lead to a hardening of personal strategic agendas, which can then frustrate decision-making action and change.

Mindsets are thus the frames of reference that provide a basis for creating shared strategic thinking.

Creating an imperative to act

It was apparent, over the course of the three workshops at BT, that although the team members moved closer to making some tangible decisions about the team's priorities, this was a slow process. The feeling that there was a need to act did not seem to be very strong (perhaps because the team was at a pause in its development or perhaps because it could not make the headway it wished to). The team's strategic debate seemed to circle slightly closer to the issues but did not really grapple with them. Perhaps what was needed was as much 'emotional vision' as 'strategic vision'.

As David says:

> Yes, we are a group of strategists who actually enjoy talking. We will talk about any issue, we will look at it from all sides, er, but actually moving it from the point of talking to actually doing something about it is really ...

Both managers and strategic management theorists alike are well aware of the frequent gaps that occur between strategic thinking and action, especially when dealing with apparently intractable problems. However, the consequence of this is that, unless the strategic behaviour within a team can create some felt a need to act (even if this action is simply 'to investigate further'), implementation may well not be mobilized, even where it is an organizational imperative.

The feeling of there being a need to act is thus the precursor to action, as a tangible behavioural outcome.

Territorial barriers may be changed

An open and cohesive style of strategic behaviour may well be more conducive to reducing territorial barriers. Some of these barriers may be mainly organizational, and some may be mainly cognitive or even emotional, especially when issues exist that individuals have attachments to, given past experiences and investment of effort.

In the BT case study, managers signalled that territorial barriers existed, and that these sometimes inhibited strategic thinking. For instance, David tells us:

> I think that Keith[B] is, I would take Keith and say that Keith is determined to get technology X implemented, that's kind of his life-goal. And, er, being pulled back from what we need to do to technology X is kind of difficult. And he will actually – he is quite happy dealing with a whole series of business issues that relate to fibre in the ground, but disconnecting them from fibre is just not viable.

The extent to which these were actually constraining (or were simply perceived to be doing so) did not come to the surface. However, it was evident that BT managers accommodated the perceived existence of territorial barriers and behaved accordingly, making strategic debate more awkward.

Shifts in territorial barriers may help to remove or reduce some of the barriers or inhibitions to action (as a behavioural outcome).

Building a platform for influencing

In the BT case study, the team did not seem to have sufficient singularity of purpose, mindsets and common style to provide a platform for influencing the rest of BT. (Elsewhere it is possible that management teams undermine their influencing capability because they find it difficult to shape their own strategic behaviour in an effective way.)

Once again, creating a platform for influencing is a precursor to achieving action elsewhere in BT. As David puts it (as a personal statement, not necessarily reflecting the views of the team):

> That's exactly the mode which we are in – the change agent mode. That is the political domain – what it is all about, mobilizing people, the people who are actually going to do the work [elaborates]. This is a really big issue. And unless we are good at doing that, we aren't going to get the change to happen.

Time expended

The amount of time expended (relative to output) appeared in the BT case study to be very substantially determined by the orchestration (or lack of it) of the team's strategic behaviour. Time expended by teams generally will obviously govern:

- the number of issues the team cover
- the depth and thoroughness of their investigations
- how many issues exist where thinking is turned into action.

As Tim puts it:

> The next consequence of that was that the discussion dragged on. The agenda slipped disastrously and, in the day, we just received half the policy statements. The consequence was that a lot of things didn't get addressed.

Time expended may have a specific impact on, for example, reducing behavioural momentum, time wasted or a narrowing down of the focus of attention.

Timeliness and utility of outcomes

Where strategic behaviour becomes increasingly chaotic, this may obviously reduce the effectiveness of the strategy process, which might be frustrating from a team's own perspective. It may result in costly organizational delays as decisions are put off and opportunities slip. While a 'task-based' perspective is by no means the only one, nevertheless, it still exists, and it should not be ignored simply because of the influence of other perspectives, such as the political. For instance, in the BT case study it is easy to imagine the team's deliberations being overtaken by events elsewhere in the organization. Here, the rate at which new strategic issues were being generated by business changes might easily have threatened to exceed the team's capacity to process them. Bonnie underlined the pressure within the wider organization as follows:

> ... Manager P is supposed to have got this job where he is supposed to solve the fact that none of the pieces will work together and he is going to expect us to help ...

The timeliness and utility of outcomes thus concerns the final outputs of strategic behaviour and how they are used by the rest of the organization.

Cognitive and emotional energy expended

Finally, a management team's mental and emotional resources may be depleted by the frustration of weak control over its strategic behaviour. Not only did this lead to personal acrimony between key individuals, but also the partial withdrawal of Keith(A) who, when he did provide input, invariably gave focus to the debate. Keith(A) explains:

> People just don't listen to other people's ideas. One of the reasons is that you find that somebody is talking and you don't agree with one item. And if you don't interrupt then you never get heard.

Potentially, unrelieved frustration levels in other teams might rise to the point at which there is an effective burn-out, especially when a particular issue becomes a 'strategic black hole'. This suggests that controlling strategic behaviour effectively requires 'energy management' activity. This concerns the less tangible and indirect effects of strategic behaviour rather than the more tangible outcomes.

In summary, strategic behaviour does appear to play a profoundly important and influential role in shaping strategic thinking. Not only does shaping strategic behaviour seem to yield potential benefits, but default behaviours do seem to have costs – for the organization, the team and also the individuals involved.

CAN STRATEGIC BEHAVIOUR BE HARNESSED AND, IF SO, HOW?

Yes it can, and many of the ways in which strategic behaviour might be harnessed more effectively have been identified already. Thus, what follows is a short summary.

- Managing the team mix so that there is a reasonably good balance of skills and style.
- Managing the interactive process (for instance, by monitoring the level of debate, as shown in Chapters 3 and 5).
- Creating a richer range of behaviours (for example, more 'questioning' and 'probing' types of behaviour).
- Improving the quality and effectiveness of meta-behaviours.
- Clearer targeting of behavioural outcomes and breakthroughs, and monitoring the delivery of these against the quality of the behavioural process.
- Surfacing and examining the less transparent aspects of behaviour.
- Orchestration of the process, including the field and duration of attention, behavioural momentum and energy levels.
- Using tools for analyzing issues and to help surface assumptions and mental maps (and feelings). Here a social interaction perspective has been seen to complement a cognitive mapping perspective in an unusual and yet powerful way.
- Being prepared to make sufficient emotional investment to achieve a strategic and/or behavioural breakthrough.

However, perhaps more important than these specific areas is the need to manage strategic behaviour as a total system (or the 'system of strategic behaviour').

The above list provides a broad range of options for any senior management team to work on – should it feel the need to shape its own strategic behaviour in an active way. However, you might now find it valuable to explore the possibilities of broadening the range of analytical tools managers might use. This obviously raises further issues (and, in effect, political ones) concerning who might do the shaping, to what ends and how.

CONCLUSION AND SUMMARY

'Strategic behaviour' is a most fruitful and relevant concept – both in management theory terms and in practice. Strategic behaviour exhibits distinctive patterns. This is insofar as their cognitive, affective, dynamic and political elements are particulary complex, dynamic and hard to manage.

Strategic behaviour appears to be important in the strategy-making process on a number of counts, yet appears neglected – an area that is seen not so much as one of 'management' or 'control', but as something to do with 'shaping'.

At the minimum, it appears that management theorists/researchers and managers should become more aware of their system of strategic behaviour as well as paying attention to strategy content, context and the more tangible aspects of strategic decision making.

MANAGING
STRATEGIC
BEHAVIOUR

When opponents present openings, you should penetrate them immediately. Get to what they want first, subtly anticipate them ... . Thus at first you are like a maiden, so the enemy opens his door; then you are like a rabbit on the loose, so the enemy can't keep you out.
Sun Tzu, *The Art of War*

INTRODUCTION

Now that the issues involved in strategic behaviour have been thoroughly explored, next comes the issue of how it can be managed. Some of the lessons learned on the journey so far are profoundly simple and some are more complicated. At its most straightforward, strategic behaviour can be managed by means of:

- direction setting
- inhibiting less desirable behaviours.

'Direction setting' involves programming those behaviours that steer the team in, more or less, the right direction. 'Inhibiting less desirable behaviours' means discouraging those behaviours that deflect the team from creating strategic outputs.

Superficially, this may feel like a rather behavioural approach (triggering memories of Pavlov's dogs, who were rewarded for performing tasks). However, it all involves a lot of determined, conscious effort on the part of managers to achieve the desired effect. To illustrate this, see Figure 7.1. The basis of this cartoon-type picture was originally drawn during workshops for the Partek Group in Finland, an engineering group with operations worldwide. In its original form, it was displayed on a massive white board with all kinds of things going on, including:

- Partek's head office – drawn as a large building bristling with antennae, reflecting strategic intelligence
- allies who would help in the combat against competitors – the enemy
- environmental turbulence – in the form of huge, electrical storms.

Figure 7.1 is, however, a much simpler and more condensed picture, which appears for instance in 'Tesco's Guide to Strategic Thinking' – used by Tesco senior management as a resource to help managers with their strategy development projects.

In Figure 7.1 the direction-setting role is played by the helicopter. The very notion of 'helicopter thinking' can act as a profound positive influence on strategic behaviour. By 'helicopter thinking' I mean:

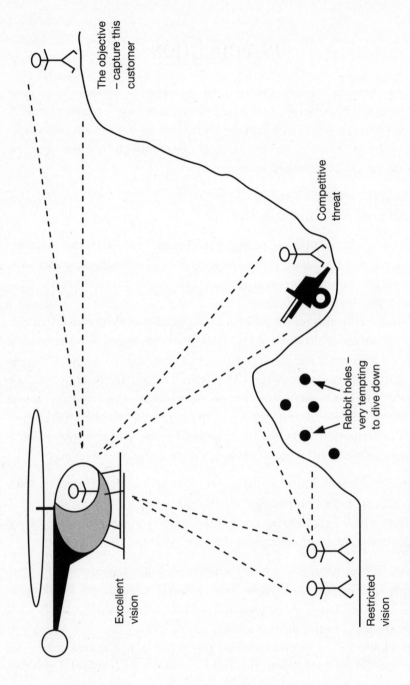

The objective – capture this customer

Competitive threat

Rabbit holes – very tempting to dive down

Excellent vision

Restricted vision

Fig 7.1 Strategic thinking – as helicopter vision

being able to focus on the really big picture – the key strategic issues – rather than merely the tactical ones – not only internally, but also externally.

The second, major ingredient (which serves an inhibiting role) is the idea of 'rabbit hole management'. You can see the rabbit holes in the hillside in Figure 7.1.

These are to remind any team discussing strategic issues to avoid going down into areas of unnecessary detail. As you will recall, in the BT case study, managers believed that they were having a strategic debate, whereas in reality they had gone down a rabbit hole. Just showing Figure 7.1 for a minute at the start of a strategic meeting has the remarkable effect of lifting the level of debate up from an everyday level. Companies such as Amerada Petroleum, Dillons, Forward Trust, NCR, Oxford University Press, Tesco and others have all benefited from using this simple picture in strategy workshops.

In addition to this simple technique, the case study has yielded even more interesting frameworks for managing strategic behaviour:

- cause of behaviour analysis (COBRA)
- stakeholder (and stakeholder agenda) analysis
- from–to (FT) analysis
- strategic agenda review (STAR)
- team roles – an alternative approach.

CAUSE OF BEHAVIOUR ANALYSIS (COBRA)

At least some managers have for many years been acquainted with the idea of 'root cause analysis', sometimes known as 'fishbone' analysis. However, it is less common to see root cause analysis applied explicitly to behavioural issues.

Cause of behaviour analysis (COBRA) is an application of root cause analysis that has been tailored to be used specifically with behavioural issues. Following the same principles as conventional fishbone analysis, you begin by describing the main symptom(s) of the problem on the right-hand-side of a piece of paper. Figure 7.2 shows an example of a management team I studied (not at BT) that struggled to evolve an effective business strategy.

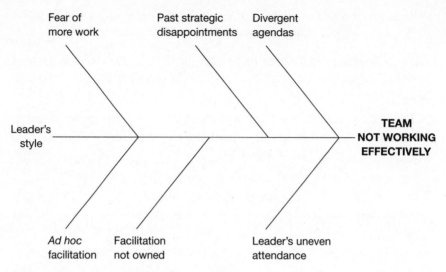

Fig 7.2 Cause of behaviour analysis (COBRA)

This COBRA picture traces this symptom back to the divergent agendas of subgroups in the team. It also highlights some sensitivities to past strategic disappointments and, unsurprisingly, the fear that agreeing a more stretching strategy will entail more work on top of the existing workload. The style of the team's leader is also a major inhibitor regarding mobilizing the team. Also, the team's strategic sessions have been facilitated in an *ad hoc* way that has not been owned by one particular camp within the team. Frequently, the team leader could not attend (or was in and out of the meetings), suggesting a partial commitment to the future path.

The outcome of this situation was that the team's strategic meetings became more and more frustrating. Those segments of the team eager for a new sense of direction decided that, at least for the time being, these strategic discussions had reached an impasse. The choice for them was really to continue to push, meeting increasing resistance, or go into a kind of suspended strategic animation. In fact, the suspended strategic animation became the option by default.

However, there was latent change still within the team. All members of the team felt that a strategic vacuum had been created and there was some embarrassment around. This embarrassment began to nudge strategy development forward in very tentative, incremental steps. Indeed, these steps were the ones that had been considered by the team in earlier, sometimes heated, deliberations.

However, the players who were now moving these changes forward were precisely the ones who were the original antagonists, not those who had sought to be change catalysts. Interestingly, it was as if these antagonists had unconsciously begun to enact the new strategy once the heat (and previous 'attack') was off.

COBRA analysis should begin (as with conventional root cause analysis) with defining the symptom of the behavioural problem. Unlike root cause analysis, the drivers of the problem are drawn in as squiggly lines, to suggest that these are less tangible and hard to observe directly – they are snake-like in operation.

Once an initial COBRA analysis has been done, it is possible to go a level deeper to explore what micro-level drivers of strategic behaviour are at work. For instance, taking a look at the divergent agendas of the subgroups within the team reflected:

- the wider organizational culture, which made it possible for people to do a lot of 'their own thing'
- the particular history of this team, which had developed around a hub of core members
- the desire for new team members to bring something new to the party, rather than be cast in the role of the audience
- the informal pecking order that existed, and which certain team members quite naturally wanted to preserve.

Piranha analysis

Before leaving fishbone analysis, let us look at a technique that is very helpful when dealing with complicated issues in piranha analysis. The idea of piranha analysis was generated by a workshop with Guardian Royal Exchange.

One particular issue that was being analyzed turned out to be not one, but several problems. When the several problems were analyzed, these became even more complicated series of problems.

Abandoning a single fishbone, I began by drawing up a series of fishbones, laid out 'around the clock'. Each fishbone was a mini fishbone, suggesting that here was not a single or even small number of problems but a veritable shoal – hence the name piranha analysis (see Figure 7.3).

217

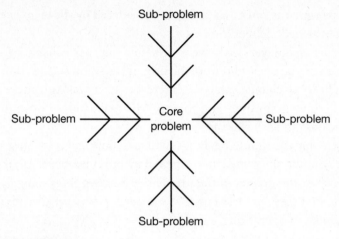

Fig 7.3 Piranha analysis

Piranha analysis is not merely applicable to analyzing a single, complicated issue. It is also highly relevant to analyzing both:

- the problems an individual manager faces in their job generally (here the 'shoal' of problems would be 'my role is simply too stretching').
- a behavioural issue (see COBRA analysis) that breaks down into a number of separate major problem strands.

Wishbone analysis

As highlighted above, fishbone analysis can help in dealing with a behavioural problem. Fishbone analysis typically deals with a problem that has developed either in the past or is with us in the present. However, is there a technique for creating future alignment within strategic behaviour?

Fortunately, the answer is 'Yes' because the notion of 'wishbone analysis' (Grundy, 1998) can be applied to aligning the system of strategic behaviour. Although originally conceived in the arena of competitive strategy, wishbone analysis is extremely helpful in identifying all the things that need to go right – and, in the future, – to create a particular behavioural pattern. Figure 7.4 depicts one example of a number of things that needed to be aligned for one particular team to behave more strategically.

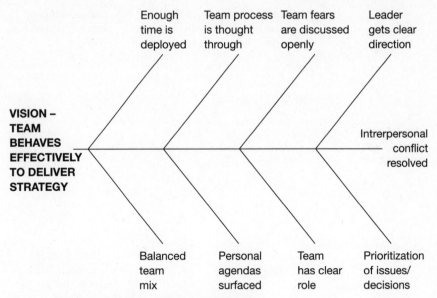

Fig 7.4 Wishbone analysis – strategic behaviour

To draw up the wishbone, it is not necessary to put the various bones in any particular order, unless you want to be particularly high tech about it. The main point is that you have covered all the key interventions and other factors needed to bring about your behavioural vision (which you write down on the left-hand side of the page). The wishbone is positioned on the page the opposite way round to the fishbone to signify that the future (to the right) is being worked out, rather than reflecting on the past (to the left).

A variant of wishbone analysis can be used to help monitor the implementation of behavioural change. Although methods for measuring change already exist – in the form of the balanced scorecard (Kaplan and Norton, 1992), the conventional types of measures do not sit easily with behavioural change. However, taking the wishbone analysis technique, it can now be used explicitly to define some measures or indicators. This leads to Figure 7.5 – the 'Scorebone', so-called as it is a cross between a wishbone and a balanced scorecard. (This tool has been devised from work by the Finance Team, Nokia Personal Communications, San Diego. 1997.)

Those who have been struggling to apply the balanced scorecard (because of the sometimes relatively inflexible categories of controls) will obviously appreciate the potential in using the scorebone to develop balanced scorecards for strategies beyond purely behavioural change.

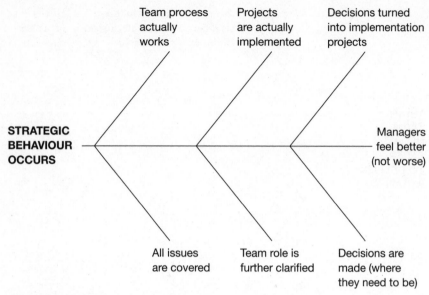

Fig 7.5 Score bone

STAKEHOLDER ANALYSIS

Stakeholder analysis is a most useful way of understanding the behavioural drivers at work in a team. While COBRA analysis focuses on a variety of drivers, both within and outside the team, stakeholder analysis looks specifically at the agendas and influence levels of key players. In Chapter 2, you will recall just how useful stakeholder analysis was in understanding patterns of political influence at Champneys.

Stakeholder analysis is the second change tool for analyzing implementation issues, and has entirely reshaped the way in which strategic development has been implemented. Although Piercey (1989) and I (1993) have drawn attention to the importance of stakeholder analysis as a practical tool, with some exceptions (for example, Goold, *et al.*, 1994, p315), it is generally seen as being more of a theoretical method.

Stakeholder analysis is the systematic identification of key stakeholders and appraisal of their influence on and posture towards implementation. It may also involve creating a strategy to reshape the influence of these or new stakeholders. Stakeholder analysis can be used after COBRA (where COBRA deals with behaviour in a group of people). Alternatively, it can be used before – to identify which stakeholders are causing behavioural difficulties.

220

Stakeholder analysis is a second method for creating organizational radar. It can be used not just on 'big picture' strategy issues, but also on much more micro-level issues, such as getting something specific done in your job.

The tool is used as follows:

1 identify who you believe the key stakeholders are for each phase of the process (the 'stakeholder brainstorm')
2 evaluate whether or not these stakeholders have a high, medium or low influence on the issue in question (you need to abstract this from the influence they generally have in the organization – Piercey, 1989)
3 evaluate whether or not at the current time they are for the project, against it or idling in neutral.

The above gives a good 'first cut' of the pattern of stakeholders. The cluster of stakeholders depicted on a stakeholder analysis grid (see Figure 7.6) should then be assessed to see what the overall picture looks like, particularly with regard to the following questions.

• Is the project an easy bet?
• Is it highlighting a long slog?
• Does it seem like *Mission Impossible*?

Following the first cut analysis, you should then move on to the next phase by asking the following.

1 Can new stakeholders be brought into play to shift the balance or can existing players be withdrawn in some way (or be subtly distracted)?
2 Is it possible to boost the influence of stakeholders who are currently in favour of the change?
3 Is it possible to reduce the influence of antagonistic stakeholders?
4 Can coalitions of stakeholders in favour be achieved so as to strengthen their combined influence?
5 Can coalitions of stakeholders antagonistic to the project be prevented?
6 Can the change itself – in appearance or substance – be reformulated to diffuse hostility to the project?
7 Are there possibilities of 'bringing on board' negative stakeholders by allowing them a role or incorporating one or more of their prized ideas?
8 Is the pattern of influence of stakeholders sufficiently hostile for the project to warrant redefinition of the project?

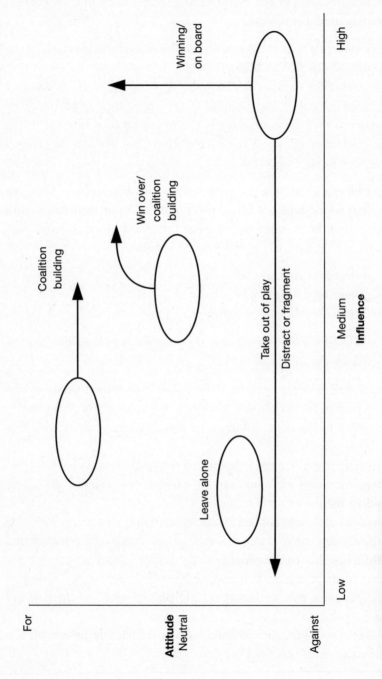

Fig 7.6 Stakeholder analysis

Stakeholder analysis involves many questions as well as answers. These questions can be used to track potential positions of stakeholders (and their agendas) in specific meetings and chance conversations. Note, too, that stakeholders change their positions – suggesting the notion of 'snakeholder analysis', the tracking of wriggly players.

Often a particular stakeholder may be difficult to position. This may be because that stakeholder's agendas are complicated. It is quite common to find that it is only one specific blocker that has made a stakeholder into an influential antagonist.

Where there are very large numbers of stakeholders at play on a particular issue, this may invite simplification of the project. The project may need to be refined – perhaps even stopped and then restarted – in order to dissolve an organizational mess.

To use stakeholder analysis effectively, you may need to set some process arrangements in place where a team project is involved. First, the analysis may be usefully done in a 'workshop' environment so as to give the analysis a 'reflective' or 'learning' feel. This helps to integrate managers' thinking on a key change issue. Also, it may be useful to devise code words for key stakeholders in order to make the outputs from this change tool feel 'safe'. On several occasions, managers have decided to adopt nicknames for the key players. The element of humour helps to diffuse the seriousness of stakeholder analysis.

Stakeholder agenda analysis

Stakeholder agenda analysis probes even deeper than stakeholder analysis. It can be even more revealing to dig down beneath the surface of stakeholder positionings to find the forces driving those key players. Figure 7.7 considers one particular stakeholder who is (overall) in favour (the 'attractor') of a particular way of dealing with an issue. However, there are several areas where this stakeholder is not attracted (and is, indeed, positively repelled – 'the repellers' – by it).

The relative balance of attractors and repellers gives a good indicator of what the overall attitude of that stakeholder is likely to be. In each case, the arrows were drawn in relative proportion to the perceived strength of the 'attractor' and 'repeller' forces.

223

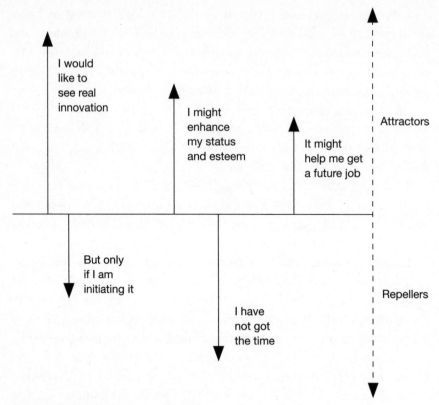

Fig 7.7 Stakeholder agenda analysis

Other individuals may also have differing levels of risk aversion, and vary in how aggressively they tend to pursue a goal if attractors exist. For instance, certain individuals may hold back from action or agreement on an issue if one repeller alone is significant. Other, more bullish types might well be happy overcoming quite significant repellers if there are major attractors.

One of the interesting aspects of stakeholder agendas is that stakeholders themselves may not be very clear about their own agendas. This is partly because they are not in just one mind, but, perhaps, several minds. Also many stakeholders do not have just a single personality, but may even have subpersonalities. So, for instance, one particular stakeholder might well be governed by two, three or even more mini-personalities. For example, they might be influenced by:

● subpersonality 1: 'I need to be in control of all situations, whatever happens' – the defensive subpersonality

- subpersonality 2: 'I want to be liked by my staff, I will do nice things to help them – at least when I don't feel this exposes me' – the 'clubby' personality
- subpersonality 3: 'I want to enjoy wielding power now and then … then and especially now' – the Nietzschean personality, after the German philosopher Frederick Nietzsche, author of *The Will to Power*.

You need to recognize, therefore, that in a management team you are not only dealing with a single 'team' but with a 'team of teams' or with a number of individuals, each with a multitude of subpersonalities and disparate agendas.

Stakeholder agenda analysis has a number of powerful uses:

- in dealing with a specific strategic issue in a team where there is a diversity of personal and strategic agendas – PASTA factors
- in working individually on a specific plan – for example, to develop a project or business plan or make an organizational structure change
- in strategic meetings, to tease out the positions of key stakeholders (which are implicit) and check out your perceptions of where they are coming from
- as part of self-management as, often, you are yourself a key stakeholder and might feel your own commitment is undermined by some repellers – stakeholder agenda analysis exposes exactly where *you* are coming from.

Stakeholder prioritization

Besides stakeholder analysis and stakeholder agenda analysis, a further technique that can be most useful in navigating organizational politics is that of stakeholder prioritization. This technique came out of work with Domino Printing Sciences, an international technology company based in Cambridge, UK.

At Domino, a team of managers was working on a particular strategic breakthrough project. Its conclusions suggested a new way of looking at things, one that needed to be skilfully positioned in top management's perceptions.

The team had a relatively tight time window in which to persuade the top team. It used a stakeholder prioritization grid to distinguish the relative importance and urgency of seeing particular stakeholders (Figure 7.8). This grid enabled them to plot the critical path through the organization, and map the spontaneous discussions that were likely to break out between stakeholders. It also enabled them to bring in at least one stakeholder early on who had not been an obvious candidate at all. Using yellow Post-its, the grid made it very easy to play around with the effects that different influencing strategies might have on the organizational network and work out which option would be the most effective one.

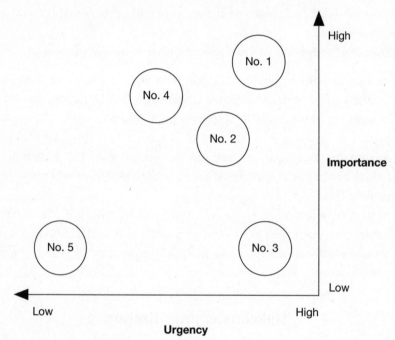

Fig 7.8 Stakeholder prioritization analysis

FROM–TO (FT) ANALYSIS

Another interesting technique for managing either a behavioural problem or stakeholder positions is to conduct from–to (FT) analysis. Figure 7.9 shows an example of how useful the FT tool can be. Taking, for instance, the example given earlier in the chapter, it can be seen that the team is trying to move from an emergent strategy to a deliberate one, from dominance by the 'gang of four' to a more open political structure and so on. FT analysis can thus be used to gather up all the strands of behavioural change and present these as a picture.

	From	To
Structures*		
Goals*		
Behaviours*		
Cost base*		
Responsiveness*		

*You need to identify shifts relevant to your own part of the business, perhaps by scoring them on a scale of 1–5 or 1–10

Fig 7.9 Using from–to analysis

FT analysis is a widely applicable strategy implementation tool, but it really comes into its own when dealing with the more behavioural side of management. It is particularly useful for monitoring and tackling behavioural change. For example, how far are you (on a scale of, say, 1–5) towards your behavioural goals? Where gaps exist, how do you propose to fill them?

From–to analysis can also be used in conjunction with stakeholder agenda analysis. To do this, you plot the existing agendas of a particular stakeholder on the left-hand side and the desired agendas on the right. This can also suggest specific action steps that need to be taken to bridge the gap between the 'from's and the 'to's. Figure 7.10 shows an example of this.

The tools which we have discussed had already been applied elsewhere (Grundy, 1993 and 1995), but were found particularly helpful in the BT intervention.

227

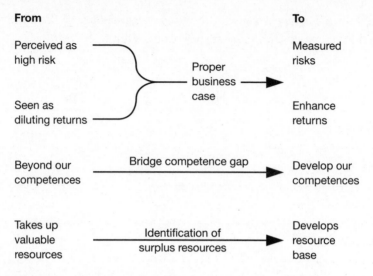

Fig 7.10 From–to analysis and stakeholder agenda analysis related to diversification

STRATEGIC AGENDA REVIEW (STAR)

The next process was created during the BT study. It was used to help BT managers review the cognitive and emotional ingredients of their strategic agendas on a particular issue. Essentially these maps (see Figure 7.11) plotted the:

- perceived strategic importance of the issue (low–high)
- perceived level of influence over the issue (high–low)
- strength of feelings (weak–strong)
- degree of anxiety (low–high)
- level of understanding (high–low)
- perceived uncertainty (low–high).

To perform a strategic agenda review (STAR) managers are asked to rate their perceptions of each ray of the star-shaped picture. Once this has been done, by linking the spots crossed on each ray of the star, the relative severity of the aspects of the strategic issue become apparent. Clearly, a very large star reflects an especially intractable issue.

However, there is more to come. To go behind why a particular point of the star is a problem, it is possible to selectively apply a fishbone

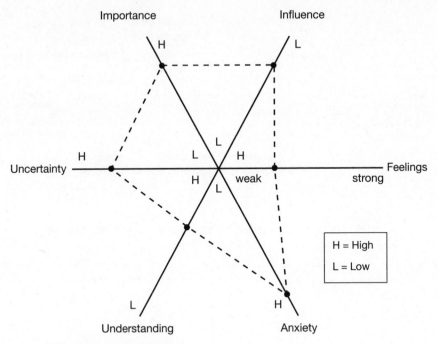

Fig 7.11 Strategic agenda review

analysis. This exposes not merely why a ray is particularly problematical, but also how it can be addressed. For instance, Figure 7.12 goes behind one point of the star, ultimately producing along its five ribs a 'starfish' analysis.

It is possible that two rays of a star will be particularly interesting to analyze together. Then, you can relate two particular rays of the star by drawing up some two-dimensional grids. Three particularly useful grids are:

- importance and influence (see Figure 7.13), which we saw earlier
- uncertainty and importance (see Figure 7.14)
- importance and understanding (see Figure 7.15).

The importance and influence grid is especially useful for identifying which issues are very important and over which there is little influence. Having identified these, the team needs to answer the question 'How can we gain more influence over these issues, using our natural cunning?' This often invites the use of stakeholder analysis or stakeholder agenda analysis, or both.

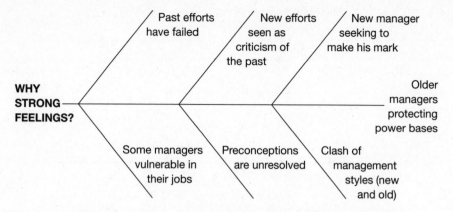

Fig 7.12 Behind the strategic agenda analysis review – a 'starfish' analysis

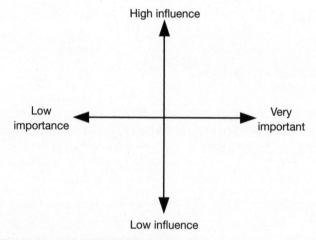

Fig 7.13 The importance and influence grid

The uncertainty and importance grid is an extremely effective way of prioritizing strategic issues for further analysis. Once again, when dealing with internal political uncertainties, using stakeholder analysis (and agenda analysis) is fruitful.

The importance and understanding grid is another useful, more cognitive tool. This helps to direct strategic attention towards the areas that are least well understood, rather than roam the terrain of greatest comfort – that where the level of understanding is high.

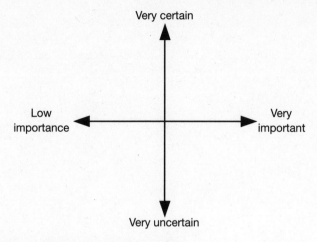

Fig 7.14 The uncertainty and importance grid

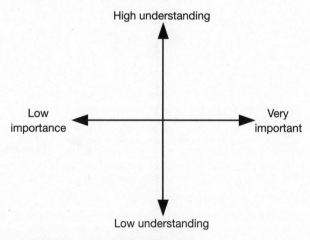

Fig 7.15 The importance and understanding grid

Next, you can use grids dealing more with emotions and feelings. These grids include:

- anxiety and understanding (see Figure 7.16)
- anxiety and importance (see Figure 7.17).

231

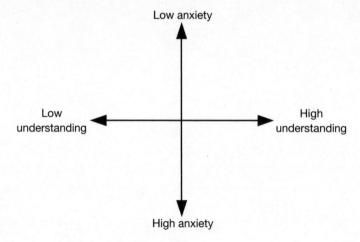

Fig 7.16 The anxiety and understanding grid

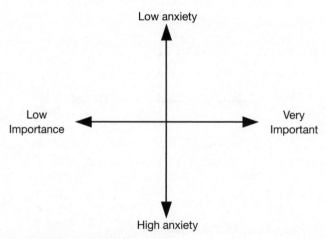

Fig 7.17 The anxiety and importance grid

The anxiety and understanding grid is useful for deciding which issues should be investigated in much greater depth. Issues about which there is high level of anxiety but low (current) level of understanding are obviously strong candidates for more work. This grid can be used not merely for looking at current levels of anxiety and understanding but also future ones.

Besides being used to look at the more tangible issues, the anxiety and understanding grid can also be used for interpersonal issues. For instance, you might be particularly anxious that your boss might make a certain kind of decision (say, changing your role), but not really understand what their likely agendas might be, and you could use this grid to explore this situation.

It is also possible that, for some issues, although you do not have a strong understanding of them, you feel little anxiety. For instance, you may not understand the plans your boss has for the organization's structure, but they are unlikely to affect you personally and so you are not particularly anxious about what will happen. Equally, there may be different shades of importance affecting an issue. While it may be common for anxiety to rise in proportion to an issue's perceived importance, this is not necessarily the case. You could be very anxious about something the real importance of which is not actually that great or you could feel very little anxiety about a very important issue.

What does 'importance' actually mean, then? Normally, this would be taken as being 'importance to the business' (in order to facilitate an objective debate). Of course, you might think of it as being to do with 'importance to me personally', but I believe it is better to stay with 'importance to the business'.

Clearly, other grids can be explored, too, if appropriate (for example, influence and anxiety, importance and feelings, and so on). As these are meant as just-in-time grids (rather than just-in-case) they are just mentioned here.

RELATING THE TECHNIQUES TO ONE ANOTHER

To understand how these various techniques fit together, take a look at Figure 7.18. This shows how problem analysis, behavioural analysis and political analysis fit together. Problem analysis can be achieved by using either conventional fishbone analysis or the grid techniques called here strategic agenda review. The refinement of fishbone analysis – COBRA –) can be applied to behavioural problems, while a number of applications of stakeholder analysis get to grips with political analysis.

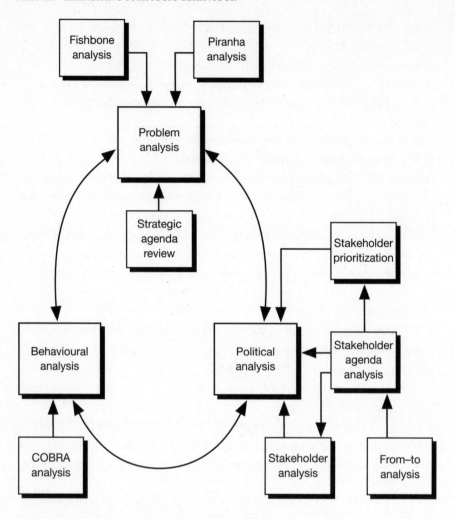

Fig 7.18 How the analysis techniques fit together

Obviously it is inappropriate to try to apply all (or even most) techniques simultaneously unless you have achieved a fluency in the techniques. Using common sense and business judgement, simply apply one, two or maybe three techniques to your first issue. Later on you can become more ambitious, applying a wider range of the techniques. In time they will become invaluable intuitive tools, hopefully shared with others in your organization.

TEAM ROLES – AN ALTERNATIVE APPROACH

Perhaps now is a good time to take a lighter look at the team roles involved in strategic behaviour. The inspiration for this comes from the famous, original *Star Trek* series, which shows the team aboard the Starship Enterprise sometimes coping well with strategic challenges, sometimes not.

The five main characters in the original series of *Star Trek* help us towards an alternative definition of team roles, these being:

- Captain Kirk
- Spock– Captain Kirk's deputy
- Scotty – the mechanic
- Bones – the doctor
- the Klingons – the enemy of the status quo.

In these alternative team roles, each member of the team brings something distinctive to the party. Running through the characters again, these are:

- Captain Kirk – the visionary
- Spock – the analyst
- Scotty – the fixer/implementer
- Bones – the facilitator
- the Klingons – the challenger.

In any strategic team, you can see different styles at work – styles that no doubt mirror these Star Trek caricatures. However, to obtain a good team mix, it is wise to obtain a variety of these styles.

Sadly, the balanced team mix does not always exist. Many teams are full of Scottys (fixer/implementers) with the occasional Spock (analyst). Otherwise, a team might be dominated by a single Captain Kirk (visionary), but lack the counterbalance of a Spock (analyst). Equally, a team might be well balanced in terms of Captain Kirks, Spocks and Scottys, but might lack an effective Bones (facilitator). Another possible mismatch in a team mix is where there is a very powerful Klingon (challenger/destroyer), but no counterbalancing Captain Kirk figure.

Figure 7.19 outlines these five team roles and their possible interrelationships. Note some particularly interesting synergies between team roles:

235

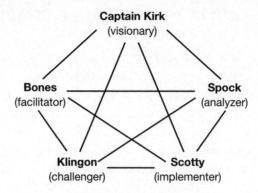

Fig 7.19 Alternative team roles – the *Star Trek* approach

- **Captain Kirk–Spock** here the analyst (Spock) helps to flesh out the logic of the strategic vision (Captain Kirk)
- **Spock–Scotty** the analyst (Spock) gives the fixer/implementer (Scotty) a clear sense of purpose and priorities
- **Captain Kirk–Bones** the visionary (Captain Kirk) relies on the facilitator (Bones) to help spread the visions
- **Bones–Klingon** the facilitator (Bones) helps to reconstruct what the challenger (Klingon) has deconstructed
- **Klingon–Scotty** the challenger (Klingon) helps to clear the ground for the fixer/implementer (Scotty)
- **Bones–Spock** the facilitator (Bones) is guided by the analyst (Spock) in identifying the really key blockages
- **Captain Kirk–Klingon** the visionary (Captain Kirk) is able to move the organization forward more easily because of the dismantling of the old brought about by the challenger (Klingon)
- **Captain Kirk–Scotty** the visionary (Captain Kirk) gives direction to the fixer/implementer (Scotty).

The advantage of these alternative team roles is that they avoid the more abstract categorizations some team role categories are hampered by. They bring in an element of humour, too, making the categorizations less threatening. Importantly, they are particularly relevant to the strategic behaviour of teams because they include the visionary and the facilitator (both of whom exemplify meta-behaviours). They also bring in the sometimes positive challenge of the Klingon.

To operationalize these *Star Trek* roles, rather than use an elaborate and tedious psychometric questionnaire, the following process is suggested.

- Each member of the team is given a number of cards with *Star Trek* roles on one side, the other side blank. They have twice as many cards each as there are members of the team (other than themselves).
- They then give each other member of the team two cards – one indicating the other person's primary team role and the other their secondary role.
- Each team member then counts up their primary and secondary roles, giving each primary card a score of two, and each secondary card a score of one.
- By adding up the scores, they can then work out their overall averaged primary and secondary scores.

Table 7.1 is a fictitious example to show how this works in practice.

Table 7.1 Example of assigning *Star Trek* team roles

			Given to		
Given by	Joe	Sue	Don	Pete	Ron
Joe	–	Spock (p)	Klingon (p)	Scotty (p)	Klingon (p)
	–	Bones (s)	Bones (s)	Klingon (s)	Kirk(s)
Sue	Scotty (p)	–	Bones (p)	Klingon (s)	Kirk (p)
	Bones (s)	–	Klingon (s)	Spock (s)	Scotty (s)
Don	Bones (p)	Bones (p)	–	Scotty (p)	Kirk (p)
	Spock (s)	Spock (s)	–	Klingon (s)	Klingon (s)
Pete	Scotty (p)	Spock (p)	Bones (p)	–	Klingon (p)
	Kirk (s)	Klingon (s)	Klingon (s)	–	Kirk (s)
Ron	Kirk (p)	Bones (p)	Klingon (p)	Klingon (p)	–
	Bones (s)	Spock (s)	Scotty (s)	Spock (s)	–
Averaged	Scotty 4	Spock 6	Klingon 6	Klingon 6	Kirk 6
scores	Bones 4	Bones 5	Bones 5	Scotty 4	Klingon 5
	Kirk 3	Klingon 1	Scotty 1	Spock 2	Scotty 1
	Spock 1				

Note: 'primary' ratings score 2 points, 'secondary' ratings score 1 point.

The overall team mix here is as follows:

Klingon	18
Bones	14
Scotty	10
Spock	9
Kirk	9

highlighting a predominance of Klingon behaviour (challenging rather than constructing).

CONCLUSION AND SUMMARY

Strategic behaviour does not have to be the unmanageable organizational turbulence portrayed by writers of the 'process' school of strategic management. Just because behavioural turbulence in strategy making is commonplace does not mean that this is inevitable. Even using a small number of techniques at BT (especially the importance and influence grid) had a calming effect.

Let us hope that, as I have discovered, you will find the inspiration to harness the power of strategic behaviour.

LESSONS FOR MANAGEMENT THEORY AND PRACTICE

Be extremely subtle, even to the point of formlessness. Be extremely mysterious, even to the point of sound-lessness. Thereby you can be the director of the opponent's fate.

Sun Tzu, *The Art of War*

INTRODUCTION

In Chapter 6 it was found that strategic behaviour did appear to be a very useful concept. So, in this final chapter, I shall relate my findings back to existing management theory. Finally, the implications for management practice shall be examined, particularly regarding efforts made to promote strategic thinking and skills development.

LESSONS FOR MANAGEMENT THEORY

The most interesting areas of the literature (from Chapter 1) to re-examine are:

- logical incrementalism
- the learning and change literature
- the role of organizational politics.

Logical incrementalism

Logical incrementalism has acted as a powerful counterbalance in the strategic management literature to the tradition that Mintzberg characterized as the 'design school' of strategy.

You will recall how (at least at BT) strategic behaviour is a very complicated, fluid and, at times, laborious set of interactive, interpersonal processes. These interpersonal processes need to be harnessed effectively in order to achieve forward momentum. However, because of the need to move cognitive, affective and territorial elements simultaneously, it becomes very difficult for managers to progress across a number of strategic issues simultaneously.

Where these strategic issues are interdependent, then incremental development of strategy on one issue may put thinking on another issue out of alignment. As a result, management teams are then forced to, as it were, 'park' their thinking at a particular point and address another area of strategic concern. Although this 'unfinishedness' is due to issues being

241

only partially thought through, it also appears to be very much due to the more opaque zone of feeling and territorial boundaries. The latter may be more difficult and take longer for managers to work through than the former.

The fact that managers may make uneven progress on different strategic issues is a natural phenomenon. However, this might well result in strategic issues being incompletely dealt with before the team parks them and moves on (because, for instance, they appear partly or completely intractable at that time). The resulting zig-zagging of debate, and continual adjustment in the focus of attention, inevitably contributes to the messiness of strategic thinking and the apparent unresolvable nature of particular strategic problems. Therefore, some of the more extreme forms of organizational politics are a consequence of poorly focused strategic debate.

The resulting process is very akin to Hickson, *et al.*'s (1986) 'vortex' in the decision-making process, rather than it taking the form of a neat, linear development. So, a natural tendency towards 'logical incrementalism' – as a style of managing strategy – might well be appreciated because of the dynamics of strategic behaviour in senior management teams. Part of this aggravation might equally be due to the perhaps apparent lack of meta-behaviour, as was the case in the BT team.

So, a strategic behaviour perspective helps to explain why a logical incrementalism style of strategic management is so prevalent. This is largely because of the perceived difficulty of establishing agreement on a particular issue area (whether this is about ends or means or both) that is sufficient to anchor it down – at least for a while.

To achieve this result would require a simultaneous realignment of cognition, feelings and territorial assumptions, which, as seen earlier, is particularly difficult. However, this 'incremental' behaviour also highlights the likely consequences of loosely controlled strategic behaviour – management teams drifting along a path, tending to only partially resolve most of their strategic issues and defaulting to those issues that appear to be either simply more urgent or easier to address. In its ultimate state, the result could be characterized as being like 'strategic indigestion'. This state inevitably aggravates organizational politics.

So, strategic behaviour routines are likely to oscillate between taking 'the path of least resistance' and short-lived and partial attempts to drive into the heart of these issues – the core of their intractability. Clearly, leadership is a positive influence on strategic behaviour. However, once again, from a strategic behaviour perspective, leadership would appear to need to be complemented by other behaviours in order to make headway on intractable issues. This line of thinking helps to explain why strategy development seems to be so inherently fluid and emergent, rather than deliberate. Of course, where strategy is left relatively undefined and open, then, unless there is very firm leadership, this can easily lead to rampant organizational politics.

Further, the BT study makes it very clear that it is necessary to distinguish between deliberate and emergent strategy content and, equally importantly, between deliberate and emergent strategy process and strategic behaviour. This helps to develop Mintzberg's (1994) notions of deliberate and emergent strategy. (Here 'strategy content' is defined as being the specific decisions, plans and ideas that are outcomes of strategic debate. 'Strategy process' is defined as being the routines, techniques and style of interaction used to generate and process strategy content.) Although it is impossible to distinguish precisely between content and process, this is still a useful distinction, particularly as strategic behaviour has been included within the strategy process.

It is possible to imagine a deliberate strategy coming out of an emergent (as opposed to a deliberate) process and set of behaviours (labelled an 'Intuitive' strategy below). Figure 8.1 represents these possibilities using a matrix of strategy styles.

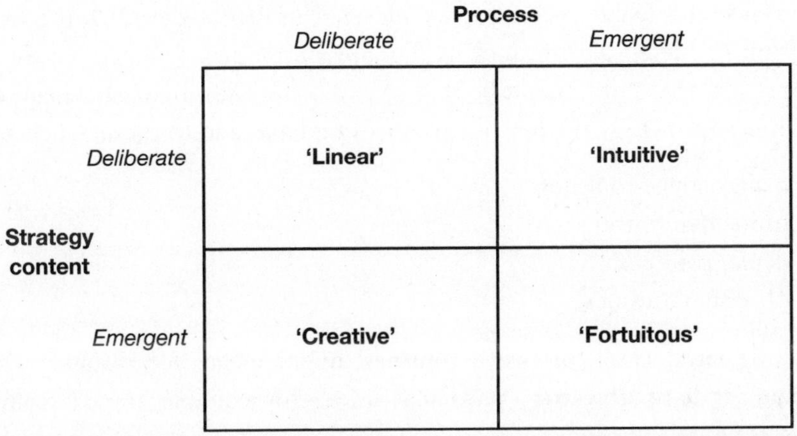

Fig 8.1 Strategy styles – deliberate and emergent strategy/process and strategic behaviour

A deliberate strategy (with an emergent process) is described here as 'intuitive' because, although a sense of strategy might be strong, this has evolved in a non-deliberate process. Equally, a different or new strategy might emerge from a deliberate process – here called 'creative'. Finally, an emergent strategy managed by means of an emergent process is called a 'fortuitous' one because outcomes are inherently subject to chance rather than design.

The learning and change literature

In the past, the learning and change literature has emphasized the significance of blocking or defensive routines that are brought into play when managers feel threatened (Argyris, 1991). Particular problem areas highlighted in the literature were the avoidance of admitting to errors of judgement. This notion of 'defensive routines' is a useful reminder of the existence of partly obvious and partly less obvious behavioural constraints on strategic action. However, Argyris' work does not move far beyond this – for instance, in exploring how the dynamics of interaction within a team may modify behaviour.

'Strategic behaviour' adds a richer set of perspectives to Argyris' earlier work. More specifically, the BT team did not particularly reveal many defensive routines. Nevertheless, the team did exhibit a tendency towards using some characteristic behavioural recipes that were well entrenched (such as 'picking apart' ideas). This may suggest that the very notion of 'defensive routines' is perhaps normative. A more powerful approach, therefore, might be that of exploring additional categories of routines (hopefully further research will find and add to these), such as:

● maintenance routines
● protective routines
● denial routines
● offensive routines.

(In the latter case, 'offensive routines' might mean, for instance, the default style of attacking a particular issue – for example, the BT team's obsessive 'picking apart'.)

In addition, the idea of 'groupthink' (Janis, 1989) is pertinent at this juncture. Janis described management behaviour as often being of a 'Wow, grab it!' mentality. (Although this obviously has more of an 'affective' than a 'cognitive' feel to it, this is in itself of interest in extending the notion of groupthink.

Besides groupthink it is useful to think about 'groupfeel', or the tendency of a team to align its feelings, as well as its thoughts about issues.) In the BT case study there was relatively little in the way of a 'Wow, grab-it' approach. The BT managers appeared to be very picky in what they decided to believe or conclude when examining complicated strategic issues.

The role of organizational politics

As a prelude to a discussion of politics, we can usefully touch on the paradigm. The paradigm has been defined as 'the deeper level of basic assumptions and beliefs shared by members of an organization that operate unconsciously and define in a basic "taken-for-granted" fashion an organization's view of itself and its environment' (Schein, 1986). Besides having some important implications for politics (via the ingredients of power, structure and control), the paradigm has been put forward as being a central concept in understanding strategic change.

Thinking back to the results of the BT case study, the idea of the paradigm is of limited help in exploring patterns in strategic behaviour. Although clearly routines (a key ingredient within the paradigm) were of some importance in shaping strategic behaviour, as has already been seen, the label 'routines' needs to be expanded. For instance, in order to embrace not only more physically obvious routines, but both behavioural and cognitive routines. Indeed, the 'paradigm' itself appears to be too general a notion to be helpful in providing a more powerful framework for understanding strategic behaviour.

More useful, perhaps, is the idea of stakeholders (and their agendas). Indeed, developing an idea into personal and strategic agendas is most helpful.

Less directly helpful, however, is Pascale's notion of contention. For, although the team did exhibit, it is fair to say, a relatively adversarial style at times, it was not at all self-evident that this was actively productive. It appeared that certain individuals in the team latched onto the notion that contention created new ideas and therefore felt able to pursue their own ideas regardless of those of others. As Keith (B) said:

> There is a tension between everyone wanting to, being creative people, and wanting to cut it into their own version of the way forward.

Contention – and particularly the assumption that good new ideas were only really likely to come out of a rigorous dialectic of ideas – actually inhibited the team's active listening capability. It also appeared to discourage the building of fresh ideas.

A particularly useful idea is that of intermingling, where a particular example of strategic behaviour can be seen from multiple-perspectives and can have a multitude of intentions. Related to this is the concept of the 'behavioural package', where a surface-level behavioural act that relates to a tangible, strategic issue simultaneously embraces a political act. Some of these intentions may even conflict and become self-cancelling, undermining the behavioural momentum of the team.

Overt expressions of power were not always easy to detect in the BT case study. By riding on the back of overtly strategic agendas, power influences were expressed in sometimes more manageable ways – by being deliberately intangible and therefore less directly threatening. At BT, there was a reticence to actually deal with politically (or territorially) sensitive issues within an open group forum in the BT team. As David and Andy put it, after the third workshop:

> *David*: The problem that we usually have is we go through this exercise, this prioritization before the real battles come through, when you are actually going through 'why'. So I think that the real contention occurs when we have to understand this. It is only then that you are really challenging people.
>
> *Andy*: Then the agony comes on ... this is an intellectual exercise at this stage. But when it applies to a budget or a departmental resource allocation, the pain comes on.

It is almost as if when a management team gets together for a formal strategic workshop meeting, it is enacting strategic options and decisions during the meeting. However, the real decisions come afterwards – otherwise this might provoke confrontation, embarrassment and a collapse in the team's system of strategic behaviour. (It is almost as if a football team were to enact a match on the pitch, but actually sort out the real score privately in the changing room. This may seem slightly strange to an observer who assumes that a real match took place and who has no knowledge of the political stakes involved.)

Summary

'Strategic behaviour' is not just a convenient 'black box' into which can be put all that is behaviourally messy in strategic management. Rather, it contains within itself some very interesting, if complicated, interactive processes that, when unravelled, produce some powerful diagnostic tools and frameworks.

The contribution to existing thinking made here can be summarized as follows:

- Strategic behaviour is a major factor encouraging a bias (whether natural or unnatural) in organizations towards incremental strategy development and emergent forms of strategy. Without visionary leadership (which seems to be in short supply), this is likely to lead to the creation of the wrong kinds of organizational politics.
- Strategic behaviour that is not very well directed may result in a backlog of undigested strategic issues and, in turn, a build-up of frustration
  - because of outputs,
  - because of the interactive process itself.
- Strategic behaviour may be shaped either deliberately or left to emerge (or both). This helps us to flesh out Mintzberg's forms of strategy to incorporate 'linear', 'creative', 'intuitive' and 'fortuitous' types.
- 'Defensive routines' can be further refined to incorporate different behavioural functions (such as 'offensive routines'), capturing the rich variety of organizational politics.
- 'Personal and strategic agendas' appear to be more helpful (at the small group level) than the notion of 'the paradigm' in explaining patterns in strategic behaviour.
- The 'behavioural package' captures the idea that cognitive, affective and territorial elements of behaviour intermingle at a both conscious and less conscious level. Particular elements of behaviour that are predominantly cognitive might be tainted with the affective and vice versa. Also, territorial elements creep into cognitive and affective elements, although they may sometimes stand out (either on the surface or deeper down) as being primary. Where the 'territorial' plays a parti-

cularly valuable explanatory role is in surfacing not merely the political ingredients of strategic behaviour, but also individuals' feelings of cognitive or affective security (or both).

- Strategic decision making in meetings and workshops may be inhibited because of the perceived need to 'do the business' off the playing field. Functionally, this may be understood to be helping to protect a potentially fragile system of strategic behaviour that managers have created.
- Finally, this very notion of a 'system of strategic behaviour' helps to explain and diagnose strategic behaviour.

LESSONS FOR MANAGEMENT PRACTICE

Clearly strategic behaviour plays a very major role in shaping strategic decisions and implementation. Yet, traditionally, top team behaviour has been associated with leadership and generic group dynamics rather than with the strategic thinking (and influencing) process. By looking at 'strategic behaviour' as a rather different element of management activity, the way in which concepts of strategy are being used in an organization acquires a fresh and clearer meaning.

Areas of strategy that, more traditionally, are seen as essentially cognitive, now appear to be much more multifaceted and concerned with generating a dynamic of strategic behaviour. Hence, the idea of strategic thinking having a more conceptual function (prevalent in some, but not all, schools of strategic management, particularly the 'design' school) recedes somewhat in terms of its practical importance. At the same time, the momentum-building and direction-giving elements of team behaviour come more to the fore. Certainly, the social interaction of the group in facilitating its own learning and that elsewhere in BT (indirectly) loomed as more important. These interactions were influenced in subtle ways by managers' feelings.

Strategic behaviour has profound implications for organizational, team or individual-level interventions aimed at improving strategic thinking. For example, it points up a very big (and obvious) gap between business school education (in certain schools) about the conduct of strategic management, which is essentially cognitive in focus, and practice. Even when exposed to process-based approaches to explaining strategic management, students are typically 'taught about' the importance of emergence, incrementalism and so on, but how to deal with this is so often left open.

Actual day-to-day strategic management is likely to be profoundly affected by strategic behaviour. It would hardly be surprising, therefore, if MBA students found that the differences between strategic management theory and the necessities of managing strategy in practice were profound.

A parallel situation is likely to occur for in-company or public business school programmes on strategic management. Once again, unless a significant element of action learning, integrating theoretical with practical application in the workplace, and this is actually positioned as a 'practical management exercise' is incorporated, the 'learning' taking place is likely to be very limited.

Equally, organizational or team-level interventions, whether these take the form of formal strategic reviews, culture change programmes or team-building exercises, may, again, suffer from being either primarily behavioural or primarily cognitive. It now seems to be absolutely essential to address cognitive, affective and territorial elements simultaneously. However difficult this may seem to be at first sight, it may well prove to be a more effective way of controlling and reshaping strategic behaviour in the longer term.

CONCLUSION

'Strategic behaviour' is a powerful and practical concept in understanding strategic management practice. This notion builds on past research management studies into the process of strategic decision making and organizational behaviour. However, most importantly of all, a better understanding of strategic behaviour should help us to begin to move beyond the undesirable elements of organizational politics.

APPENDIX 1
Checklist for managing strategic behaviour

The following brief checklists are a quick *aide-mémoire* to allow busy managers to do a health check on present and future strategic behaviour in their management team. The checklists are structured along the lines of the model in Figure 3.2, page 76. They therefore include:

- strategic tasks and problem analysis
- analytical and interpersonal processes
- team mix and individual characteristics
- team interaction and dynamic processes
- meta-behaviour
- organizational context
- outputs.

Strategic tasks and problem analysis

Strategic tasks are, essentially, the major strategic activities a team under-takes. These can include, for example:

- acquisitions
- business development programmes
- business performance reviews
- cost reviews
- divestment/rationalization decisions
- key management appointments
- reacting to external change
- resource allocation
- restructuring decisions.

During these activities, many problems can arise, including, for example, deciding whether to make a senior appointment internally or recruit externally, or, where there are many business development projects, determining which should be given priority.

Key questions

- What are the key strategy activities our team faces over the next 6 to 12 months?
- Which of these activities are most critical to the business in the:
  - medium term?
  - longer term?
- How time-intensive are these activities likely to be, and how should they be programmed?
- What does the team need to do less of – or stop doing altogether – to devote sufficient time to its truly strategic activities?
- Which of these activities is liable to generate the most behavioural tur-bulence?
- What roles should key individuals within the team play (for a specific activity)?
- What specific problems and dilemmas are likely to come up, and how can these be addressed?

- What personal and strategic agendas (PASTA) factors are likely to come into play, and how should these be managed?
- What major constraints are likely to be faced, and what options for getting around these are likely to exist?
- Where are these constraints likely to become virtually impossible to deal with, and how can these be headed off?

Analytical and interpersonal processes

To address these strategic tasks and problems requires both analytical and interpersonal processes.

Key questions

- How can problems and dilemmas be anticipated well in advance by the management team?

- How can the team ensure that it clarifies issues before debating situations, let alone creating options?

- How can the team avoid tunnel vision and achieve some genuine creative thinking when generating options?

- How will solutions be challenged and probed, without destructive picking apart?

- Who will summarize and synthesize a conclusion?

- How will the team ensure that where people do agree, they say that they agree?

- When members of the team disagree, will they be expected to also say, in the same breath, why they disagree?

- How will interruptions be managed so as not to disturb the flow of debate, yet still allow valuable, but lateral, thoughts to be heard?

- How will key team members allow themselves to be influenced and won over (where appropriate), rather than taking up fixed positions?

Team mix and individual characteristics

Key questions

- Is the team mix genuinely in balance or is there a preponderance of one or two styles (for example, in Belbin terms, too many plants or chairmen; in *Star Trek* terms, too many Spocks or Klingons)?

- Is it worth while to get the team to check out its team styles (using some psychometrics)?

- Do individuals with pronounced team styles require one-to-one support (off-line, as it were) to adapt their behaviour or could they fruitfully simply try out another role?

- Where the team recruits someone new, what are their preferred team roles, and, assuming this replaces someone leaving the team, will this inadvertently unbalance the team mix?

- What other characteristics of particular individuals might distort the strategic behaviour of the team (for example, their idiosyncratic cognitive style or other personal traits)?

- Does the professional background of team members bias them towards certain types of behaviours (for example, towards picking apart)?

- Are there particularly acute 'power contours' surrounding a particular individual (or individuals) and how can these be toned down?

- What are the personal career ambitions of individuals, and how might they influence or distort their behaviours?

- Are there particular anxious, vulnerable or sensitive individuals, and how does this need to be managed?

- Are the team members (either as a group or individually) just that little bit too serious, and is it necessary to oil the flow?

- Who is likely to succumb to strategic frustration, and on which issues? How can this be headed off?

Team interaction and dynamic processes

Key questions

- What is likely to generate a particularly high level of behavioural turbulence and how can these issues or interactions be navigated?

- If there are specific threats of team breakdown, how can this be facilitated? (What could give rise to these breakdowns? Consider using cause of behaviour (COBRA) analysis.)

- Where known or likely areas of conflict or personality clash exist, how can these be averted or controlled? In which behavioural scenarios are these likely to arise?

- How can levels of excitement be managed so that the team neither flags nor burns up too much energy? What is its 'energy over time' curve expected to look like?

- Where there is real threat of one or more individuals dominating the conversation (and probably withdrawing), how can this be minimized?

- Is there a tendency to dive into or rush the discussion of issues so that problem analysis is incomplete? If so, how can this be averted (for example, by more helicopter-like reflection)?

- Can team time be managed more effectively to avoid both slippage and allow sufficient time to debate the really big issues?

Meta-behaviour

Key questions

- What facilitation is the team likely to need – when and how should this be provided?
- Would it be wise to ask the team (before discussing a particularly sensitive topic) what 'P' behaviours it wants to avoid (for example, being political, picky, pessimistic and so on)?
- Should the team use any strategic analysis tools or methodologies, and how can it learn to use these consistently? (For example, consider using fishbone analysis for any strategic problem.)
- Could the team benefit by consciously trying to avoid 'rabbit hole management' and strive instead towards 'helicopter vision'?
- Would stakeholder analysis or stakeholder agenda analysis be useful in surfacing agendas in the team?
- How can the team target (in advance) the value of its outputs and monitor these subsequently (for example, by using the 'value over time' curve)?
- How can the team take up the idea of value destruction and use this idea on an everyday basis to steer debate towards value added?
- How should the team prioritize its decisions? (For example, by using 'AID' – attractiveness–implementation difficulty – analysis.)
- How can the team build in time to reflect on the process (even if this is just five minutes at the end of a two-hour meeting)?
- Can the team usefully introduce more humour to lighten its heavier strategic debates (without being frivolous)?

Organizational context

Key questions

- Who are the key stakeholders (outside the team) with an influence on the team's strategic activities? What is on their agendas and how should these agendas be taken into account or proactively influenced?
- How does the wider organizational and political structure influence what goes on in the team?
- What factors outside the team are likely to result in inaction, inertia or distraction, and how can these be managed?
- How does the team interact with strategic processes elsewhere in the organization, and how can these processes be managed more proactively?

Outputs

Key questions

- What specific outputs will be needed from key team meetings (for example, decisions to do things, new projects, decisions not to do things and so on)?
- How will these outputs be communicated to the rest of the organization?
- How will the likely reaction of other stakeholders outside the organization be gauged? Will this cause the team to think through its positioning of those messages most carefully?
- At the end of the day, what are those outputs worth – what value have they really added?

APPENDIX 2
Strategic behaviour – exploring the energy dimension

During the BT study, the theme of management energy came up a number of times. The energy of the team itself was an important determinant of how effective they were in their strategic interactions. This energy also helped to build their strategic momentum, thus enabling them to take on a number of strategic issues virtually simultaneously.

Energy is also clearly important at an individual level, too. Specific individuals can generate a lot of energy (for example, Bonnie) or be particularly good at channelling other people's energy (for example, Keith (A) or Andy). To most of us, this energy is a relatively intangible thing, but we perhaps feel that somehow it must be important.

I believe that it is very important indeed in strategic teams. Sadly, at the time of the study, I was not especially trained to observe, feel, intuit individuals' energy – not only quantitatively, but qualitatively. Since the study, however, I have become aware not only of the energy fields that human beings – like it or not – 'give off', but especially those of managers.

With some special training it has been possible to detect, and also to subtly influence, the energy levels of teams (or individual) managers. Probably the means by which this is done will seem peculiar in a management book, so for those who find this whole idea less than credible, do go back to reading the checklists!

For others who are more curious, when you have just had a good (or difficult) experience of interacting with other managers, ask yourself the following questions.

- What did their energy feel like – light, confused, heavy/lethargic, negative?

- How did being exposed to this energy make you feel?
- How did the energy itself seem to influence managers' thinking and behaviour?
- Were there specific issues that seemed to generate their own energy field?

If you have noticed something here, it may be useful to know that, with training, you can become at least ten times more sensitized. Perhaps also, detecting these energies might start you on a journey exploring how your own energy is influenced by, and influences, other people – and managers.

For those who are still intrigued, then you might find it interesting to learn more about something called Reiki, which is a process for sensing (and healing) human energy. I discovered Reiki myself in seeking to cure a minor back problem (probably brought on by too much research analysis at my desk). Since then I have used Reiki to:

- help set a positive lightness in otherwise difficult strategic meetings and workshops
- help align the managers in a team with those things they value most
- bring out the most positive energies in individuals who otherwise threaten to be 'very difficult'.

Reiki itself focuses on energy that is channelled by a number of energy channels surrounding the meridian system, which is central to acupuncture techniques. Reiki was (re)discovered by Dr Usui in Japan over a hundred years ago.

In Japan today, many businessmen practise Reiki to bring harmony to business relationships. It is beginning to spread now quite quickly through the West and, hitherto, has gone unnoticed by management (except perhaps in Australia, where it is increasingly used by managers).

I would be delighted to hear from anyone (especially if you are a manager) whose curiosity has been aroused and who wants to learn more. Do contact me (telephone 01954 251569) and help bring a new sense of lightness to the conduct of strategy and management generally by means of organizational Reiki.

Postscript

For a good introduction to Reiki, see *Essential Reiki* by Diane Stein, The Crossing Press, 1995.

REFERENCES

Chapter 1

Ansoff, H. I. (1965) *Corporate Strategy*. New York: McGraw-Hill.

Ansoff, H. I. (1987) 'The Emerging Paradigm of Strategic Behaviour', *Strategic Management Journal*, 8, 501–15.

Argyris, C. (1991) 'Teaching Smart People How to Learn', *Harvard Business Review*, May–June.

Argyris, C. (1989) 'Strategy Implementation: An Experience in Learning', *Organizational Dynamics*, 18 (2), 5–15, Autumn.

Argyris, C. (1986) *Strategy, Change and Defensive Routines*. London: Pitman.

Barwise, P., Marsh, P., Wensley, R., and Thomas K. (1988) *Managing Strategic Investment Decisions in Large Diversified Companies*. London: London Business School.

Braybrooke, D., and Lindblom, C. E. (1963) *A Strategy of Decision*. New York: The Free Press.

Brunsson, N. (1982) 'The Irrationality of Action and Action Rationality: Decisions, Ideologies and Organizational Actions', *Journal of Management Studies*, 198 (1), 29–44.

Chilingerian, J. A. (1994) 'Managing Strategic Issues and Stakeholders: How Modes of Executive Attention Enact Crisis Management', in Thomas, H., Neal, D. O., and Hurst, D. (eds), *Building the Strategically Responsive Organization*. Chichester: John Wiley, pp198–213.

Cohen, M. D., March, J., and Olsen, J. P. (1972) 'A Garbage Can Model of Organization Choice', *Administrative Science Quarterly*, 7, 1–25.

Cyert, R. M., and March, J. (1963) *A Behaviour Theory of the Firm*. Englewood Cliffs, New Jersey: Prentice Hall.

Dixit, A. K., and Nalib, B. J. (1991) *Thinking Strategically*. New York: W. W. Norton and Company.

Goold, M., Alexander, M., and Campbell, A. (1994) *Corporate-level Strategy*. Chichester: John Wiley.

Grundy, A. N. (1992) *Corporate Strategy and Financial Decisions*. London: Kogan Page.

Hickson, D. H., Butler, R. J., *et al.* (1986) *Top Decisions: Strategic decision-making in Organizations*. Oxford: Basil Blackwell.

Janis, I. L. (1989) *Crucial Decisions*. New York: The Free Press.

Johnson, G. J. (1986) *Strategic Change and the Management Process*. Oxford: Basil Blackwell.

Johnson, G. J. (1992) *The Challenge of Strategic Management*. London: Kogan Page.

Johnson, G. J., and Scholes, K. (1987) *Exploring Corporate Strategy*. London: Pitman.

Kanter, R. M. (1983) *The Change Masters*. London: Unwin.

March, J. E., and Simon, H. A. (1958). *Organizations*. New York: John Wiley.

Miller, P., and Freisen, P. (1978). 'Archetypes of Strategy Formulation', *Management Science*, 24, 921–33.

Mintzberg, H. (1978) 'Patterns in Strategy Formation', *Management Science*, 934–48.

Mintzberg, H. (1994) *The Rise and Fall of Strategic Planning*. Englewood Cliffs, New Jersey, Prentice Hall.

Mitroff, I. I., and Linstone, H. A. (1993) *The Unbounded Mind*. Oxford: Oxford University Press.

Pascale, R. (1990) *Managing on the Edge*. London: Penguin.

Pettigrew, A. M. (1977) 'Strategy Formulation as a Political Process', *International Studies of Management and Organization*, 7 (2), 78–87.

Piercey, N. (1989) 'Diagnosing and Solving Implementation Problems of Strategic Planning', *Journal of General Management*, 15 (1), Autumn.

Porter, E. M. (1980) *Competitive Strategy*. New York: The Free Press.

Porter, E. M. (1985) *Competitive Advantage*. New York: The Free Press.

Quinn, J. B. (1980) *Strategies for Change: Logical incrementalism*. Illinois: Richard D. Unwin.

Schein, E. H. (1986) *Organizational Culture and Leadership*. San Francisco: Jossey-Bass, p6.

Senge, P. (1990) *The Fifth Discipline: The art and practise of the learning organization*. New York: Doubleday.

Spender, J. C. (1989) *Industry Recipes*. Oxford: Basil Blackwell, p32.

Stacey, R. D. (1993) *Strategic Management and Organizational Dynamics*. London: Pitman.

Sun Tzu (1991) *The Art of War*. London and Boston: Shambhala.

Chapter 3

Boland, R. J. (1995) *Narrating Accountability*. Working papers. Case Western Reserve University, Cleveland, USA.

Milliken, F. J., and Vollrath, D. A. (1991) 'Strategic Decision-making Tasks and Group Effectiveness', *Human Relations*, 44 (12), 1229–53.

Chapter 4

Grundy, A. N. (1998) *Exploring Strategic Financial Management*. Englewood Cliffs, New Jersey: Prentice Hall.

Chapter 5

Grundy, A. N. (1998) *Exploring Strategic Financial Management*. Englewood Cliffs, New Jersey: Prentice Hall.

Chapter 6

Boland, R. J. (1995) *Narrating Accountability*. Working papers. Case Western Reserve University, Cleveland, USA.

Chilingerian, J. A. (1994) 'Managing Strategic Issues and Stakeholders: How Modes of Executive Action Enact Crisis Management', in Thomas, H., Neal, D. O., and Hurst, D. (eds), *Building the Strategically Responsive Organization*. Chichester: John Wiley, pp198–213.

Milliken, F. J., and D. A. Vollrath (1991) 'Strategic Decision-making Tasks and Group Effectiveness', *Human Relations*, 44 (12), 1229–53.

Mintzberg, H. (1987) 'Crafting Strategy', *Harvard Business Review*, 66–75, July–August.

Pettigrew, A. M. (1977) 'Strategy Formulation as a Political Process', *International Studies of Management and Organization*, 7 (2), 78–87.

Chapter 7

Grundy, A. N. (1993) *Implementing Strategic Change*. London: Kogan Page.

Grundy, A. N. (1998) *Exploring Strategic Financial Management*. Englewood Cliffs, New Jersey: Prentice Hall.

Goold, M., Alexander, M. and Campbell, A., (1994) *Corporate-level Strategy*. Chichester: John Wiley.

Kaplan, R. S., and Norton, D. P. (1992) 'The Balanced Scorecard: Measures That Drive Performance', *Harvard Business Review*, 71–9, January–February.

Piercey, N. (1989) 'Diagnosing and Solving Implementation Problems in Strategic Planning', *Journal of General Management*, 15 (1), 19–39, Autumn.

Chapter 8

Ansoff, H. I. (1965) *Corporate Strategy*. New York: McGraw-HIll.

Ansoff, H. I. (1987) 'The Emerging Paradigm of Strategic Behaviour', *Strategic Management Journal*, 8, 501–15.

Agyris, C. (1989) 'Strategy Implementation: An Experience in Learning', *Organizational Dynamics*, 18 (2), 5–15, Autumn.

Argyris, C. (1991) 'Teaching Smart People How to Learn', *Harvard Business Review*, May–June.

Agyris, C. (1986) *Strategy, Change and Defensive Routines*. London: Pitman

Barwise, P., Marsh, P., Wensley, R., and Thomas, K. (1988) *Managing Strategic Investment Decisions in Large Diversified Companies*. London: London Business School.

Boland, R. J. (1995) *Narrating Accountability*. Working papers. Case Western Reserve University, Cleveland, USA.

Braybrooke, D., and Lindblom, C. E. (1963) *A Strategy of Decision*. New York: The Free Press.

Brunsson, N. (1982) 'The Irrationality of Action and Action Rationality: Decisions, Ideologies and Organizational Actions', *Journal of Management Studies*, 198 (1), 29–44.

Chilingerian, J. A. (1994) 'Managing Strategic Issues and Stakeholders: How Modes of Executive Attention Enact Crisis Management', in Thomas, H., Neal, D. O., and Hurst, D. (eds), *Building the Strategically Responsive Organization*. Chichester: John Wiley, pp190–213.

Cohen, M. D., March, J. C., and Olsen, J. P. (1972) 'A Garbage Can Model of Organization Choice', *Administrative Science Quarterly*, 7, 1–25.

Cyert, R. M., and March, J. G. (1963) *A Behaviour Theory of the Firm*. Englewood Cliffs, New Jersey: Prentice Hall.

Dixit, A. K., and Nalib, B. J. (1991) *Thinking Strategically*. New York: W. W. Norton and Company.

Goold, M., Alexander, M., and Campbell, A. (1994) *Corperate-level Strategy*. Chichester: John Wiley.

Grundy, A. N. (1992) *Corporate Strategy and Financial Decisions*. London: Kogan Page.

Grundy, A. N. (1993) *Implementing Strategic Change*. London: Kogan Page.

Grundy, A. N. (1998) *Exploring Strategic Financial Management*. Englewood Cliffs, New Jersey: Prentice Hall.

Hickson, D. H., Butler, R. J., *et al.* (1986) *Top Decisions: Strategic decision-making in Organizations*. Oxford: Basil Blackwell.

Janis, I. L. (1989) *Crucial Decisions*. New York: The Free Press.

Johnson, G. J. (1986) *Strategic Change and the Management Process*. Oxford: Basil Blackwell.

Johnson, G. J. (1992) *The Challenge of Strategic Management*. London: Kogan Page.

Johnson, G. J., and Scholes, K. (1987) *Exploring Corporate Strategy*. London: Pitman.

Kanter, R. M. (1983) *The Change Masters*. London: Unwin.

Kaplan, R. S., and Norton, D. P. (1992) 'The Balanced Scorecard: Measures That Drive Performance', *Harvard Business Review*, 71–9, January–February.

March, J. E., and Simon, H. A. (1958) *Organizations*. New York: John Wiley.

Miller, P., and Freisen, P. (1978) 'Archetypes of Strategy Formulation', *Management Science*, 24, 921–33.

Milliken, F. J., and Vollrath, D. A. (1991) 'Strategic Decision-making Tasks and Group Effectiveness', *Human Relations*, 44 (12), 1229–53.

Mintzberg, H. (1978) 'Patterns in Strategy Formation', *Management Science*, 934–48.

Mintzberg, H. (1987) 'Crafting Strategy', *Harvard Business Review*, 66–75, July–August.

Mintzberg, H. (1994) *The Rise and Fall of Strategic Planning*. Englewood Cliffs, New Jersey: Prentice Hall.

Mitroff, I. I., and Linstone, H. A. (1993) *The Unbounded Mind*. Oxford: Oxford University Press.

Pascale, R. (1990) *Managing on the Edge*. London: Penguin.

Pettigrew, A. M. (1977) 'Strategy Formulation as a Political Process', *International Studies of Management and Organization*, 7 (2), 78–87.

Piercey, N. (1989) 'Diagnosing and Solving Implementation Problems of Strategic Planning', *Journal of General Management*, 15 (1), Autumn.

Porter, E. M. (1980) *Competitive Strategy*. New York: The Free Press.

Porter, E. M. (1985) *Competitive Advantage*. New York: The Free Press.

Quinn, J. B. (1980) *Strategies for Change: Logical incrementalism*. Illinois: Richard D. Irwin.

Schein, E. H. (1986) *Organizational Culture and Leadership*. San Francisco: Jossey-Bass, p6.

Senge, P. (1990) *The Fifth Discipline: The art and practise of the learning organization*. New York: Doubleday.

Spender, J. C. (1989) *Industry Recipes*. Oxford: Basil Blackwell, p32.

Stacey, R. D. (1993) *Strategic Management and Organizational Dynamics*. London: Pitman.

Stein, D. (1995) *Essential Reiki*. The Crossing Press Inc., Freedom CA.

Sun Tzu (1991) *The Art of War*. London and Boston: Shambhala.

INDEX

269